# Monteverdi

# Monteverdi

## *Music in Transition*

SILKE LEOPOLD
Translated from the German by
ANNE SMITH

CLARENDON PRESS · OXFORD
1991

Oxford University Press, Walton Street, Oxford OX2 6DP
Oxford  New York  Toronto
Delhi  Bombay  Calcutta  Madras  Karachi
Petaling Jaya  Singapore  Hong Kong  Tokyo
Nairobi  Dar es Salaam  Cape Town
Melbourne  Auckland
and associated companies in
Berlin  Ibadan

Oxford is a trade mark of Oxford University Press

Published in the United States
by Oxford University Press, New York

English translation ©
Oxford University Press 1991
Translated from the original German publication
Claudio Monteverdi und seine Zeit
© 1982 by Laaber-Verlag

British Library Cataloguing in Publication Data
Leopold, Silke
Monteverdi: music in transition.
1. Italian music. Monteverdi, Claudio, 1567–1643
I. Title II. Claudio Monteverdi und seine Zeit. English 780.92
ISBN 0–19–315248–7

Library of Congress Cataloging in Publication Data
Monteverdi: music in transition/Silke Leopold;
translated from the German by Anne Smith.
Translation of: Claudio Monteverdi und seine Zeit.
Includes bibliographical references.
1. Monteverdi, Claudio, 1567–1643—Criticism and interpretation.
I. Title.
ML410.M77L513   1990      780'.92—dc20      90–7074
ISBN 0–19–315248–7

Set by
Pentacor PLC, High Wycombe, Bucks
Printed in Great Britain by
Biddles Ltd., Guildford and King's Lynn

Dedicated to

ANNA AMALIE ABERT

on the Occasion of her Seventy-fifth Birthday

# FOREWORD TO THE ENGLISH TRANSLATION

This book, dedicated to Anna Amalie Abert on the occasion of her seventy-fifth birthday and published in 1982 in the series Große Komponisten und ihre Zeit, was the first Monteverdi monograph to appear in the German language since Hans Ferdinand Redlich's small volume, *Monteverdi: Leben und Werk*, was published in 1949; it was, indeed, the first large Monteverdi monograph in German. It might seem that justification is needed for the appearance of this book now, six years later, in an English translation, not only because there were already a number of English biographies about Monteverdi, but also because, in the meantime, particularly in England, several new books on Monteverdi have been published: *The New Monteverdi Companion*, edited by Arnold and Fortune; *The Cambridge Opera Handbook* about *L'Orfeo*, edited by Whenham; Bianconi's *Seicento*; Fabbri's *Monteverdi*; and, finally, Tomlinson's *Monteverdi and the End of the Renaissance*. Monteverdi's letters have been available to the English language reader since 1980, when Denis Stevens published his careful translations with detailed commentary. The fact that this book presents its own translations rather than utilizing Stevens's should not be understood as a criticism of Stevens's work. Monteverdi's letter style, at times extremely highflown, at times as spontaneous as a few snatches of conversation, often admits of several interpretations; the translations in this book are thus intended to do nothing more than extend the spectrum of possible interpretations.

This book, however, is not a study of some special aspect of Monteverdi's music, but a comprehensive monograph which is directed chiefly towards a lay audience but also in part towards specialists. It is so indebted to previous Monteverdi studies that in the footnotes I have limited myself to mentioning the sources of the quotations, following the example of Denis Arnold in his Monteverdi study in the Master Musicians Series, in order to keep the critical apparatus from growing unwieldy. None the less, this book also aspires to do more than just reflect upon and supplement the current state of research on Monteverdi. By means of a different disposition it attempts to place in the foreground the connections, links, and interrelations in Monteverdi's work which would of necessity be pushed to the side with the usual grouping according to genre. Superficially, the life of the composer may be divided into three stages (Cremona, Mantua, Venice) and his music into three categories (madrigals, operas, and sacred works). This grouping has been used until now by all Monteverdi biographers; it suggests, however, a clarity that is not substantiated by the music itself. This book, on the other hand, endeavours to meet the challenge of the riddles posed by the genres, compositional techniques, and styles which Monteverdi's music reveals upon closer inspection. It may seem with this organization of the material as if Monteverdi's music, seen as a whole, is wilfully torn asunder and the chronologies of his works confounded; but the recognition that there are more points in common than differences in the groups of music more than makes up for not proceeding in a strictly chronological order, for not presenting the operas from a single point of view.

I wish to thank the publisher of the Laaber-Verlag, Henning Müller-Buscher, and the representative of Oxford University Press, Bruce Phillips, who have made the translation of this book into English possible.

My particular thanks, however, go to Anne Smith, who, with patience and tenacity, with painstakingness and generosity, with sympathy and critical distance, made the thankless job of translation into a new, joint review of the material.

S.L.

*Berlin, 1989*

# CONTENTS

# LIST OF MUSIC EXAMPLES

# LIST OF FIGURES

# LIST OF PLATES

# CHRONOLOGY

1565    Baldassare Monteverdi married Maddalena Zignani, a gold-smith's daughter, in Cremona. He was born in 1542 and, like his father and his grandfather before him, was a barber-surgeon. Like them he had his practice on the market-place at the foot of the Cremonese cathedral alongside vegetable and fish vendors. It may be assumed from this occupation that his origins were modest. Immediately after his marriage, however, he moved to another area of Cremona which promised greater earnings and esteem. The social status of the family improved decisively over the course of the following twenty years. Forced by a Milanese decree that forbade the practice of surgery to those who had not been recognized and tested by a council, Baldassare Monteverdi became a founding member and the president of an association of surgeons whose statutes were approved officially in 1587. From that moment on the members were allowed to bear the title of doctor.

1567    On 15 May Claudio Zuan Antonio Monteverdi was baptized in the Church of SS. Nazzaro e Celso.

Palestrina's *Missa Papae Marcelli* appeared in print.

1568    Birth of Tommaso Campanella, the Italian philosopher and social utopian.

1569    Birth of Giambattista Marino, one of the most important seventeenth-century poets, whose texts were set, not only by Monteverdi, but by almost all the madrigal and monody composers.

1571    Birth of Johannes Kepler.

The Turkish fleet was destroyed in the battle of Lepanto.

1572    St Bartholomew's Day Massacre in Paris.

1573    Monteverdi's brother, Giulio Cesare, was born. He also
        became a musician at the Mantuan court and later the director
        of music at the cathedral of Salò.

        Alessandro Striggio was born. His father, Alessandro, was an
        important madrigal composer. The son studied law and had a
        brilliant diplomatic career at the court of Mantua: secretary of
        state, ducal advisor, ambassador to Milan, as well as to the
        Spanish and papal courts, high chancellor of Mantua. He
        served five Mantuan dukes and was named first a count and
        then later a margrave. A lifelong friendship bound him to
        Monteverdi.

        The Turks took Cyprus from Venice.

        Tasso's pastoral drama, *Aminta*, was performed in Ferrara.

1575    Birth of Marco da Gagliano.

        Tasso completed *Gerusalemme liberata*.

1576    Following the death of his first wife, Baldassare Monteverdi
        married Giovanna Gadio, who bore him three children.

        Death of Titian in Venice.

1577    Birth of Peter Paul Rubens.

1580    First edition of Tasso's *Aminta*.

        Death of Andrea Palladio.

1581    First edition of Tasso's *Gerusalemme liberata*.

1582    At the age of fifteen, Monteverdi arranged for the first printed
        publication of his music: the three-part *Sacrae cantiunculae*. In
        the title he called himself a pupil of Marc'Antonio Ingegneri.
        This Veronese musician came to Cremona in the 1570s and
        soon received the position of director of music at the cathedral.
        His works—sacred compositions and madrigals—show that,
        although he was no innovator, he was a solid exponent of the
        Venetian polyphonic style. His indebtedness to Cipriano de
        Rore is demonstrated further by his interest in strict contra-
        puntal writing as well as in chromatic richness. Just when
        Monteverdi began studying with him cannot be said with any
        certainty. It may be assumed, however, that he began studying
        with him in the middle of the 1570s, shortly after Ingegneri

became the director of music at the cathedral. Monteverdi's early publications indicate that he received thorough instruction in contemporary compositional techniques. In addition, Ingegneri seems to have been an excellent player and teacher of string instruments. Throughout his life, Monteverdi paid particular attention to these instruments.

In Florence the Accademia della Crusca was founded, which devoted itself to the cultivation of the Italian language.

1583   Monteverdi published a volume of four-part *Madrigali spirituali*.

1584   Following the death of his second wife, Baldassare Monteverdi married Francesca Como.

Vincenzo Gonzaga, son of the duke of Mantua, married Eleonora de' Medici.

Monteverdi published a volume of *Canzonette a tre voci . . libro primo*. His intention to publish further volumes (why else did he call the print 'Book One'?) was not carried out.

1585   Birth of Heinrich Schütz.

In Vicenza the Teatro Olimpico was inaugurated with the Sophocles tragedy, *Edipo re*. Andrea Gabrieli composed the music for the choruses.

1586   Death of Andrea Gabrieli.

Birth of Francesco Gonzaga, Vincenzo's and Eleonora's son.

1587   Following the death of his father Guglielmo, Vincenzo Gonzaga became the duke of Mantua.

Birth of Ferdinando Gonzaga, Vincenzo's and Eleonora's second son.

Monteverdi's first book of five-part madrigals was published; in the title he still called himself a pupil of Ingegneri.

1588   The English fleet destroyed the Spanish Armada.

1589   The high point of the wedding festivities for Ferdinando I de' Medici and Christine of Lorraine, a granddaughter of Caterina de' Medici, queen of France, was a performance of the comedy *La pellegrina* with musical intermedi by Giovanni de' Bardi, Emilio de' Cavalieri, Cristofano Malvezzi, Luca Marenzio,

Jacopo Peri, and Giulio Caccini, for scenes conceived by Bernardo Buontalenti. These *intermedi* are among opera's most important forerunners.

Taking along a few compositions, Monteverdi went to Milan in the hope of obtaining the vacant position of director of music at the cathedral, or perhaps some other situation. These hopes remained unfulfilled, in spite of the recommendations from Cremona and a warm reception in the house of the President of the Milan Senate.

Galileo Galilei (born 1564) became professor of mathematics in Pisa.

In Paris Henry III of France was murdered. Henry IV of Navarre turned Catholic and became king of France.

The first edition of Battista Guarini's *tragicommedia pastorale, Il pastor fido*, was published (dated 1590).

1590   Monteverdi published his second book of five-part madrigals. In the same year—the exact date is not known—he received a position as a string player (*suonatore di viuola*) at the court of Duke Vincenzo I of Mantua.

1591   Birth of Margherita Gonzaga, Vincenzo's and Eleonora's first daughter.

Death of Gioseffo Zarlino, director of music at S. Marco in Venice.

1592   The first plans were drawn up for a performance of Guarini's *Il pastor fido* at the Mantuan court.

Death of Marc'Antonio Ingegneri.

Monteverdi's third book of madrigals was dedicated to his new master, Vincenzo.

1594   Deaths of Pierluigi da Palestrina and of Orlando di Lasso.

1595   After the Turks had forced their way to Hungary and were a serious threat to Vienna, Emperor Rudolph II of Habsburg sent an envoy to Italy to ask for help from the pope and the Italian princes. Except for Mantua, none of the city-states was willing to respond to the summons. Vincenzo, however, who had read his protégé Tasso's crusader epic with enthusiasm, immediately armed himself for a campaign against the infidels. Political concerns may have played a far smaller role in this decision than his desire to participate in this almost theatrical adventure. Although Mantua was constantly on the brink of financial ruin and was only brought nearer to the edge by this campaign, the duke not only sent troops, but also took along the courtiers, pages, chamberlains, chancellors, secretaries, lord high steward and seneschal, squires, doctors, cooks, cellarers, and armourers deemed suitable for his rank and prestige, as well as some singers. A great lover of music, he did not want to forgo his nightly entertainment. He named Monteverdi the *maestro di cappella* of this group. Giovanni Battista Marinoni was among these singers; Marinoni remained closely connected with Monteverdi and gave homage to him after his death. Passing through Vienna and Prague (where they were welcomed with splendid receptions and magnificient banquets), they advanced to Whyserad. There the Mantuan cavalry, together with the papal artillery, laid siege to the fortress. The war was soon over for Vincenzo. He left the imperial army and returned to Mantua in November. Monteverdi's financial situation, which at the rate of twelve and a half scudi a month was certainly nothing to brag about, worsened as a result of this expedition, as he had to equip himself. In Mantua the verbal generosity of the duke was one thing; the hole in the treasury and the trustworthiness of the financial officials were something else indeed.

Torquato Tasso died in the hospital of S. Onofrio in Rome shortly before he was to receive his laurels as a poet at the Capitol.

1596   Giaches de Wert, Duke Vincenzo's director of music, died. Although Monteverdi aspired to this position, the duke chose Benedetto Pallavicino of Cremona as Giaches de Wert's successor. There may have been objective reasons for this choice: Pallavicino had already been at the Mantuan court for more than ten years and was older and more experienced than the twenty-nine-year-old Claudio. There may, however, also have been some intrigue. Monteverdi himself at least was convinced of this.

1597   One of the many pre-operatic forms was published in Venice: Orazio Vecchi's madrigal comedy, *L'amfiparnasso*.

1598    Ottavio Rinuccini's pastoral drama, *Dafne*, with music by
        Jacopo Peri and Jacopo Corsi, was performed in Florence.

        Adriano Banchieri's madrigal comedy, *La pazzia senile*, was
        published in Bologna.

        *Il pastor fido* was performed with musical intermedi in Mantua.

        Birth of Eleonora Gonzaga, the second daughter of the duke
        and later the empress of Austria.

        The Edict of Nantes guaranteed religious freedom to the French.

        Death of Philip II of Spain.

        Birth of the baroque sculptor Lorenzo Bernini.

1599    On 20 May Monteverdi married the court singer Claudia
        Cattaneo, the daughter of the string player Giacomo Cattaneo.
        Shortly thereafter, on 7 June, he set off to Flanders in
        Vincenzo's entourage. During this trip he was granted once
        again the provisional title of *maestro di cappella*. The journey
        led from Basle and Nancy to Spa, where the duke stayed for a
        month. It then continued via Liège and Antwerp to Brussels.
        Here they remained for three weeks before Vincenzo set off for
        home on 20 September. In spite of his numerous official duties
        involved with providing music for the banquets and receptions
        which were held by Vincenzo, particularly in Spa and Brussels,
        Monteverdi still managed to find time to cast an eye on the
        French music. The fruit of this study, even if it was of
        necessity superficial, was the application of a new style of
        singing to Italian vocal music. Giulio Cesare protested with
        great indignation on his brother's behalf about the introduction
        of this style in the foreword to the *Scherzi musicali* of 1607:

        particularly the *canto alla francese* in this modern style, which has
        been seen now for three or four years in prints, to the words of
        motets, of madrigals, of canzonettas, or of arias—who was the first
        one before him who brought it back to Italy when he returned from
        the baths of Spa in the year 1599? And who began to apply it to Latin
        and Italian texts before him? Did he not compose these scherzos at
        that time?[1]

        Death of Luca Marenzio.

        Gabriello Chiabrera's collection of poems, *Le maniere dei versi
        toscani*, was published; it revolutionized the metre of Italian
        poetry.

---

[1] *Claudio Monteverdi: Lettere, dediche e prefazioni*, ed. Domenico de'Paoli (Rome, 1973; cited
below as *Lettere*), 402.

1600 Emilio de' Cavalieri's sacred opera, *La rappresentatione di anima, et di corpo*, was performed in Rome during the carnival season.

The great event of this year was the marriage of Henry IV of France and Maria de' Medici, which was celebrated with enormous pomp in Florence. On 6 October (the day after the nuptials, a ball, and a banquet) Jacopo Corsi presented Ottavio Rinuccini's *Euridice* with music by Jacopo Peri to a small select circle in the Palazzo Pitti. Three days later the official dramatic production of the festitivies took place in the Uffizi theatre: *Il rapimento di Cefalo* (text by Gabriello Chiabrera, music mainly by Giulio Caccini, and stage design by Bernardo Buontalenti). It cost the grand duke the colossal sum of 60,000 scudi.

In Venice a treatise appeared with the title *L'Artusi Overo delle Imperfettioni della moderna musica. Ragionamenti dui. Ne' quali si ragiona di molte cose utili et necessarie alli Moderni Compositori* (Artusi or the Imperfections of Modern Music. Two discussions in which many things useful and necessary to modern composers are discussed). The author of this polemic text against modern music was a Bolognese priest, Giovanni Maria Artusi, a student of Zarlino. Although he criticized only compositions by Monteverdi, though without mentioning his name, he objected to the new direction in its entirety, as is seen by the way he introduced his criticism:

I was invited to hear some new madrigals . . . in the house of Signor Antonio Goretti; there I met Signor Luzzasco [Luzzaschi] and Signor Ippolito Fiorini, distinguished men, and many noble and musically trained minds had gathered together with them. The madrigals were sung once and then once more; . . . the style was not bad, even though it introduced new rules, new modes, and new declamatory expression. But they are raw and of little pleasure to the ear; and they cannot be otherwise, for when one transgresses the good rules, which are partly based on experience—the mother of all things— partly drawn from nature, and partly proved by demonstration, one must believe that the result must be things that deviate from nature and from the essence of actual music harmony, and are far from the musician's task of pleasing.[2]

The controversy that was kindled by this treatise dragged on for years, even decades; Monteverdi concerned himself in detail with Artusi's attacks one last time in a letter of 22 October 1633, at a time when the subject had long been decided in practice.

Giordano Bruno was burned publically in Rome as a heretic.

[2] Quoted from Domenico de' Paoli, *Monteverdi* (Milan, 1979), 110–11.

1601    On 27 August Monteverdi's son, Francesco Baldassare, was
        born. One of the godfathers was the successor to the Mantuan
        throne, Francesco Gonzaga.

        On 26 November Benedetto Pallavicino died. Two days later
        Monteverdi wrote a letter to Vincenzo in which he requested,
        using an almost untranslatable, stilted rhetoric, the now vacant
        position of *maestro et de la camera et de la chiesa sopra la musica*:

> If I did not hurry to request myself from the great graciousness of
> Your Excellency on this occasion of Pallavicino's death the title for
> music that was once possessed by Signor Giaches, perhaps the envy
> in the designs of others could come to my misfortune, more by means
> of words than music, in such a way that it could tarnish the favour
> with which Your Excellency regards me; they could make Your
> Excellency believe that my silence was a consequence of a fear of my
> own inadequacy or of an overweening opinion of myself, on the basis
> of which I was waiting ambitiously for that which I, being the
> miserable servant that I am, actually have to request and ask for with
> particular humility. Furthermore, if I did not most urgently and
> humbly beseech to be able to continue to serve you, whenever the
> occasion presents itself, you would have particular reason to
> complain justifiably about my negligence.[3]

        Vincenzo, who was returning from his third Hungarian
        campaign, chose Monteverdi this time, in spite of all the
        intriguing which went on. Monteverdi appeared for the first
        time as the *Maestro della Musica del Ser.mo Sig.r Duca di
        Mantova* in the title-page of the fourth madrigal book.

        Guarini's *Compendio della poesia tragicomica tratto dai due
        Verrati* presented a defence of the new dramatic genre, the
        pastoral tragi-comedy, refuting the objection that it transgressed
        the rules of ancient poetry.

1602    Death of Emilio de' Cavalieri in Rome.

        Caccini's *Le nuove musiche* was published. In its foreword the
        author claims that he was the inventor of the solo song
        accompanied by a thorough-bass.

        Lodovico Grossi da Viadana published his *Cento concerti
        ecclesiastici*. In its foreword the thorough-bass receives a
        theoretical grounding.

        Rubens came to Mantua.

1603    On 20 February Monteverdi's daughter, Leonora Camilla, was
        born, but lived only for a short time.

---

[3] *Lettere*, pp. 17–18.

Caterina Martinelli, thirteen years of age, came from Rome to the Mantuan court. She was trained as a singer by Monteverdi.

The dedication of the fourth book of five-part madrigals, which appeared eleven years after the third, to the Signori Accademici Intrepidi di Ferrara shows that Monteverdi had connections with the Ferrarese court.

1604   On 10 May Monteverdi's second son, Massimiliano Giacomo, was born.

1605   The publication of the fifth book of five-part madrigals; in its foreword to the readers, Monteverdi refutes Artusi's criticism:

> Learned Readers, do not be surprised that I am having these madrigals published without first having responded to the objections which Artusi has raised concerning several very short passages of them, for in the service of his Highness [duke] of Mantua I am not master of the time which I would need. Nevertheless I have written this answer in order to make it clear that I do not write my things in a haphazard manner, and as soon as I have revised this answer, it will appear in print under the title of *Seconda pratica overo perfetione della moderna musica*, which perhaps will surprise some people who do not believe that there is any style of composition other than that taught by Zarlino. But they should be assured that there is an idea concerning consonances and dissonances other than the established one which, if regarded calmly, speaks for the modern style of composition. I wanted to inform you of this, first of all so that the term *seconda pratica* will not at some time be used by somebody else, but also so that imaginative people will reflect upon other 'second things' in reference to the musical style and may believe that the modern composer works in accordance with the foundations of truth.

This last thought is a direct allusion to Artusi's declaration that his concern lay not with specific people, but with serving art and truth.

Camillo Borghese ascended the papal throne as Paul VI.

1606   Monteverdi began composing *L'Orfeo: favola in musica* on a text by Alessandro Striggio.

1607   On 24 February *L'Orfeo* was performed for the first time for members of the Accademia degli Invaghiti, whose seat was in the Palazzo Ducale. Francesco, the heir to the throne in Mantua and a member of the Accademia, wrote to his brother Ferdinando, who was studying in Pisa:

Tomorrow the sung favola will be performed in our academy, for Giovanni Gualberto [Magli, a Florentine singer] has applied himself so well that, in the short time that he has been here, he has not only learnt his whole part well by heart, but also speaks it with great elegance and effect, so that I am most pleased with it. And as the text has been printed so that each of the spectators may have one to read during the performance, I am sending you a copy.[4]

The great success of the performance is shown by a further letter from Francesco to his brother written a week later:

The favola meets with so much approval from all those who hear it that the duke, not satisfied with having listened to it at many rehearsals, has given the order that it be performed once again, and that will happen today in the presence of all the ladies of this city, and for that reason Giovanni Gualberto remains here; he has performed very well and has given everyone great satisfaction with his singing, and particularly the Princess.[5]

In July Monteverdi went with his wife to his father's home in Cremona. His wife was already very ill, and he needed respite from the exertions of the spring. The move to a more wholesome climate, however, brought no improvement to Claudia's health. She died on 10 September and was buried in S. Nazzaro. There was little time for mourning. In a letter of 24 September the court chamberlain Federico Follino summoned Monteverdi back to Mantua, for now the opportunity presented itself 'to acquire the greatest fame that man can have on earth'.[6] The marriage of Francesco, the successor to the throne, to Margherita of Savoy was to be celebrated during the following carnival season. Two operas were planned for this occasion. In accordance with Follino's letter, Monteverdi went to Francesco, who wrote to his father on 10 October:

Yesterday evening Monteverdi came to me to talk and expressed his desire to serve Your Excellency with the festivities for this wedding, in particular with the *pastorale in musica*; he requested me to write to you because he would need to have the text within seven or eight days in order to be able to begin to compose; he fears that otherwise, in the short time left until the carnival celebration, he will not be able to deliver good work.[7]

---

[4] Angelo Solerti, *Gli albori del melodramma* (Milan, etc., 1904; repr. Hildesheim, 1969), i. 68–9.

[5] Ibid. i. 69–70.

[6] Quoted from de' Paoli, *Monteverdi*, p. 206.

[7] Ibid. 209.

Shortly after Monteverdi returned to Mantua, Rinuccini also arrived there and presented him with his libretto, *L'Arianna*. At the bidding of the duke, Monteverdi began composing immediately.

In August the *Scherzi musicali a tre voci* was published. The edition was prepared by Claudio's brother, Giulio Cesare, and contains the famous *Dichiaratione*—the exegesis of Monteverdi's foreword to the readers in the fifth book of madrigals about the *prima* and *seconda pratica*.

On 24 December Ferdinando Gonzaga was named a cardinal.

1608    By the end of 1607 the duke had decided for political reasons to postpone the celebration of the wedding until May. Monteverdi thus had a bit more time to compose and rehearse. So that the carnival season might not be totally without musical entertainment, however, Vincenzo arranged for a performance of Marco da Gagliano's *La Dafne*. It was on the same text by Rinuccini used by Peri and Corsi for their setting. The singer Antonio Brandi, as well as Marco, came from Florence. The role of Venus was sung by Caterina Martinelli, who, in the meantime, had become the duke's favourite. The role of Arianna had been intended for her as well; rehearsals were set to begin in February. Things turned out differently, however. As early as 2 February Cardinal Ferdinando wrote to his brother: 'Things are not well with *L'Arianna*, for it is not sure that Caterina can be saved; she is actually in no little danger. Apart from that, Monteverdi has shown great dispatch and has finished almost the entire composition.'[8] Caterina had smallpox. On 17 February the duke travelled with the crown prince to Turin, where the wedding was to take place. On 9 March Caterina died; the performance of the opera was endangered. After some debate, the actress Virginia Andreini was chosen as a substitute. She was the star of the Compagnia dei Fedeli, a famous *commedia dell'arte* troupe, which was also in Mantua for the festivities. Virginia was just as talented a singer as an actress, and was apparently very intelligent, as is shown by a letter from a courtier to the duke: 'She has memorized the role very well in six days, and sings it with such grace and feeling that she has won the admiration of the duchess, Rinuccini, and of all the other gentlemen who have heard her.'[9] All the difficulties were finally overcome. On 24 May the newly-weds

[8] Solerti, *Albori*, i. 91.    [9] Ibid. i. 95.

entered Mantua with great ceremony and the festivities began. On 28 May *L'Arianna* was performed with great success. The legate from Modena wrote the following about it to his prince:

Then the opera was performed, which began before the 'Ave Maria' and lasted until the third hour of the evening, and all of the beautifully dressed singers did their job very well, best of all though Arianna, the *commedia dell'arte* actress; and it was the story of Ariadne and Theseus, and in her *lamento in musica*, which was accompanied by viols and violins, she brought many people to tears with her misfortune. A singer by the name of Rasi also appeared, who sang divinely; but compared to the part of Arianna, the castrati and the others appeared to be nothing.[10]

In addition to this opera, which brought Monteverdi 'almost to death's edge because of the brevity of the time',[11] he had to contribute other compositions to the festivities: *Il ballo delle ingrate* (performed on 4 June) on a text by Rinuccini and the prologue to the Guarini comedy, *L'Idropica* (performed on 2 June), for which the Compagnia dei Fedeli had come to Mantua.

The excessive workload did indeed bring Monteverdi to the brink of total exhaustion and was exacerbated by the fact that the recompense for his labours was limited to compliments. In addition he was offended by the court's sudden exorbitant interest in the Florentine musicians. Exhausted and bitter, he once again returned home to Cremona, where he was received by his father, who was appalled by his appearance. It was decided that the duke should be requested to release him from his services; Baldassare's letter to Vincenzo, however, remained unanswered. A second letter to the duchess shows the seriousness with which Baldassare regarded his decision. It also sheds light on the miserable condition of his son, although the description was certain exaggerated for sake of expedience:

Claudio Monteverdi, my son, immediately after the conclusion of the festivities in Mantua, came to Cremona, seriously ill, with debts, poorly dressed, and without the salary of Signora Claudia, with two poor children whom he has to support since her death, for whom he has nothing other than the usual twenty scudi per month. Because of this—being convinced that the Mantuan climate, which is very bad for him, is responsible for everything together with the large amount of work that he has had and will continue to have if he remains in

---

[10] Solerti, *Albori*, i. 99.
[11] Letter of 1 May 1627 (*Lettere*, p 241).

service, as well as the bad fortune that has always plagued him throughout the nineteen years he has been in service to the duke of Mantua—a few days ago I decided to write to His Highness on my knees, imploring that he, for the love of God, grant my son an honourable dismissal, for, if he returns to Mantua with this workload and this climate, he will soon die. And I will be left to support the poor children, I who am myself old, weak, and poor, and I myself have a wife, children, servants, and maids, and in addition I have had on several occasions to give Claudio a total of 500 ducats and more, when he had to follow His Highness to Hungary and Flanders and when he came to Cremona with his wife, servants and maid, children and carriage, and on other occasions about which I will for brevity's sake say nothing—I therefore beg Your Highness, as I have received no reply from your husband, that you ask him to fulfil my request.[12]

This letter crossed with one from the chancellor summoning Monteverdi back to court. That was the last straw for Claudio. Normally extremely prudent and diplomatic in his contact with the duke, he sent an angry reply, in which he poured out all the pent-up feelings of humiliation and rage which had built up over the years.

The letter had an unexpected success: instead of granting Monteverdi's requested dismissal, the duke gave the order to raise his salary to 300 scudi an year, and shortly thereafter bestowed an inheritable pension of 100 Mantuan scudi upon him. Although these were only promises and Monteverdi once again had to fight for their fulfilment in the following years, he let himself be talked into continuing his service with the duke of Mantua. He did, however, extend his stay in Cremona for a while in order to regain his strength fully.

1609   In addition to smaller works for the duke, Monteverdi prepared the edition of *L'Orfeo* which was published in August. In September he returned to Mantua.

      Vincenzo bestowed Mantuan citizenship upon him.

      Kepler's *Astronomia nova* was published.

      Heinrich Schütz studied with Giovanni Gabrieli in Venice.

      Giacomo Gastoldi died; he had been director of music in the Mantuan palace church, Sta Barbara.

1610   At the duke's bidding, Monteverdi set a madrigal cycle which Scipione Agnelli had written on the occasion of Caterina

---

[12] Emil Vogel, 'Claudio Monteverdi', *Vierteljahrsschrift für Musikwissenschaft*, 3 (1887), 428.

Martinelli's death, 'Lagrime d'amante al sepolcro dell'amata';
he also made a five-part madrigal setting of the by then famous
'Lamento d'Arianna' (published in 1614). A third lament on
Marino's verses about Hero and Leander remained unexecuted.
At the beginning of the autumn Monteverdi requested
permission to go to Rome to present the pope with a collection
of sacred works dedicated to him. Francesco Gonzaga informed
his brother, Cardinal Ferdinando Gonzaga, of the intended
visit, and, equipped with letters of introduction from the duke
to the Cardinals Borghese and Montalto, Monteverdi set out
for Rome. In his luggage he had the printed edition of the
parody mass, *Missa 'In illo tempore'* and the *Marian Vespers*.
Monteverdi had concealed from the duke at least one and
perhaps even two of the reasons for this trip: he wanted to
obtain a free place for his son at the Seminario Romano and he
no doubt wanted to offer his services to the pope. After the
fatigue and vexation of the recent past, a desire to leave the
Mantuan court may have grown in him. The trip, however,
was not at all successful, although he was welcomed warmly by
the cardinals, as he received neither an audience with the pope,
nor a place in the Seminario for the nine-year-old Francesco.
He thus had to return to Mantua without having accomplished
what he had set out to do.

1611   After the failure of this trip, Monteverdi continued to devote
himself to his duties at the court and composed sacred and
secular music for the duke. In the meantime Vincenzo had
brought another famous singer to his court, Adriana Basile
from Naples. Her extraordinary talent was extolled enthusi-
astically by the most important poets of the time. Her
engagement in Mantua was preceded by diplomatic negoti-
ations of such delicacy that they bear witness not only to the
artist's allures, but also to Vincenzo's fanatic zeal in regard to
art (and women) at his court. It was not only the duke who was
delighted by her charm, Monteverdi also was much impressed
by her artistic ability:

Before I left Rome, I heard Sig.ra Hippolita [Recupito Marotta] sing
very well, in Florence I heard the daughter of Giulio Romano
[Caccini] sing and play the chitarrone-lute [leutto chitaronata] and
harpsichord very well, but in Mantua I have heard Sig.ra Adriana
[Basile] sing most beautifully, play most beautifully, and declaim
most beautifully.[13]

[13] Letter of 28 Dec. 1610 (*Lettere*, p. 52).

Adriana became the attraction of the Friday evening concerts, which were held at that time in the palace's hall of mirrors and eagerly attended by all of the local nobility. Monteverdi was the director and organizer of these soirées and wrote the following to Cardinal Ferdinando:

Every Friday evening music is performed in the hall of mirrors, Signora Adriana comes to sing in concert, and she gives the music so much strength and particular grace and thereby delights the senses that this location has almost become a new theatre, and I believe that the carnival of concerts will not end without the duke having to place guards at the entrance, for I swear to Your Highness that last Friday not only the duke and duchess came to listen, and Donna Isabella of San Martino, the Marquis and Marquise of Solferino, ladies and knights from the entire court, but also more than a hundred other gentlemen from the city; on such a good occasion I will make use of chitarrones played by the Casaleschi and an *organo da legno*, which has a very beautiful sound, and in that manner Adriana and Giovanni Battista will sing the wonderful madrigal 'Ah che morir mi sento' and the other madrigal to the organ alone.[14]

Heinrich Schütz published his nineteen Italian madrigals.

On 8 December the Duchess Eleonora of Mantua died of a stroke.

1612 Broken by the effects of a wild life, Vincenzo died on 18 February after a short illness, leaving his small city-state horrendously in debt. Francesco, the godfather of Monteverdi's elder son, was his successor and began a big clean-up campaign against the flunkeys, comedians, and alchemists whom Vincenzo had collected around himself, particularly in his later years. Indirectly Monteverdi also became a victim of the great physical and psychological stress which Francesco assumed with his inheritance. Although Monteverdi's relationship with the new duke remained excellent, Monteverdi and his brother Giulio Cesare were dismissed from his service on 31 July. Nothing is known about the reasons behind this sudden decision; everything suggests that it was a rash act executed in a fit of temper. Monteverdi left Mantua at the beginning of August and returned to Cremona to his father. The news of his dismissal spread like wildfire and the hyenas immediately made their presence known. Only a month later Francesco received a letter in which the director of music at the cathedral of Ferrara offered his services as a successor. Cardinal Ferdinando placed

[14] Letter of 22 June 1611 (*Lettere*, pp. 57–8).

his own director of music, Sante Orlandi, at his brother's service. Nasty rumours were also heard from Milan, where Monteverdi had gone, perhaps hoping for a position. Francesco, who apparently already rued his decision to dismiss Monteverdi, asked Striggio, at that time his ambassador to Milan, for an explanation of the rumour that Monteverdi had applied for the position of director of music at the cathedral, but had failed so miserably in directing the choir that he had had to retreat in disgrace to Cremona. Striggio's answer is clear:

It is completely untrue that Monteverdi left this city [Milan] in disrepute; to the contrary he was highly honoured by the nobility of the city as well as received most heartily and with flattery by the musicians, and his works are sung here with great success in the important assemblies. Nor is it true that it ever occurred to him to become director of music at the cathedral here, he never strove for this position, in order not to damage the man that has the position, for it is occupied.[15]

This answer seemed to have relieved Francesco, for he ordered a performance of *L'Arianna*, perhaps in the hope of winning back the composer. He also left the position of director of music open. There was, however, no performance. A devastating smallpox epidemic broke out in Mantua, which first took Francesco's only son Lodovico and finally Francesco himself on 22 December, after a reign of only ten months full of financial and political burdens. He was succeeded to the throne by his brother, Cardinal Ferdinando.

The first edition of the *Vocabolario italiano* of the Accademia della Crusca appeared.

1613    Gesualdo's collected madrigals appeared in a printed score.

Death of Carlo Gesualdo.

The director of music at the cathedral of S. Marco in Venice, Giulio Cesare Martinengo, died on 22 July. Monteverdi's name was among those suggested as possible successors. The procurators of Venice had their ambassadors collect information, then invited Monteverdi to Venice for an audition, and finally decided in his favour on 19 August. He was given a yearly salary of 300 scudi—100 more than Martinengo—and received an apartment in the prebend of S. Marco as well as the 'usual gifts'.

---

[15] Quoted from de' Paoli, *Monteverdi*, pp. 270–1.

1614    Monteverdi published his sixth book of madrigals, which contains the five-part madrigal version of the 'Lamento d'Arianna' and the 'Lagrime d'amante'.

1615    After a break of two and a half years—years of great affliction for the dukedom—the Mantuan court again began to seek cautious contact with Monteverdi. After the death of Francesco in 1612, his father-in-law Carlo Emmanuele I of Savoy had taken over the Mantuan possession of Monferrato. Thereupon Ferdinando abandoned his cardinal's hat and, with the help of France, Spain, Tuscany, and Venice, forced restitution of Monferrato to Mantua. This was an action desired by all of Europe in order that political stability might be maintained. Soon after the treaty between Mantua and Savoy of November 1614, Ferdinando had Alessandro Striggio request Monteverdi to come to Mantua and write an opera on a text by the duke. Monteverdi replied cautiously that he would ask the procurators for a leave of absence, but clearly implied that he did not wish to return to Mantua. Ferdinando then had to pull back the feelers he had extended towards Monteverdi, because the conflict with Savoy broke out once again. Monteverdi, however, used the opportunity to request prompt payment from Ferdinando of the pension that Vincenzo had granted him in 1608, but to no avail. Instead, after several months of silence, Monteverdi was commissioned in November to write a *ballo*. Monteverdi, having received no detailed instructions, suggested the ballet *Tirsi e Clori*, which he had already composed, and sent it to Mantua. He was glad that the duke was pleased with it, and expressed his willingness to take on other projects. *Tirsi e Clori* was presumably performed for Ferdinando's coronation ceremonies in January 1616 and was published almost four years later in the seventh madrigal book.

1616    Because of all he had done for the choir of S. Marco, the Serenissima raised Monteverdi's yearly salary to 400 ducats. The laxity which Monteverdi had first encountered at S. Marco had gained ground slowly after Zarlino's death; during the time of his successors, the singers, with the consent of the doge, had organized themselves into a guild. Too many engagements in other churches or patrician's palaces had undermined the choir's discipline and had caused its quality to sink noticeably. Having been provided with all the authority necessary, Monteverdi saw to it not only that rehearsals were attended regularly, but also that his singers received solid training in unaccompanied choral singing, an art that had been lost in the thorough-bass euphoria of the previous years. Within a short time the choir had regained the high standards which had made it world famous decades ago under Willaert, de Rore, and Zarlino. Although the singers' rights were thus circumscribed, they accepted Monteverdi's authority; he conducted the rehearsals not so much with strictness as with the power of conviction.

Mantua also made itself known in this year. In February 1617 Ferdinando's wedding with Caterina de' Medici was to be celebrated. Striggio sent Monteverdi Scipione Agnelli's *Favola di Teti e di Peleo*, which was to be performed, together with Francesco Rasi's *Favola di Aci e di Cibele* and Ferdinando Gonzaga's *Favola di Endimione*. The piece did not please Monteverdi for various reasons. He thought that it was impossible to set to music because, first of all, instead of people only natural elements appear, such as the wind who cannot speak, and, secondly, because the instrumental accompaniment would cause difficulties. None the less at the duke's bidding he began work on the composition.

1617    In January Monteverdi learned to his relief that *Le nozze di Tetide* was intended not as an opera but as intermedi. This simplified the composition considerably, as he could in this context replace the human emotions missing in the text with mechanical stage effects, decorative music, and ballets. He had already composed all the monologues when he heard from Striggio that the duke had recognized the weaknesses of the fable and had withdrawn the commission. In the end only Gabriello Chiabrera's *Galatea* with music by Sante Orlandi was performed at the wedding ceremonies.

Giambattista Andreini's *La Maddalena* was performed, for which Monteverdi composed the prologue.

Death of Monteverdi's father Baldassare.

1618    A new commission came from Mantua: Monteverdi's patron, the ducal secretary Ercole Marigliani, sent him a libretto of his own, *Andromeda*, which Monteverdi had little desire to set. As a well-versed courtier, however, he did not decline the job outright, but at first merely offered his excuses, saying that he had little time because of his duties as director of music at S. Marco, which were particularly burdensome in spring:

My obligations for the Easter celebrations in S. Marco have kept me so busy that I have not yet been able to send Your Excellency the music to the Andromeda text. I have also received with the present post other lines on the same subject of Andromeda, but I do not know whether I can do as much by Ascension Day as Your Excellency commands and I myself desire, for next Thursday, on the Day of the Holy Cross, there will be exposition of the Holiest of Blood, and I will have to be ready with a concerted mass, as well as motets for the entire day, for the Blood will also be displayed for the whole day on an altar specially built high for it in the middle of S. Marco; after that I have to rehearse a certain cantata in praise of the doge, which is sung each year in the Bucintoro when he celebrates the marriage with the sea with the entire Signoria on Ascension Day; and I must also work up the mass and the solemn vespers that are sung at that time in S. Marco. I thus fear, Your Excellency, that I will not be able to do what I desire, but will none the less try to do everything that I can.[16]

Every now and then Monteverdi sent a completed portion of *Andromeda* to Mantua. He delayed the matter for over three years, coming up continually with new, wordy excuses. In 1620 Marigliani's *Andromeda* was finally performed in Mantua during the carnival season. It remains unknown, however, in spite of the recent rediscovery of the libretto, how much of the music used in this performance was by Monteverdi.

Beginning of the Thirty Years War.

Death of Giulio Caccini.

Ranuccio Farnese had a theatre built in a hall of the Palazzo della Pilotta in Parma. Its inauguration, however, did not take place until 1628.

1619    Monteverdi's sons, Francesco and Massimiliano, were 17 and 14 years of age respectively, and their father was concerned that they receive a solid education, one which would not only enable them to provide well for themselves but also give them an acceptable social status. This, however, was not accomplished without difficulties. First he had to exert himself for his elder and musically talented son, for whom he desired a career in law.

I went to accompany my elder son Francesco to Bologna as soon as the first festivities for Christmas were over, and take the opportunity to remove him from Padua, to release him from the good time which the illustrious Abbot Morosini had granted him in his goodness that

---

[16] Letter of 21 Apr. 1618 (*Lettere*, pp. 106–7).

he might enjoy a little of the boy's singing, whereby in the end he would have become a good singer, with everything that, so to speak, involves (but I think it would be better to say nothing of this), rather than an average doctor; to my way of thinking I would prefer that he be good in the second profession and average in the first, and this as an adornment, thus I have lodged him in Bologna at the priory of the Servites where there is daily reading and discussion.[17]

Although Francesco began to study jurisprudence, the paternal foresight was to no avail. Francesco's musical talent was greater than his interest in law. He was spared his father's fate, however, which was Claudio's primary objective. Francesco joined the Carmelite Order a year later and never became a court musician.

In addition to the compositions for Ercole Marigliani, Monteverdi set Striggio's eclogue, 'Lamento di Apollo'.

In December the seventh madrigal book was published, with the title of *Concerto*. It was dedicated to the duchess of Mantua. Originally Monteverdi had wanted to come to Mantua himself and present the duchess with his work. The printer, however, did not meet his deadlines and thus Monteverdi had to go to Mantua without the collection, presumably to make a further attempt to receive payment of his pension.

1620    After the death of Sante Orlandi, who had temporarily taken over the position of director of music after Monteverdi had been dismissed, Ferdinando made a new attempt to bring Monteverdi back to the Mantuan court. His answer, however, was clear: in comparison with his duties, his position, his reputation, and last but not least his generous (and punctual) salary in Venice, Mantua was of no interest to him. The duke, however, did not give up so quickly. Unperturbed by this obvious rebuff, he continued to give Monteverdi commissions, for Mantua again had new plans: the duchess's birthday was to be celebrated with great pomp on 2 May. Peri's opera *Adone* was to be performed as well as Monteverdi's *L'Arianna*. Monteverdi sent the opera to Mantua; he would have liked to revise it had he heard of the plan somewhat sooner. He promised to come to Mantua himself after Easter for the performance of *L'Arianna*. Once again the plans remained unfulfilled. Because of the short rehearsal time, both projects were dropped and the birthday was celebrated merely with a ballet.

[17] Letter of 9 Feb. 1619 (*Lettere*, pp. 110–11).

1621 Cosimo II, the grand duke of Tuscany, died on 28 February. The Florentines who lived in Venice organized a funeral service, for which Monteverdi composed the responsories and, with the collaboration of an organist at S. Marco, a mass which made a deep impression: 'After the very mournful *Sinfonia*, moving to tears, perhaps even arousing sorrow, imitating the old Mixolydian mode, which was once invented by Sappho, Francesco Monteverdi, Claudio's son, sang "O vos omnes attendite" with the sweetest voice . . . ' After the Dies irae, the De profundis made perhaps the greatest impression, 'a dialogue as of souls suffering the torments of purgatory and being visited by angels . . . '.[18]

Monteverdi received a commission from the Duchess Caterina, for which he expressed his thanks; at the same time he requested a recommendation to Cardinal Montalto's seminary in Bologna, where Massimiliano was to reside during his studies.

1622 In response to the duchess's recommendation, Massimiliano received a place in the seminar and began to study medicine in Bologna.

1623 On 1 July Francesco Monteverdi was taken on as a tenor in the choir of S. Marco.

The 'Lamento d'Arianna' was published, fifteen years after its première and nine years after the publication of its five-part arrangement.

Maffeo Barberini ascended the papal throne as Urban VIII.

The first edition of Giambattista Marino's epic appeared, *Adone*, one of the main poetic works of the Baroque.

1624 On Shrove Tuesday, in the palace of Girolamo Mocenigo, a Venetian patrician, Monteverdi's *Combattimento di Tancredi e Clorinda*, on a text from Tasso's *Gerusalemme liberata*, was performed as a musical drama.

Monteverdi's father-in-law, Giacomo Cattaneo, died; he left his Mantuan house to his grandsons, but a legal conflict with other heirs broke out over this inheritance.

1625 Monteverdi's contact with Ercole Marigliani was not limited solely to the legal conflict concerning Cattaneo's house, but

[18] Quoted from de' Paoli, *Monteverdi*, p. 367.

extended to a common hobby: alchemy. At this time when experimental methods had begun to prevail in the natural sciences, it had turned more and more into a secret lore. Monteverdi discussed methods of melting gold and lead, of transforming mercury into water, and other things of similar nature with Marigliani. In the process of his experiments, however, he seems to have lost real conviction, as is shown by the last letter to Marigliani on this subject: 'And I give you news of how I am just making fire under a glass retort with a lid on it, to extract an I-don't-know-what for producing an I-don't-know-what, so that with the help of God I can explain this I-don't-know-what joyfully to my Signor Marigliani . . . '[19]

Death of Giambattista Marino.

1626   Massimiliano finished his studies in Bologna and returned to Mantua as a doctor. A restless soul, he frequented the scientific circles there and discussed astrology with a Jesuit priest. This all disturbed his father very much, for he would not allow his son to come to Venice until 'he had begun another and more useful life than before'.[20] Justification of his parental concern was soon made manifest, as the society in which Massimiliano moved was to bring him to misfortune in the near future.

Under the influence of Marino, the opera *La catena d'Adone* (text by Ottavio Tronsarelli, music by Domenico Mazzocchi) was published in Rome as a musical adaptation of the Adonis legend.

Duke Ferdinando of Mantua died on 29 October. He was succeeded by Vincenzo's sickly youngest son, who ascended to the throne as Vincenzo II.

1627   The new duke also tried to bring Claudio back to the Mantuan court. This time it was done secretly and with the request that Monteverdi say nothing about it. Monteverdi, who could respond only with tired irony to this offer ('my misfortune would again play its tricks on me, . . . that for nine of ten months wages no money would be found for me in the treasury.'[21]), agreed willingly to secrecy as such a rumour would be a source of disquiet to his singers. First, however, the duke tried to entice the composer with a commission and had Striggio

[19] Letter of 26 Mar. 1626 (*Lettere*, p. 236).
[20] Ibid.
[21] Letter of 10 Sept. 1627 (*Lettere*, p. 274).

ask him whether he would be willing to set an opera text. The proud assurance of his response makes it clear that in the meantime he had learned how to deal with princes. At the same time he brought up a project, whose realization seemed to be quite important to him:

I wish, however, to pray and beseech Your Grace to clarify that, if His Highness deigns to have me compose the play indicated by him to me, that he deign to consider two things: first, that I would have to have enough time for composing it and, second, that the text would have to be written by an excellent poet, even more so as it would cause me much work and little pleasure and great affliction to have to set excellent poetry to music in a short time. For the brevity of the time was the reason that I was almost reduced to death during the composition of *L'Arianna*. I know that one could compose quickly, but fast and good together are impossible. If there were enough time, however, and if the text were to come from your talented pen, then rest assured, I would be infinitely pleased with it, for I know how easy it would be to set a text of yours and how special it would be. If it involved the intermedi for a play, then the work would not be so difficult nor last so long, but a sung play, which means as much as an epic poem, cannot—believe me—be done in a short time without committing one of the two mistakes: working badly or getting sick. However, I have completed many stanzas by Tasso where Armida begins 'O tu che parti, parte tuo di me parte ne lassi', followed by the entire lament and the rage, with Rinaldo's [Monteverdi wrote Ruggiero] responses, which would perhaps meet with pleasure. And I have completed the *Combattimento di Tancredi e Clorinda*, and in addition I have a small work by Giulio Strozzi in mind, extraordinarily beautiful and curious, which consists of 400 lines; it is entitled *Licori finta pazzi innamorata d'Aminta*, which after a thousand ridiculous small scenes with excellent deceptive manoevres leads to a wedding. And similar things of this nature could serve for little episodes between other well-composed music and I know that it would please Your Grace.[22]

The duke actually agreed to this and Monteverdi began with the composition of *La finta pazza Licori* with the knowledge that Margherita Basile, Adriana's sister, would be a suitable lead singer and that he could tailor the part to suit her. Until September he worked together with the librettist on the opera and sent scene after scene to Mantua. Striggio made suggestions on how it might be improved and requested other compositions. Further events in Mantua, however, prevented a performance of all these works, one of which was to have been the *Armida* which

---

[22] Letter of 1 May 1627 (*Lettere*, p. 241).

Monteverdi had mentioned in the letter: Duke Vincenzo II died on Christmas Day. The direct lineage of the Gonzaga family died out with the last son of Vincenzo I. He was succeeded by Carlo di Nevers from the French line of the Gonzagas, who was quickly married to Maria Gonzaga, the daughter of the late Duke Francesco, at Vincenzo's deathbed. Spain and the emperor, however, did not recognize this line of succession, which linked Mantua with France.

Monteverdi had barely finished *La finta pazza Licori* for Mantua before he received another commission so important that he would even turn down a future commission from Mantua. There was to be a celebration in Parma for the wedding of Duke Odoardo Farnese and the eldest daughter of the duke of Tuscany. In August Monteverdi received an offer to set several intermedi by Ascanio Pio di Savoia from Marquis Enzo Bentivoglio, an old Ferrarese acquaintance and the organizer of the festivities in Parma. The first one came in September and by the next day he had already composed half of it—easy work, 'for they are almost all soliloquies'.[23] Indeed time was really very short, for the wedding was supposed to take place in October. It did not, however, take place. While the theatre machines from 1618 were being hurriedly put into shape, the grand duke of Tuscany accepted the suit of Gaston d'Orléans, the brother of the French king, for the eldest Medici daughter. As a substitute Odoardo was offered Margherita, the daughter next in age. His assent appeared to save the ceremony. Gaston d'Orléans, however, suddenly retracted his suit; perhaps someone had informed him that Maria Christina de' Medici was a hunchback. Only after Maria Christina had retreated to a cloister was the second daughter free to marry. The ceremonies were postponed for a year. This gave Monteverdi more time, and he went to Parma in order to devote himself better to the composition. In the meanwhile he had also received the commission to set the tourney *Mercurio e Marte* by Claudio Achillini. Before Monteverdi could leave Venice, he had much work to accomplish:

[that he deign to do me the favour of allowing me to] remain in Venice until 7 October, because on that day the doge goes in a procession to Santa Giustina in order to give thanks to the Lord for the fortunate naval victory [at Lepanto] and the whole senate goes with him and there solemn music will be sung; but immediately after this service I will get on the boat with the courier and will come to obey Your

---

[23] Letter of 10 Sept. 1627 (*Lettere*, p. 273).

Highness's commands, and it will be prudent to go and look at the theatre in Parma, so that I can adapt the instrumentation as much as possible to the large location, and in my opinion it will not be an easy thing to set to music the diverse and varied texts which I see in these most beautiful intermedi.[24]

He arrived in Parma with Antonio Goretti, the musician in whose home Artusi had once heard Monteverdi's new madrigals, and began to compose and rehearse immediately. Goretti appears to have lent him a hand as a scribe and collaborator. This did not particularly please Goretti, as he had already composed a work for the festivities planned for 1618. It was not performed then nor tranferred to the later festivities. He tried to improve his subordinate position in these preparations by writing nasty letters to Marquis Bentivoglio: 'The parts still must be copied, and I have already written a good part of Signor Claudio's composition, which, as it comes from under his hands, is so entangled and mixed up and confused that I protest to Your Highness that he makes me guess.'[25] He made use of Bentivoglio's demand that they should push ahead with the work for another gibe:

Signor Claudio composes only in the morning and in the evening, and after lunch he does not want to do anything; I urge him on and relieve him from work, that is I take away the compositions from under his hands after we have discussed them and played them through, and they are so entangled and mixed up that I—I assure Your Excellency—have more work than if I were to compose them all myself . . . and if I were not there at his side he would have finished only half of what he has done; it is true that it is a long and large work, but he is a man who likes to talk things over at length in company . . . and so I leave him no opportunity to do so.[26]

It would be difficult to determine how much of this description is true. In any case Goretti let no chance of taunting his colleagues pass by, as is illustrated by what he had to say about Sigismondo d'India in a letter to Bentivoglio:

[He believes that he is] the foremost man in the world, and that no one but he knows anything; and whoever wishes to be his friend, and deal with him, has to puff him up with this wind; a thing one might tolerate, and give him this pleasure, if he were satisfied with a little of it; but he then becomes so saturated with this delirium that he does

[24] Letter of 25 Sept. 1627 (*Lettere*, pp. 287–8).
[25] Quoted from de' Paoli, *Monteverdi*, p. 399.
[26] Ibid. 400.

not wish ever to hear anything else—in such a fashion that he puffs up with it and bounds away like a balloon.[27]

Although the procurators of Venice had extended Monteverdi's leave of absence for the work in Parma, they did demand that he come back to Venice for the Christmas festivities so that he might fulfil his duties at S. Marco. He returned at the beginning of December.

An unfortunate occurrence cast a shadow over this year, which had been one of the most productive and successful in the composer's life: Massimiliano was arrested by the Inquisition in Mantua because he was in possession of a prohibited book. He had been denounced by the owner of the book, who had also been arrested. Monteverdi was willing to pay 100 scudi as bail so that his son would be free until the trial and could come to him in Venice. Although he was now much better off financially, he could raise such a large sum only by pawning a valuable necklace. Striggio, however, paid the bail himself and refused to take any guarantee.

Monteverdi published a volume of four-part madrigals by Jacques Arcadelt.

The first German-language opera was performed in Torgau. Its text was by Martin Opitz (an adaptation of Rinuccini's *Dafne*) and its music by Heinrich Schütz.

1628    Massimiliano was released and was allowed to go to Venice, where he probably continued to practise medicine.

At the beginning of the year Monteverdi went once more to Parma, where the preparations for the wedding were in high gear, although no one was really sure when and if it would take place. Monteverdi, in any case, had heard rumours from the Procurator Contarini: '[He believes] that this wedding will not take place in this carnival season, nor in May, the time, as I have heard from Ferrara, that it will take place; perhaps not at all; nevertheless I will go and put in order the music which I have been commissioned to write; I can nor must do no more.'[28] Truly Monteverdi could not complain about a lack of work:

Here in Parma my music is being rehearsed in haste, for their Highnesses believe that their wedding will take place much sooner

---

[27] Stuart Reiner, 'Preparations in Parma 1618, 1627–28', *Music Review*, 25 (1964), 287.
[28] Letter of 9 Jan. 1628 (*Lettere*, p. 302).

than is thought, and these rehearsals are held because at the moment there are singers from Rome and Modena in Parma and instrument- alists from Piacenza and elsewhere . . . and there will be two very beautiful entertainments; one is a spoken play with musical intermedi and none of the intermedi is shorter than three hundred lines and the texts have a different character, the words to which were written by Ascanio Pio . . . ; the other will be a tourney, in which four squadrons of knights will participate, and the leader will be the duke himself. The text for this tourney was written by Signor Aquilini, and there are more than a thousand lines, which may be nice for the tourney but are very difficult to set to music; they have given me a lot to do. They are now rehearsing this music for the tourney, and where I could not find diversity in the affects, I have attempted to vary the instrumentation, and I hope that the works will give pleasure . . . [29]

Finally in December everything was ready to go: on the 13th the intermedi were performed and on the 21st the festivities were brought to a close with the magnificent tourney. Notwithstanding the splendour of the sets and the spectacular effects created with stage machinery, the audience was most taken with Monteverdi's music. A secretary to the Tuscan grand duke described him as being 'the greatest Italian composer'. Monteverdi could enjoy only half of his triumph, for the procurators had ordered him clearly, albeit politely, to return to Venice for the Christmas celebrations.

The nuptials of Odoardo with Margherita de' Medici had begun in Florence in October. On 14 October Andrea Salvadori's opera *La Flora*, with music by Marco da Gagliano and Jacopo Peri, was performed in the Uffizi.

1629    Heinrich Schütz, who had come to Venice in the autumn of the previous year, remained in the city until the summer. He probably met Monteverdi there. In the same year his *Symphoniae sacrae* appeared in print.

In Rome Giovanni Francesco Parisani's opera, *Diana schernita*, with music by Giacinto Cornacchioli, was performed in the home of the Baron von Hohen Rechberg. It was the first opera performance sponsored by the Barberini family; it was also one of the first operas with comic scenes, in which, among other things, Galilei's newest invention, the telescope, was ridiculed.

1630    After the death of Vincenzo II, a conflict concerning the succession and thus also the possession of the dukedom of

[29] Letter of 4 Feb. 1628 (*Lettere*, p. 304).

Mantua and Monferrato broke out. As a result, Austrian troops conquered Mantua after a short seige and plundered it for three days. Not even the ducal palace was spared; all the paintings that Vincenzo II had not already sold were destroyed, as were the library and archives. Presumably the loss of all of Monteverdi's works which were written for Mantua but did not appear in print may be attributed to this sack of Mantua.

The Mantuan war of succession also had a terrible consequence for Venice. Venice had entered an alliance with France, Mantua, and the papal territory in 1629 which resulted not only in military and diplomatic defeats for the city-state, but also in something worse: on 8 June the ambassador of the duke of Mantua to the emperor came to Venice and brought with him the plague. Although the authorities, experienced in contending with epidemics, did everything to limit the damage of the plague, it raged for more than a year and took a third of the population. In November alone more than 14,000 people died.

Monteverdi set Giulio Strozzi's 'Anatopismo', *Proserpina rapita*, which was performed with great visual and musical splendour for the wedding festivities of Giustiniana Mocenigo and Lorenzo Giustiniani.

Death of Johannes Kepler.

1631   The plague abated a bit in January so that the republic began to think of carrying out its solemn vow to build a church for the Holy Virgin; the doge was to visit it each year on the anniversary of the end of the plague. In March, however, with hot and humid south winds, the plague flared up again, and a few months later another prominent Mantuan fell victim to it: the Marquis Alessandro Striggio, Monteverdi's friend and librettist. Mantua, besieged by imperial troops, had sent him as an ambassador to ask for help from the republic. The epidemic's strength, however, was finally on the wane. In July the republic prepared a ceremonial public reception for a legate of the Swedish king. In October the senate decided to open the depopulated city to immigrants, particularly those from north Italy. A month later the senate even opened the guilds for three years to foreign immigrants. On 28 November the end of the plague was officially commemorated with a ceremonial procession of the Signoria to the site where later the promised church was to be built. All of the large churches held services of thanksgiving. Monteverdi wrote a mass for the service in S. Marco, which took place before a procession.

1632  The events of the previous years had brought to a head Monteverdi's decision to join the clergy. He appeared for the first time as *reverendo* Signor Monteverdi in the print of the *Scherzi musicali* collected and published by Bartolomeo Magni.

King Gustav Adolf of Sweden died in the battle of Lützen. He was succeeded to the throne by his daughter Christine.

Birth of Jean-Baptiste Lully (actually Giovanni Battista Lulli).

Giulio Rospigliosi's *Il S. Alessio*, with music by Stefano Landi, was performed in the Teatro Barberini in Rome.

Galilei's *Dialogo sopra i due massimi sistemi del mondo* was published (a dialogue on the advantages of the Copernican world view over that of Ptolemy).

1633  Monteverdi once again took up the idea of publishing a book on the *seconda pratica*.

Death of Jacopo Peri.

Galilei's *Dialogo* was put on the list of books prohibited by the church (until 1822).

1634  Wallenstein was killed.

1637  At the instigation of the Trons, a Venetian patrician family, the first public opera theatre in history, S. Cassiano, was inaugurated in Venice on 6 March with a performance of the opera *L'Andromeda*. It was well-known outside artists who brought opera to Venice: Benedetto Ferrari, composer and poet, who wrote the libretto of *L'Andromeda*, and Francesco Manelli, a pupil of Stefano Landi, who provided the music. Other Roman singers came with Manelli and his wife, the singer Maddalena Manelli, to north Italy; they performed the first operas there with colleagues from Venice, among them Francesco Monteverdi.

After the death of his father, Ferdinand II, Ferdinand III became the Holy Roman Emperor.

1638  The eighth book of madrigals, entitled *Madrigali guerrieri et amorosi* was published. In addition to solo and polyphonic compositions, it also contained several works *in genere rappresentativo*—such as *Il ballo delle ingrate*, which had been

performed at the wedding festivities for Francesco Gonzaga
and Margherita of Savoy, or the *Combattimento di Tancredi e
Clorinda* of 1624—some of which were several decades old.
The dedication to Emperor Ferdinand III, Eleonora Gongzaga's
stepson, gives an insight into the unhappy circumstances
surrounding this publication, which had actually been intended
for Ferdinand's father:

I lay these my musical compositions at Your Majesty's feet, as a
tutelary god of virtue. Ferdinand, the great father of Your Majesty,
who in his innate goodness deigned to accept and honour them in
manuscript, had given me authorative permission to have them
published. And now I publish them boldly, dedicating them to the
revered name of Your Majesty, heir not only to the throne and
empire, but also to his valour and his benevolence.

1639    On 20 January the Teatro SS. Giovanni e Paulo was opened
        under the patronage of the Grimani family.

        Monteverdi's sixth book of madrigals was published by Pierre
        Phalèse in Antwerp.

        During the carnival season Giulio Rospigliosi's opera, *Chi
        soffre, speri*, with music by Marco Marazzoli and Virgilio
        Mazzochi, was performed in the Palazzo Barberini in Rome. It
        is continuous musical comedy, from beginning to end, the first
        such piece. Many masque figures from the *commedia dell'arte*
        appear in it, among others, speaking at times in a Bergamesque
        or Neapolitan dialect.

        A second opera, *La Galatea*, with text and music by Loreto
        Vittori, was dedicated to the Barberini family during this year.

        Monteverdi had a new edition of the *Arianna* libretto published.

1640    After a break of thirty years, Monteverdi once again published
        a collection of sacred music: the *Selva morale e spirituale*, a
        selection of Latin and Italian compositions, among them a
        sacred *contrafactum* of the famous 'Lamento d'Arianna'. He
        dedicated the edition to Eleonora Gonzaga, the widow of
        Emperor Ferdinand II.

        *L'Arianna* was performed in the Teatro S. Moisé, which had
        recently been opened.

1641    Before Monteverdi's opera *Il ritorno d'Ulisse in patria* was
        performed in the Teatro S. Cassiano in the autumn, the work
        was played by Francesco Manelli's troupe in Bologna. In the
        same year the Teatro SS. Giovanni e Paolo performed

Monteverdi's opera *Le nozze d'Enea con Lavinia*. As with *Il ritorno d'Ulisse*, the text is by Giacomo Badoaro.

Francesco Cavalli's *La Didone* was played during the carnival season at S. Cassiano.

Giulio Rospigliosi's *Il palazzo incantato*, with music by Luigi Rossi, was staged in the Teatro Barberini in Rome.

Monteverdi composed a ballet to the text *La vittoria di amore*, which was performed at the court of Piacenza.

1643　*L'incoronazione di Poppea*, Monteverdi's last opera, on a text by Francesco Busenello, was performed in the Teatro SS. Giovanni e Paolo.

In September Monteverdi went to Cremona and Mantua, where he tried one last time to get due payment of the pension which Vincenzo had bestowed upon him in 1609, this time from the reigning Duke Carlo I Gonzaga di Nevers and his wife Maria Gonzaga. He returned to Venice weakened by the trip. He died there of a 'malign fever' on 29 November at the age of 76. The solemn funeral service in S. Marco was attended by the city's leaders, princes, and a large number of common people. The music was directed by Giovanni Rovetta, Monteverdi's successor as *maestro di cappella*. Another burial service was organized by Monteverdi's old friend, Giovanni Battista Marinoni, in the church of Sta Maria Gloriosa dei Frari, where Titian is also buried. Monteverdi was interred in this church's S. Ambrogio chapel.

Deaths of Galileo Galilei and of Marco da Gagliano.

Louis XIV became King of France.

Birth of Isaac Newton.

1644　Marinoni published a collection of texts that were written on the occasion of Monteverdi's burial: *Fiori poetici*. The engraved title-page of this anthology contains the only portrait of the composer in his old age which is not anonymous. It is a copperplate copy of the portrait attributed to Bernardo Strozzi, which was reversed during the printing process. It was by means of this copy that the subject of the oil painting could be identified.

Monteverdi's fourth book of madrigals was published for the second time by Pierre Phalèse in Antwerp.

Death of Pope Urban VIII.

1646 *L'incoronazione di Poppea* was performed in the Teatro Grimani under the direction of Cavalli.

1650 The posthumous collection, *Messa a quattro voci e Salmi,* was published by Alessandro Vincenti.

1651 *Madrigali e canzonette a due e tre voci . . . Libro nono* was published by Alessandro Vincenti.

# I

# A CHANGE IN STYLE

Monteverdi lived during a period of pervasive upheaval which violently shook the very foundations of the world in all realms of life. It was a time of radical change: the religious and political developments of the previous decades began to affect the intellectual and cultural life, and the political landscape of war-scarred Europe both caused and resulted from the destruction of the individual's sense of emotional security. Certainly, the times at the turn of the sixteenth to the seventeenth century were no worse than any others; wars, recessions, famine, epidemics, and religious controversies were not inventions of the sixteenth century. Even so, the permanent political insecurity of the sixteenth century had succeeded in shaking the self-confidence of Renaissance man to such a degree that the awareness of an inescapable crisis, of the absurdity of all human endeavour could effectively replace his faith in the creative forces of man as a rational creature. Throughout the entire sixteenth century Italy was the exercise-ground and booty of foreign powers, it was oppressed, ruled, and plundered by Spain, France, and the German Empire. Even in 1561 the consequences of such invasions were recognized by Guicciardini in his history of Italy:

Charles VIII [of France] bore the seed of innumerable calamities with him, of the most horrible vicissitudes, and of changes in practically everything. Not only did the changes in the borders, the upheavals in the states, the devastation of villages, the massacres in the cities, the extremely cruel murders begin with his first campaign [1494], but also the new clothing, the new customs, the new bloody method of waging war, the illnesses that were unknown up until this time.[1]

The Peace of Cateau-Cambrésis of 1559, which placed most Italian states under foreign rule, temporarily mitigated the situation. Monteverdi himself, however, was to experience on numerous occasions, the last time at the terrible sack of Mantua, that Guicciardini was also only too right about the future.

[1] Francesco Guicciardini, *Storia d'Italia*, ed. C. Panigada (Bari, 1929), i. 9, 67.

The political crisis was accompanied by an economic one, which culminated in the first half of the seventeenth century. The sense of confidence in religion was also disturbed. The Reformation had split Central-European Christians into Catholics and Protestants and religious denomination became a favourite pretext in power politics; the Catholic Church retaliated with the Counter-Reformation, relentlessly insinuating itself into the conscience and minds of its believers. Finally, man's last secure foothold was eroded away by the natural sciences, which just at that time began to change from speculative into experimental ones, and brought to light results that in the end robbed the individual of his fixed place in the cosmos. The newly-discovered microscope showed man things and structures that he had never even imagined before. With the telescope, developed roughly simultaneously, it was possible to prove claims that the universe was infinite; just a few years previously the Dominican monk, Giordano Bruno, had been burned publicly as a heretic for this belief. It was perceived that things did not have a fixed place in a well-disposed cosmic order, but rather that no limits were placed on largeness and smallness, that the world was immeasurable, and that the earth was not its centre, but only one of countless planets in the universe.

Man had to react to these shocks in some way. In all of this political and economic turmoil there had still been oases of peace in which the pursuit of the arts and sciences could be carried out with the harmony and balance of Renaissance man, born of rational pride and wise self-restraint. With the new scientific knowledge, however, the ordering framework, the system of convictions, also collapsed. Pessimism, insecurity, tension, inner strife, opposition to rationalism, rejection of commonly accepted limitations, sudden changes of mood, and polarization of feelings were the result—literally eccentricity; the atmosphere bore greater resemblance to a dance on a volcano than to the quiet rocking of the ship of life. Falling into one extreme only provoked another: the recognition of the absurdity of all earthly endeavour encouraged vigorous enjoyment of the here and now; the impossibility of finding oneself in the confusion of the world stimulated a dramatic portrayal of one's self; the loss of norms awakened pleasure in effulgent artistry.

This change in attitude towards life is most tangibly apparent in the graphic arts, where man portrays himself, not as he is, but as he sees himself. Heinrich Wölfflin, one of the first to study the history of baroque art, summarized the differences between Renaissance and baroque art in five antithetic pairs, whose connection with the mood of the times is evident: linear–planet, surface–depth, closed form–open form, unity–variety, clarity–obscurity. These concepts, of course, cannot be directly transferred to other arts. In literature, however, similar developments may be distinguished which, at the very least, have the same roots, although they lie outside the visually oriented interpretation. The preference for exaggerated metaphors is completely in line with the gushing opulence of baroque décor. Where Petrarch only allows a brook to swell with the tears of love, Marino's tears cause the Tiber to overflow and flood the seven hills of Rome: the same bulkiness, the same impetuous movement as in baroque painting. The stylistic means were different though, more artificial. If the essence of Renaissance poetics was *imitatio*, the imitation of classical models, which could originate from both ancient and Italian literature, baroque poetics was based on *meraviglia*, wonder, astonishment, amazement: mystification instead of comprehensibility, surprise instead of satisfaction, effect instead of depth of feeling.

It is likewise obvious that Wölfflin's concepts cannot be directly applied to music, since every proof of simultaneity is fraught with great difficulty. We are also not concerned with a comprehensive classification of eras in the sense of determining exact time periods, an analysis which is particularly difficult at points of change. In spite of this, it is worth investigating whether developments similar to those in literature and the graphic arts show themselves in music, phenomena which are not directly connected with those in other arts, but like them are based on a *tertium comparationis*—the emotional attitude towards life at the time. Friedrich Blume, in his attempt to describe the general characteristics of baroque music, perceived one quality in the epoch as a whole which is also characteristic for its music: a unity that consists of nothing but contradictions. Its most prominent feature is its tendency towards antitheses: towards extremes as far as the instrumentation, the duration, and expression are concerned; towards structural contrasts, which exhibit themselves in metric changes and the alternation between recitative and aria, between tutti and solo; a division between an old and a new style, between *stile antico* and *stile moderno*, between *prima* and *seconda pratica*; idiomatic language dependent on the scoring—in other words, for example, a specific style of writing for vocal and for instrumental parts.

If one were to apply Blume's definitions also to poetry, then one could certainly find more similarities than with the graphic arts. This is due partly to their intrinsic nature, for, in their conjunction in vocal music, poetry and music must continually rub against, take stock of one another. None the less, the importance of such similarities should not be overestimated. If, on the one hand, in the Renaissance, we observe in both arts the desire for balanced harmony, for unity, and, on the other hand, in the baroque, we perceive the propensity for antithesis, for contrast, for the surprising turn of phrase, this cannot be attributed to anything more than the flux of the general spirit of the time, the outgrowth of a common emotional sustenance. Nor can it be seen as anything less than this; Monteverdi, who was about the same age as Kepler and Galilei, and who had studied Plato and alchemy, who began with madrigals and ended with vocal *concerti*, who renounced the world in his old age and yet wrote a highly erotic opera, captured much of what went on about him in his music and in his choice of subject-matter. Thus in comparing two madrigals about nature in this connection, 'Ecco mormorar l'onde' from Book II (1590) and 'Hor che il ciel e la terra' from Book VIII (1638), as examples for two epochs, it is inappropriate to make generalizations about Renaissance and baroque music. They are only meant to show how a different attitude towards life, a different basic mood, can exhibit itself in one and the same genre at a time when other, much more essential things changed than the musical style alone.

The madrigal 'Ecco mormorar l'onde' is a masterpiece of the lyrical interweaving of sensual feeling, and of descriptions of nature and of the soul, so characteristic of the late sixteenth-century madrigal and particularly of Tasso. It comes from a group of poems for Laura Peperara, a rich merchant's daughter, with whom Tasso had fallen in love in Mantua.

> Ecco mormorar l'onde
> e tremolar le fronde
> a l'aura mattutina e gli arboscelli
> e sovra i verdi rami i vaghi augelli
> cantar soavemente
> e rider l'oriente:
> Ecco già l'alba appare
> e si specchia nel mare,
> e rasserena il cielo
> e le campagne imperla il dolce gelo,
> e gli alti monti indora.
> O bella e vaga Aurora,
> l'aura è tua messaggera, e tu de l'aura
> ch'ogni arso cor ristaura.

> Hark, how the waves murmur
> and the leaves tremble
> and the bushes in the morning air,
> and on green branches the lovely birds
> sing suavely and the East laughs:
> Lo, already the morning light is rising
> and is reflected in the sea
> and lights up the heavens,

and the sweet morning dew bespangles the meadows
and gilds the high mountains.
O beautiful and lovely Aurora,
the morning breeze is your messenger and you hers
which refreshes every burnt heart.

Tasso rejects all wit, all poetic subtlety. The madrigal is of almost disconcerting simplicity; its ingenious architecture is revealed only at a second glance. What at first appears to be a succession of short-winded phrases is in reality a gradual intensification leading towards the evocation of Aurora, who at the apparent high point remains enveloped by paronomasias rich with connotation. First comes a syntactically indifferent section, in which four infinitive verb forms— 'mormorar', 'tremolar', 'cantar', 'rider'—only imperceptibly refer to the introductory 'Ecco'; this is followed by a second, in which the dawn takes on shape and the description makes use of finite verb forms—'appare', 'indora'—and finally by a third which invokes Aurora and at the same time embeds her in the sound of Laura's name (Laura = l'aura). This poem lives from the sound of the language, the buoyant content, and the syntactical balance. The metrically loose generic form of the madrigal is restrained by the strict parallelism of the sentence structure, which on the other hand avoids all symmetry, for example placing the verb sometimes in front of the subject, sometimes after it. The description of nature is offered for its own sake but then reveals itself in the last line as the means to an end. The poetic ego, although just as present as the addressee, Laura Peperara, is totally integrated in a timeless occurrence of nature, with no direct reference to a specific situation. In this rapture the madrigal has something utterly stable; nothing and no one is there that could disturb the peace of the breaking dawn, that could destroy the equilibrium of its content or its structure, in which the poetic elements support one another.

It is manifest that Tasso's madrigals, in particular the poems for Laura, were of great musicality. 'Ecco mormorar l'onde' not only assembles an entire arsenal of words which just cry out for a musical setting, such as 'mormorar', 'tremolar', 'cantar', and 'rider', but is in itself a musical painting, with its play on the words *Laura—l'aura— Aurora*, with the way the same vowel is emphasized within a single verse—m*o*rm*o*rar l'*o*nde, già l'*a*lba *a*ppare'—etc. All who have praised Monteverdi's setting—and that includes everybody who has studied the work—have called special attention to its pictorial writing: the quiet, almost soundless murmur of the waves at the beginning; the slow awakening of nature, with the gradual increase in the number of voices, in the tempo of the declamation, and in the melodic range; the ethereal weightless passages in thirds, with which Monteverdi surrounds the 'airy' references; the singing of the birds; the dawn. All of this certainly contributes greatly to the charm of the composition, a musical description of nature which does justice to the tonal magic of the text. The secret of this madrigal, however, is not revealed by such observations. Descriptions of nature were among the most popular madrigalistic devices of the late sixteenth-century. Monteverdi himself opened his second book of madrigals with 'Non si levava ancor l'alba novella', which has a similar, equally subtle image of the breaking day (Ex. 1.1).

Ex. 1.1.    'Non si levava ancor l'alba novella'
            (The new day has not yet dawned)

In 'Ecco mormorar l'onde' the word-painting madrigalisms, the circular quaver movement at 'tremolar', the coloratura at 'cantar', the ascending motion at 'rasserena', the octave leap at 'alti monti', are all based on an old, widespread madrigal tradition. The effect, the marvel, of this composition, however, lies in the unique balance which exists between all of the individual components of the piece. Stability and inner peace are guaranteed to begin with by the imperturbable adherence to the main key of F, with only one surreptitious cadence on C (bars 64–5). Its perseverance is, nevertheless, nothing robust; even the poetic ambiguity of the word *l'aura* can be integrated in a similarly vague manner—with parallel progressions full of hidden fifths, in which the same chords are repeatedly juxtaposed. The composition maintains a balance between the polyphonic structure and the themes which are perceived as being monodic, between a prevailing general mood and madrigalistic word-painting, between the motet principle of giving each line a new *soggetto* and motivic interrelationships. Describing the first line, with its almost monotonous recitation, as a precursor of the solo song is just as correct as the observation that it constitutes a regularly executed polyphonic section. The above-mentioned madrigalisms are certainly present, but are not so excessively emphasized that the picture of the awakening of nature as a whole disintegrates into details. This is in part because they are embedded in a motivic context which conceives of them, above and beyond the mere *imitare le parole*, as purely musical material. Thus 'rider l'oriente' and 'rasserena il cielo' are melodically almost the same, 'Ecco già l'alba appare' and 'O bella e vaga Aurora' are rhythmically the same and melodically similar, and even the opening line with its strongly recitative nature, which so sensitively mirrors the rhythm of the spoken language, has its rhythmic counterpart in 'e si specchia nel mare'. As they do in Tasso's poem, the constituent elements provide support for one another in the music: an arch whose keystone is the text. The inner balance and the lively composure of this madrigal represent the culmination of the Renaissance spirit, the outcome of an emotional attitude towards life which derives its strength from the consciousness of having a fixed place in the universe, and which manifests itself in harmonious equilibrium and measured serenity.

The idea that a composition on a Petrarch sonnet should reflect the baroque spirit at first seems paradoxical; this fourteenth-century poet is considered to be one of the founders of the Renaissance and his works were set innumerable times, particularly by madrigal composers of the sixteenth century. This idea, however, is documented, not only in Monteverdi's music, but also by the text itself and by the special recognition Monteverdi granted this poet in his choice of texts. As opposed to most of his contemporaries, he set only a few of Petrarch's texts, a total of six, of which the first two appeared in his sixth book of madrigals (1614) and the others in his last two publications, the eighth book of madrigals (1638) and the *Selva morale e spirituale* (1641). Both of the texts which open the *Selva morale* would be sufficient in themselves as proof of Petrarch's kinship to the new spirit, for which Monteverdi's personal fate would seem to serve as a parable: an adaptation of the 'Trionfo della morte', which begins with 'O ciechi, ciechi, il tanto affaticar che giova' (O you blind ones, what use are all of your efforts) and ends with 'Miser chi speme in cosa mortal pone' (Miserable is he who places hope in mortal things); and the opening sonnet of the *Canzoniere*, which bewails the 'giovenil errore', the juvenile error of putting too much value in feelings of a worldly nature. However one does not even need texts of such confessional content to show the change in attitude. Sonnet CXXIX of the *Canzoniere* demonstrates that an apparently peaceful description of nature can also hide baroque traits full of suspense.

> Hor che il ciel e la terra e 'l vento tace,
> e le fere e gli augelli il sonno affrena,
> notte il carro stellato in giro mena
> e nel suo letto il mar senz'onda giace;

veglio, penso, ardo, piango, e chi mi sface
sempre m'è innanzi per mia dolce pena;
guerra è il mio stato, d'ira e di duol piena,
e sol di lei pensando ho qualche pace.

Così sol d'una chiara fonte viva
move 'l dolce e l'amaro ond'io mi pasco;
una man sola mi risana e punge;

e perchè 'l mio martir non giunga a riva
mille volte il dì moro e mille nasco:
tanto da la salute mia son lunge!

Now that the heavens, the earth, and the wind are silent
and sleep has overcome the animals and the birds,
[now that the] night guides the starry wagon in its course
and the sea rests in its bed without waves;

I am awake, think, burn, weep, and she who consumes me
is always before me to my sweet pain;
war is my state of mind, full of rage and grief,
and only when thinking of her do I find peace.

Thus only from a clear, lively fountain
do the sweetness and bitterness flow, on which I nourish myself;
one hand alone heals and punishes me.

And so that my torment never ends,
I die a thousand times a day and am born a thousand times:
I am still that far away from my salvation!

As opposed to Tasso's madrigal, which from its first to its last line depicts a natural event, Petrarch's description of nature constitutes only the first stanza of the whole. From the outset it serves a different purpose, that of a contrast to the psychic state of the poetic ego, an abrupt change of mood between the first and second quatrain. Whereas Tasso's poetic ego peeps out of the last line, incognito as it were, Petrarch's assumes the stage at the very beginning of the second quatrain and dominates the poem from then on. The description of nature does not appear here for its own sake; it is the curtain-raiser, it sets the scene for the ensuing 'drama of the soul'. There is a certain theatricality in the opening two quatrains, something similar to the confrontation between stage sets and the appearance of the actors or between the décor and scenic gestures, a theatricality that is also evident in the syntax: the entire first quatrain is a subordinate clause dependent on 'Hor che'; the principal clause opens with the sudden outburst of the poetic ego, the climax of which, 'veglio, penso, ardo, piango', displays great rapidity in the declamation.

The impression of contrast, which at the beginning of the sonnet results from the juxtaposition of quiet and agitated images, becomes, in the second section, a predominant element of the mental state, whose description is characterized by antithetical pairs of words (*dolce/amaro, risana/punge, moro/nasco*). They not only serve as stylistic devices but depict an inner conflict, emotional polarity, instability, a broken spirit, pessimism. Nothing makes the difference in mood of the two poems clearer than a comparison of their respective last lines: in Tasso gentle faith, in Petrarch restless pain. In this last tercet in particular, with its unsettled nature, its tension between life and death, Petrarch wears a baroque mask; it embodies the mood in which the seventeenth century consumed itself. Petrarch was, of course, by no means a baroque poet, but his poetry is so multifaceted in regard to form and content that each age could find its own in it.

What primarily inspired Monteverdi about this poem was the antithetical beginning, the opposition of quiescent nature and a highly charged soul. He divided the sonnet into two sections, the second of which, the two tercets, is composed much more conventionally, in a more balanced way, based on traditional madrigalisms. The first section, however, makes the differences from the late sixteenth-century madrigal more than obvious, the change in the attitude towards descriptions of nature and of the heart. One is first struck by the outward aspects in the compositional technique. Independently from the text, they reveal the radical change in the method of presentation: 'Ecco mormorar l'onde' is characterized by five-part, polyphonic, *a cappella* writing; in 'Hor che il ciel e la terra', the eight-part vocal and instrumental writing is homophonic throughout long sections and accompanied by a thorough-bass. The basso continuo allows for solo passages or ones with fewer parts within the composition; the string writing has become sufficiently independent so that it no longer serves only as additional colour for the voice parts, but also as an autonomous, instrumentally conceived, non-vocal accompaniment. Far more important than these outward aspects, however, is the formal conception of the first quatrain. It opens with a smooth carpet of chords without any great harmonic changes, a monotonous murmur, almost like psalmody, just as motionless as the first line of 'Ecco mormorar l'onde'. Nevertheless a different kind of stillness is evoked here, not a contented quiescence, but one which has to lead to an outburst. The polyphonic writing of 'Ecco mormorar l'onde' could continue for a long time in the same manner without losing its sense of balance, without becoming boring. The uneventful melody of the first stanza of 'Hor che il ciel e la terra' seems balanced for only a few bars at most before our curiousity about what is to follow gains the upper hand; the stillness of quiescent nature becomes the highly charged calm before a storm. The outburst therefore stands in great contrast to the opening murmur, but is not unexpected, although the musical gestures of the short, breathlessly uttered sentence-fragments deviates greatly from that of the first section. The desperation of the poetic ego, which expresses itself with 'veglio, penso, ardo, piango', overshadows the next line as well, which is conceived as a tenor duet, with agitated interjections; the literary contrast between the scenery and the drama is thus skilfully caught. The extreme opposites in the poetic concept also dominate the setting of the last two lines of the first section. Here the violins are distinguished from the vocal writing, simple homophonic music associated with the word 'pace', by means of excited dotted and semiquaver figures which depict the emotional tumult of the 'guerra è il mio stato' (the only justification for including this composition in the *madrigali guerrieri*). In the already antiquated genre of the madrigal Monteverdi assembled everything which characterized the new attitude towards life in the epoch we call the Baroque: contrast, tension, instability, theatricality—the turmoil of feelings that was a consequence of the wavering image of the world, of the emotional insecurity of the time.

## *SECONDA PRATICA* OR THE PREDOMINANCE OF TEXT OVER MUSIC

Seeing one madrigal as an example for an entire age, branding another as typical for another—speculations of this sort can only be made from a historical distance. For the people of the time, questions about compositional techniques and stylistic changes had a different significance. A controversy sprang up shortly after the middle of the sixteenth century about the treatment of dissonances and the changing of modes. Monteverdi was drawn into it as a result of the attacks made by Giovanni Maria Artusi, a Bolognese clergyman. It was the culmination of a sense of unease concerning the neglect of the madrigal's text, and manifested itself, on the one hand, in the dissolution of structural elements of the polyphonic style and, on the other, in the effort to revive ancient music. Contrapuntal writing was regarded increasingly as the enemy of words: the imitative style obstructed the comprehension of the text, the expressive means allowed in strict counterpoint no longer seemed sufficient for the interpretation of the textual content, and the nature of the polyphonic *soggetti* appeared to take too little account of the textual form. In the preface to *Le nuove musiche*, Caccini could only express his contempt for the polyphonic madrigal with the words 'laceration of poetry' (*laceramento della poesia*).[2] Monteverdi considered it an outright presumption to judge his compositions solely by the rules of strict counterpoint, 'as if they were written by a child who is beginning to learn the note-against-note style'.[3] The deliberate transgression of musical rules for the benefit of textual interpretation was soon held to be preferable. Pietro Della Valle, a highly educated, widely travelled diplomat, man of letters, and lover of music, published *Della musica dell'età nostra che non è punto inferiore, anzi è migliore di quella dell'età passata* (About the Music of our Time, which is not Worse but Better than that of Previous Ages) in 1640. He wrote with disgust of composers who had gone so far in the neglect of the text that one 'knew of some of them, even among the best, who first wrote their compositions in simple notes, to which, after they were finished, the words which best fitted were added'.[4]

The underlying reasons for these trends are as manifold as the situations in which the changes in the practice were made manifest. It is necessary to distinguish between them clearly if one wants to understand what Monteverdi was concerned with in his definition of the *seconda pratica*, which still haunts musicological literature as the solo song's manifesto. The cutting polemics on both sides represented not just the fight between traditionalists and modernists which may be found in any time period; it is also the dispute between theorists and practical musicians, between musicians and literary men, between the demands of scholarship and of entertainment. Although Monteverdi was not involved in the debates about ancient music nor in the development of monody, it was he who was drawn against his will into the battle between the conservatives and the progressives; it was thus largely out of a sense of self defence that he formulated his famous thesis about the predominance of the text over the musical setting.

Two lines of development, independent from one another, led to the radical change which took place around 1600. In the 1570s a group of patricians, scholars, musicians, literary men, and philosophers was formed which met regularly in the house of Count Bardi and discussed the most diverse problems in an entertaining and learned manner. The count was particularly interested in antiquity as well as in music, and he also composed; thus it was only natural that ancient music was discussed at these meetings. One of the members of the group—which musicologists later called the 'Florentine Camerata'—was Vincenzo Galilei, the father of Galileo Galilei. Based on his correspondence with Girolamo Mei, a Florentine philologist living in Rome, he wrote the

---

[2] Angelo Solerti, *Le origini del melodramma* (Turin, 1903; repr. Hildesheim, 1969), 56.
[3] Letter of 22 Oct. 1633 (*Lettere*, p. 321).
[4] Solerti, *Origini*, p. 152.

*Dialogo della musica antica, et della moderna*, published in 1581. In it the primary requirements for the development of the solo song are formulated: the return to ancient monody and the union of a recitation of the text with its affective content, thereby creating a new form of song. Galilei demonstrated his theory on two texts, one from the Bible, the other from Dante; the compositions are lost, and it is not certain to what degree the practical musician in Galilei was able to meet the demands of the theorist. Two other musicians, however, seized upon the new possibilities of passing over the dictates of strict counterpoint and of singing a text over a long sustained single chord in accordance with its formal structure and its affective content: Jacopo Peri and Giulio Caccini. Both of them justified dissonances by the recitation of the text:

I caused the bass to move in the tempo of those [changes in the text's contents], sometimes more, sometimes less, in accordance with the affects, and I held it steadily throughout the false and true intervals.[5]

I had the idea of introducing a kind of music in which one could speak musically as it were [*in armonia favellare*], employing in it . . . a certain noble nonchalance [*nobile sprezzatura*] of song, sometimes passing through some forbidden intervals while holding, however, the bass note.[6]

The rules of counterpoint, seemingly of their own accord, lost their significance for this new soloistic style of writing, for this new kind of musical recitation: when the polyphonic style of writing was negated, it was also no longer necessary to observe its rules. The solo song was therefore never an object of criticism for the advocates of strict counterpoint. The development of monody based on ancient models—or on what the members of the Bardi circle understood them to be—was in itself more of a polemic than something that produced a polemic from the contrapuntalists' side.

For Monteverdi, whose work stands at the end of the other line of development, dissonance had another meaning. Around the middle of the century, the madrigal, in the hands of Cipriano de Rore, began to absorb chromaticisms which were able to render the text's content more sensitively. (This was independent from the academic pastimes of the Camerata, which was both geographically and sociologically isolated.) Although usually only the simple alteration of individual notes was involved, this procedure paved the way for what would henceforth become the main characteristic of the madrigal: an increase in the intensity of the power of the musical expression through the use of chromaticisms in the graphic presentation of descriptions of nature

[5] J. Peri, *L'Euridice* (1600), in Solerti, *Origini*, p. 46.
[6] G. Caccini, *Le nuove musiche* (1601), in Solerti, *Origini*, p. 51.

(*imitazione della natura*) and in the interpretation of individual words (*imitare le parole*). It was a question not of a musical imitation of a spoken recitation here, in which some dissonances were tolerated for the sake of the comprehension of the text and the unity of affect of the composition, but rather—quite to the contrary—of a delineation of the affective content by means of these dissonant progressions. They had already been a standard method of textual interpretation even within strict counterpoint when the stick-in-the-muds threw themselves on Monteverdi's madrigals and used them as a target for their critique.

In the year 1600 the above-mentioned Artusi published his treatise, *L'Artusi Ovvero delle Imperfettioni della moderna musica*. In its second part, even if Monteverdi's name is never mentioned, several of his madrigals are taken as an excuse for a sharp polemic against the new way of treating dissonances. Monteverdi did indeed differ from his predecessors in that he did not always prepare his dissonances as passing notes or suspensions, as would be permitted in strict counterpoint, but allowed them to enter freely. Artusi was a respected musician, a student of Zarlino's, whose *Istitutioni harmoniche* (1558) constituted the main theoretical work about counterpoint in the century. Artusi himself was the author of an important treatise on counterpoint and in addition a conservative critic of all of the musical trends of his time. The controversy with Monteverdi is only one of many, but it is the most significant one for the present-day spectator as it is exemplary of the generation gap in regard to the change of style around 1600. In addition, the record of this dispute shows the extent of the aversion Monteverdi had towards getting involved in the argument at all—he placed far greater value in real music than in abstract intellectual constructs. He did not react at all to the first attack in the treatise of 1600. Rather, when he had his fourth book of madrigals published in 1603, it included one of the madrigals criticized by Artusi. In the same year Artusi published a continuation of his critique of Monteverdi, again without mentioning his name. Only then did the latter react: two years later, in the declaratory preface to the fifth book of madrigals, he announced a forthcoming answer in the form of a book that was to deal with the 'perfection of modern music'. But this short preface (see above, Chronology 1605) was the only thing which Monteverdi himself contributed to the dispute. Artusi then struck back under a pseudonym. The reply thereto came from Monteverdi's brother Giulio Cesare, who delivered a detailed interpretation of the terse preface of 1605 in the foreword to the *Scherzi musicali* (1607). This is the manifesto of the *seconda pratica*, in which reference is once again made to the previously announced treatise. Artusi had the last word, however: in a second *Discorso*, appearing a year after the *Scherzi musicali*, he found fault with the rhythm of some of the *scherzi*—this time using the full name of their composer.

The book about the *seconda pratica* was never written. When Monteverdi last spoke of it in 1633 it had become superfluous. The dispute had long been decided by musical practice, the development had long passed it by, and Artusi himself had acquiesced and was even one of Monteverdi's admirers.

'Imperfection' on the one hand, 'perfection' on the other—what were the ideas that lay behind Artusi's and Monteverdi's disagreement? On the surface, the dispute was about two things: the treatment of dissonances and changing the mode. Artusi accused Monteverdi of violating the rules of strict counterpoint: for example, he allowed the soprano to enter at a ninth to the bass, as in 'Cruda Amarilli' (Ex. 1.2*a*), and did not tie syncopated dissonances, but re-articulated

Ex. 1.2*a*.   'Cruda Amarilli'
              (Alas)

them, as in 'Anima mia perdona', *seconda parte* (Ex. 1.2*b*). The second complaint of changing the mode within a composition—as in 'O Mirtillo Mirtillo', which begins in F and ends in D—is based on the opinion, already expressed by Zarlino, that each mode has its own character. A change in mode therefore also meant a change in the affective content, which was contrary to the unity required of a composition. This requirement was by no means universal; Nicola Vicentino, another important theorist although not highly thought of

Ex. 1.2*b*. 'Anima mia, perdona'
(not your torments)

by Zarlino, had permitted a change of mode in his treatise *L'antica
musica ridotta alla moderna prattica* (1555), when the affective content
of the texts took a turn, for example, from cheerful to sad.

The real dispute, however, was about the question of how far vocal
music, with its union of words and sonorities, was allowed to lay claim
to a special status in regard to the rules of counterpoint. Monteverdi's
answer therefore does not even respond to Artusi's arguments. It is
not a defence of his style of composition at Artusi's intellectual level,
but an exposition of the principles of his own musical perception. For
him the deviations for which he was criticized were not merely
'minutiae', but were based primarily on a completely different idea of
vocal music. It is at this moment that this supposed quarrel about
trifles is revealed to be a discussion at cross-purposes. As far as Artusi
was concerned, it was not about vocal music at all; characteristic of
this is the fact that he quotes Monteverdi's examples without text. He
is solely concerned about strict contrapuntal style. According to its
rules, the cited passages really are composed 'incorrectly'. Monteverdi,
on the other hand, only wanted to see the problem of the treatment of
dissonances in relation to the setting of its text. He thereby came to
the maxim, which sounded revolutionary but which had long been
realized in practice, 'that the declamation of the text is the mistress of
the music and not its servant' (*che l'oratione sia padrona dell'armonia e
non serva*).[7]

The definition of the *seconda pratica* is not based on a compositional
principle; it is not concerned with the discussion about vocal

---

[7] In the foreword to *Scherzi musicali* (1607) (*Lettere*, p. 396).

polyphony versus monody, about several parts versus a single part. It means nothing more than a certain attitude towards the text and can be the basis for a polyphonic madrigal just as much as for an opera recitative. As authorities for the *seconda pratica*, Monteverdi mentions, among others, Cipriano de Rore, who died in 1565, his teacher Marc'Antonio Ingegneri, and the Florentine monodists, Peri and Caccini. The *seconda pratica* is not a momentous doctrine consisting of laws and rules, but a simple attempt to do complete justice to the text when composing. Monteverdi quite consciously chose the title *Pratica*: '[My brother] said 'practice' and not 'theory' because he intends to speak about the way in which one uses consonances and dissonances in composing [*nel atto prattico*]. He did not say 'Institutioni Melodiche' because he does not believe it is a topic for such a great undertaking.'[8]

Thus the controversy is finally reduced to two different points of view which do not even necessarily exclude one another: on the one hand, the esteem for musical rules, and, on the other, the respect for the text. The comprehensibility of the text and its form, two points which were just as influential in the change in musical style, were not even questioned. It is significant that in this whole dispute about the polyphonic madrigal, no mention is made of Luca Marenzio's efforts or of those of his Roman colleagues to achieve greater text comprehensibility by means of extended homophonic sections, nor of the endeavour on Monteverdi's part, as well as on that of many of his contemporaries, to achieve a text declamation that was already very close to that of a recitative. Artusi's problem was solely that of the melodic progressions and the vertical intervals resulting from them.

However pedantic Artusi's individual objections may sound, even he was moved by greater worries than forbidden dissonances. Monteverdi's style of composition shook the foundations of all traditional musical values. Ultimately the dispute about the unprepared entrance at a ninth was about nothing less than a change in the concept of art. Up until then scholars were in agreement that the intellect (*intelletto*) and not the feelings (*senso*) were the last resort when judging a work of art. Monteverdi, however, perceived the goal of music as being an appeal to the emotions of the audience, not to their understanding. In order to attain this goal, music was justified in using any means, even that of infringing on the rules. For Artusi 'art' meant artistic skill, a craft at the highest level, constrained by a theory which established its rules and thus made it teachable and learnable, debatable and controllable. 'Art' for Artusi was on the same plane as science.

[8] In the foreword to *Scherzi musicali* (1607) (*Lettere*, p. 399).

For Monteverdi, however, the true art (he spoke again and again of the *verità dell'arte*) lay in practice and not in theory. It began for him at the point where it stopped for Artusi. For Monteverdi the ingenious idea, the non-verifiable, the non-teachable, the step past the boundaries of instruction, was the essence of art—based, however on an otherwise compulsory codex of rules, so that a transgression against it could be recognized as such. For Monteverdi 'art' was a private artistic expression, wherein rational criteria such as 'right' or 'wrong' lost ground in relation to emotional ones such as 'moving' or 'stirring'. A perfect approach to a work for Artusi lay in being able to understand it, if one were only at the same intellectual level as the composer; for Monteverdi, on the other hand, a work of art distinguished itself by the very fact that it could not be completely understood, that it possessed something disconcerting, mysterious, not entirely explicable. It is significant that neither Monteverdi nor the Florentines replaced the old rules with new ones, but only with wilful transgressions against them. Within the idea of the *seconda pratica* are found the origins of the later aesthetic theory of genius in which the genius breaks the shackles of tradition and creates his own rules.

It is curious, as well as typical for the time, that the same ancient philosopher is used as a point of reference by both sides. Monteverdi cites him directly, Artusi indirectly through the definitions of his teacher Zarlino. The source was Plato and his discussion of music in the third chapter of *The Republic*. Its central sentence is quoted in the following manner by Giulio Cesare Monteverdi: 'Melodiam ex tribus constare, oratione, harmonia, rithmo'. It is from this order and from a further passage which Zarlino prudently passed over in silence—'Rithmus et Harmonia orationem sequitur non ipsa oratio Rithmum et Harmoniam sequitur'—that Guilio Cesare derives his seemingly revolutionary sentence about the predominance of the text over the music. Zarlino, however, proceeds from 'harmonia', from the simultaneous sounding of two or more voices: 'From all these three things together, i.e. the proper harmony [*harmonia propria*], the rhythm, and the text [*oratione*], the melody, as Plato says, is born [*nasce*].'[9] Plato, however, is concerned not with the origins of melody, but with its definition; this implies the opposite and would therefore seem more to justify Monteverdi's interpretation. Further he does not even speak of melody, and *oratio* is a restrictive translation of an ambiguous Greek word: *melodia* is *melos* in the Greek original, *oratio* is *logos*, a word which may be translated cautiously but insufficiently as

[9] Gioseffo Zarlino, *Istitutioni harmoniche* (Venice, 1573; repr. Ridgewood, NJ, 1966), vol ii, chapter 12, p. 95.

'text'. For *oratio*, as well as the Greek *logos*, can mean two things: on the one hand the words as such, and, on the other, the delivery of the words. Vincenzo Galilei in his work had already pointed out the importance of the delivery: 'Before the ancient musician sang any poem, he most diligently examined the quality of the speaking person, his age, his sex . . . and these concepts . . . could then be expressed by the musician in that intonation, with those inflections and gestures, with that quantity and quality of sound, and that rhythm which was suited to that action of such a person.'[10]

In Monteverdi's treatment of dissonances the meaning of *oratio* is revealed to be the delivery of the words. The composition 'Cruda Amarilli', for example, is not a discourse on Mirtillo's sorrows of love from the distance of the observer, but the musical presentation of a tormented person who—to put it extremely—in his sorrow is no longer able to take Zarlino's treatment of dissonances into consideration. Again Monteverdi used Plato as proof: 'Does not the way of speaking and the delivery itself follow the state of the soul?' (*Quid vero loquendi modus ipsaque oratio non ne animi affectionem sequitur?*) For the moment it is not important what Plato himself may have meant; his comments were made, moreover, in a completely different context. Far more important are the ideals which served as a basis for Artusi's and Monteverdi's respective interpretations of Plato's text. They are both concerned less with understanding the source than with providing support for their own persuasions by means of a reference to an ancient authority, even at the risk of having to mould it to make it fit. Monteverdi envisioned the following disposition for the book he never wrote: 'The title of the book will be: Melody or the *seconda pratica musicale*. With *seconda* I mean in numerical order the modern, with *prima* the ancient [practice]. I will divide the book into three sections, corresponding to the three aspects of melody: in the first I will discuss *oratione*, in the second *armonia*, and in the third *ritmo*.'[11] Zarlino would have had nothing to object to in such a disposition, and at the same time would have come to completely different conclusions. For him *melodia* was the self-engendering result of the union of two or more voices in consonant sonorities, of the text, and of the rhythm— the work seen as a whole where none of the three elements prevails over the others. For Monteverdi *melodia* was the result of a style of composition which subjugates the sonorities and rhythm to the presentation of the text, a procedure which concerned polyphony just as much as the chordally accompanied solo song. As a result of this

---

[10] Vincenzo Galilei, *Dialogo della musica antica et della moderna* (Florence, 1581; repr. New York, 1967), 90.

[11] Letter of 22 Oct. 1633 (*Lettere*, p. 321).

style of composition, centred on the affects, 'forbidden' dissonances with the other voices could arise, which were none the less justified by the content of the text in that specific passage. Monteverdi was very careful to employ such dissonances only for emphatic expressions or exclamations of sorrow (such as *Ahi, Ohimé, tormento,* etc.). Subordination instead of co-ordination is the principal difference between the two interpretations; opinions were divided on the ranking of the three aspects of melody. Monteverdi's innovation lay not so much in the recognition of the fact that the contents of the text should determine the composition, but in daring to stretch or even to break the rules in the process of interpretation.

This is not the fighting spirit of a revolutionary. Peri, Caccini, and Cavalieri were more courageous in their break with tradition. Monteverdi was never an avant-garde composer, and no one other than Artusi ever characterized him as such. To the contrary, only the manner in which Monteverdi cautiously furnished the Florentine pioneer achievements with a solid musical basis, with its inherent set of laws, made further development possible. He also never wanted to be an innovator; it was his extraordinary sensitivity towards the texts he set, a basic characteristic of all his compositions, which led him to break these rules. His definition of the *seconda pratica* is more of a confession than a message. The experiments of Bardi's circle passed him by at first; he was not interested in the restoration of ancient music; he had no time for controversies about theory. Monteverdi was much too much of a practical musician and was too creative musically to want to restrict himself to mere imitation of models that were not even sufficiently well known. From the beginning his study of the ancient world had a different objective, that of applying the theoretical reflections of ancient philosophers to his own music, not of reconstructing ancient music.

In a letter written in 1634 to the theorist Giovanni Battista Doni, who decades later vehemently defended the goals of the Camerata, Monteverdi revealed the only way in which the ancient world influenced him:

I have however seen—not just now, but twenty years ago—the Galilei where he notated that little bit of ancient music; it was valuable to me at the time to have seen it and to have observed in this piece how the ancient [musicians] used their musical symbols differently from how we employ ours, but I did not try to go any further in understanding them, for I am sure they would have remained very obscure ciphers, or even worse, for this ancient practice has disappeared totally. I therefore turned to other paths in my studies, which I based on the knowledge of the best philosophers, who investigated nature, and because, on the one hand according to what I read there, I see that the affects agree with their reasonings and with the needs of nature, when I write practical music based on these observations; and because I, on the other hand, truly notice that the present rules have nothing to do with conforming to nature, I have therefore chosen the name of *seconda pratica* for my book, and I hope to make it so clear that one will not censure it, but consider it worthy of consideration. In my essay I will avoid the method used by the Greeks with their words and signs and will adopt the words and characters in use today, because it is my intention to show with the means of our present practice, what I was able to draw from the reflections of these philosophers to put to the service of good art, and not for the principles of the *prima pratica*, which only takes the *armonia* into account.[12]

In this way both lines of development of the time could meet in the works of Monteverdi—in music which did complete justice to the text.

### THE METAMORPHOSIS OF THE MADRIGAL

The year 1600 is a key date in the classification of musical epochs. It is accepted as the division between vocal polyphony and the instrumentally accompanied solo song, between the polyphonically and the instrumentally conceived musical style, and as the year in which opera and thorough-bass were born. To the superficial observer, the predominant vocal genres before 1600 were sophisticated polyphonic madrigals and pseudo-folkloristic villanellas or canzonettas; after this date solo madrigals and scherzos, arias, duets, and terzettos prevailed. Between 1600 and 1602 a series of vocal compositions appeared in print which document this change: 1600, the first operas by Cavalieri, Peri, and Caccini; 1601, Luzzasco Luzzaschi's solo madrigals; 1602 Caccini's solo madrigals and arias, whose very title *Le nuove musiche* (The New Music) constituted a rather pugnacious declaration, and in the same year Lodovico Viadana's *Cento concerti ecclesiastici* (One Hundred Ecclesiastical Concertos), with the new-fangled term 'concerto' in its very title, which announced the transfer of the new style to sacred music. As different as all of these pieces may be from one another in intention, in the compositional techniques employed, and in style, they share one thing: the presence of an instrumental bass part.

Neither the instrumental accompaniment, nor the solo singing, nor the union of music and drama was as new as could be inferred from Caccini's title and, to an even greater degree, from his strident tirades in the forewords to the printed editions of his music. The publications around 1600 were preceded by many years of experimentation and,

---

[12] Letter of 2 Feb. 1634 (*Lettere*, p. 326).

although not documented in writing, by decades of solo singing to instrumental accompaniment based on polyphonic vocal compositions. The transition from vocal polyphony to the chordally accompanied solo song took place gradually, not abruptly. Around 1600 this compositional style had simply reached such a state in its development that one could present it to a larger public and dare to disply it openly alongside the well-worn and mature polyphony.

It is not for a didactic purpose that Monteverdi's name does not appear on the list of innovators in this introduction; he just was not one of them. Monody, the instrumentally accompanied solo song, remained foreign to him outside opera, although he praised both the composers of polyphonic madrigals and those of the *seconda pratica*, Luzzaschi, Peri, and Caccini. He did not publish a single solo madrigal with a simple chordal accompaniment, and even the number of his solo scherzos is very small compared to other composers of the time.

Monteverdi did not need a new genre to acquire new compositional techniques or styles. All his life he remained united with the genre which already seemed near perfection when he began to compose: the madrigal. Those objectives which Caccini and many others strove for in their solo compositions—the union of the song with an instrumental accompaniment, a new kind of text declamation, a new vocal style, the presence of new virtuoso elements—were attained by Monteverdi in his polyphonic madrigals.

The madrigal, the predominant secular genre in the second half of the sixteenth century, had its origins around 1530, as did the poetic genre of the same name. This does not mean that musical madrigals were composed only on poetic madrigal texts. From the very beginning, sonnets, canzonas, octaves, and other poetic forms served as texts. The madrigal united the Franco-Flemish style with Italian poetry and replaced the frottola as the literary–musical form cultivated by society. It became an area of experimentation in compositional technique. The genre, which with its free grouping of verse and musical themes had taken the field against the schematism of the frottola, proved again and again to be suited to allowing new freedoms and absorbing new ideas; and, while the emergence of the madrigal can be rather precisely dated, its end, the dividing line between 'still' and 'no longer', can scarcely be determined.

Monteverdi's madrigal production is at one and the same time the mirror and pacemaker for the musical development of his time. When he published his first books of madrigals, the classical five- and six-voice polyphonic, *a cappella* madrigal was at its zenith. Orlando di Lasso, Filippo de Monte, and Giaches de Wert had published most of their immense madrigal output; Luca Marenzio's star was rising. Monteverdi was to receive many a new idea from him and from de Wert. Up until his fifth book of madrigals Monteverdi stayed with the traditional five voices, but still laid much of the groundwork for what would later characterize the madrigals with fewer voices and lead to the trademark of the new style: the instrumental bass. This basso continuo was at first a basso seguente which simply doubled instrumentally whichever part was lowest; as an independent bass part it then took on functions of a completely different nature. For one thing, it allowed solo passages in polyphonic compositions, and secondly it permitted a new compositional style within the traditional full sonorities, which would have been impossible without it.

This change in style becomes clear when one compares the beginning of the four-part 'Tu dormi? Ah crudo core' from Book VII (1619) with a madrigal from one of the first books. The difference is particularly obvious if one looks at the beginning of 'Cantai un tempo' from Book II. It is the most archaic of Monteverdi's madrigals and appears like a swan song at the end of this collection; it is certainly not without reason that he chose to compose it on a text by Pietro Bembo, who had died in 1547. It was, in 1590, a consciously antiquated composition, in which regularly imitating *soggetti* are formed from the lines (or segments of them) of the text, written from a distant point of view, long after this style had been passed by (Ex. 1.3). This

Ex. 1.3.    'Cantai un tempo'
                   (I sang one time)

compositional technique stands in contrast to that found at the beginning of 'Tu dormi? Ah crudo core' of 1619, in which four melodic fragments are presented one after the other in the upper three voices and then set contrapuntally against one another, never in imitation nor joined together in full-voiced writing. The bass voice does not even enter until the next section. Such a broken compositional style is possible only over a continuous bass part which unites the seemingly vagabond elements (Ex. 1.4).

In 1605, when the production and publication of solo songs with solo accompaniment were in full swing and began to be fashionable, Monteverdi for the first time, in the second part of his fifth madrigal book, published compositions whose compositional style made a thorough-bass necessary. Alternating between sections using only some of the voices and those using all of them was quite usual for the sixteenth-century madrigal, but here it has become a formal structural principle. The musical organization of a traditional madrigal as a succession of ever-new *soggetti* worked out in imitation was replaced by a juxtaposition of diverse sections, blocks, in which not only the thematic subjects were new, but also the range, the rhythmic gestures, and the type of declamation, and the selection of voices used in each section. It makes much more of an impression when a ritornello form develops from this simple alternation, when a line of the text is taken out of its context and used as a refrain, a technique that was completely new for the madrigal. Book V contains several compositions of this kind: 'Ahi come a un vago sol', in which the last line, the final conceit of the

Ex. 1.4.    'Tu dormi? Ah crudo core'
            (You are sleeping? O cruel heart
            you can sleep because love sleeps in you)

poem, interrupts the tenor duet three times with a three-to five-voice
refrain, and 'T'amo mia vita', a madrigal by Guarini of a dramatic
nature, which embodies the confrontation between polyphony and
monody:

> 'T'amo mia vita', la mia cara vita
> dolcemente mi dice; e 'n questa sola
> sì soave parola

par che trasformi lietamente il core,
per farmene signore.
O voce di dolcezza e di diletto!
Prendila tosto Amore,
stampala nel mio petto,
spiri solo per lei l'anima mia.
'T'amo mia vita' la mia vita sia.

'I love you, my life,' says my dear life
sweetly to me; and to this one
so sweet word
my heart seems to transform itself joyfully
in order to make me its master.
O utterance of sweetness and of delight!
Take it quickly Amor,
impress it on my heart,
my spirit shall only breathe for it.
'I love you, my life' shall be my life.

Monteverdi takes the life-giving device with which the madrigal opens and closes out of its poetic context and sets it four times as a motto against the *raisonnement* of the rest of the text, before the beginning of the last line. The *soggetto* of this device is practically the sole thematic material of the composition. It is a classical polyphonic theme; the simplicity of its stepwise descent of a fifth lends itself exceptionally well to musical imitation, as is shown by the last five-part section (Ex. 1.5*a*). It is also, however, a melody of monodic quality which follows the gesture of the spoken language, a melody which stands in relief, theatrically as it were, to a chordal, reciting murmur of the lower three voices (Ex. 1.5*b*). Thus there are two styles here, both based on the same thematic material. This composition demonstrates more clearly than all of the loquacious Florentine counterarguments that the stylistic change around 1600 was not a break with tradition; rather the new was gradually whittled out of the old.

In his polyphonic madrigals Monteverdi seemed to have tried out what it was like to write with fewer voices, before taking them out of the context of a larger ensemble. In the form of self-sufficient duets and trios, however, where it was no longer possible to alternate between passages with a few and all of the voices, this style required different structural principles. There were two sources from which Monteverdi gathered the elements of his new vocal style: firstly, the traditional vocal ornaments, with which every polyphonic work was adorned, often to the point of nonrecognition, and, secondly, the art of instrumental improvisation. The novelty, however, did not lie only in the fact that the *ad hoc* ornaments, up till then the responsibility of the singer, were now notated and thereby clearly dictated. Coloraturas, which until then were perceived as nothing more nor less than the

Ex. 1.5.    'T'amo mia vita'
            ('I love you, my life,')
            ('I love you, my life,' [says] my dear life)

possibility of embellishing the interval between one structural note in the melody and the next—compositionally speaking, irrelevant melodic variation—now became constituent elements of the composition and began to act as structural notes themselves.

'Mentre vaga Angioletta' from Book VIII is one of those Janus-headed compositions in which old is joined with new. The text of this tenor duet is a madrigal by Guarini which praises the singer's vocal technique. It is an inventory of the requisites of the art of singing, a description of the extraordinary technical abilities of the artist:

Mentre vaga Angioletta
ogni anima gentil cantando alletta,
corre il mio core e pende
tutto dal suon di quel soave canto.
E non so come intanto
musico spirto prende
fauci canore e seco forma e finge,
per non usata via,
garrula e maestrevole armonia.
Tempra d'arguto suon pieghevol voce,
e la volve e la spinge,
con rotti accenti e con ritorti giri,
qui tarda e là veloce;
e talor mormorando
in basso e mobil suono et alternando
fughe e riposi e placidi respiri,
or la sospende e libra,
or la preme, or la frange, or la raffrena;
or la saetta e vibra,
or in giro la mena,
quando con modi tremoli e vaganti,
quando fermi e sonanti.
Così cantando e ricantando il core,
o miracol d'amore,
è fatto usignolo,
e spiega già per non star mesto il volo.

While lovely Angioletta
entices every noble soul with her singing,
my heart races and hangs
completely on the sound of this sweet song.
And I do not know how in the meantime
the spirit of music seizes
her musical throat and forms and shapes therein
in an unusual way
various and masterful harmonies.
It tempers the supple voice with a metallic sound
and turns it and drives it
with broken notes and twisted circles,
slowly here and quickly there,
at times murmuring
with a low and mobile sound and alternating
between fugues and rests and quiet breaths;

now the spirit suspends it and holds it,
now it presses, now breaks, now curbs it;
now it shoots and hurls it,
· now it leads it in a circle,
at times trembling and rambling,
at times firm and sonorous.
Thus with singing and singing over and over again the heart,
O miracle of love,
becomes a nightingale
and already takes its flight so as not to be sad.

From this list of vocal ornaments Monteverdi forms a catalogue of musical figures that apparently are all madrigalisms. None is lacking, neither the circular movements at 'giri' nor the sighing rests at 'placidi respiri', the interruptions at 'rotti accenti' nor the chromatically descending line of the 'pieghevol voce'; these are all techniques of word-painting that one can discover in any sixteenth-century madrigal. Each term is associated with the corresponding musical figure, regardless of whether Angioletta's voice sings fugues, trembles, murmurs, shoots, or hurls. Even the ornamental figuration at 'garrula', 'volve', and 'veloce' represents, in principle, a return to madrigalistic word-painting. In it, however, a new compositional style is revealed, in which a coloratura is understood not as a mere embellishment within a chord progression, but as an independent melody which in its course demands chord progressions of its own. The difference becomes clear when one compares the 'volo' of the last line (Ex. 1.6a) with 'volve' in the eleventh (Ex. 1.6b). The former is nothing more than an embellished cadence; none of the notes of the coloratura constitutes an important structural tone for the harmonic progression. In the second case, however, the first note of each group of semiquavers is itself a harmonically constituent structural tone.

Such ornamental passages, made up of much smaller melodic units, are based on a compositional technique which was used only rarely in classical vocal polyphony and then only for word-painting purposes. It was rejected completely by Palestrina and was obviously avoided in the diminution treatises of the sixteenth century. This technique was the sequence, the repetition of a short melodic entity at neighbouring pitches. It crept into vocal music from instrumental improvisation, from *ad hoc* extemporization on a melodic structure, something particularly common in dance music; its simplest form consisted of a sequence in which a single melodic figure was repeated on each of the structural notes. In the early seventeenth-century diminution treatises, which document in retrospect the development of ornamental practices, the sequence had become the main characteristic of the

Ex. 1.6.  'Mentre vaga Angioletta'
(flight)
(turns it)

coloratura. The fact that the best structural melodies for this purpose
were stepwise ascending and descending progressions lies in the
nature of the sequential technique. A direct line leads from the parallel

sonorities of the second-to-last line of 'Ecco mormorar l'onde' in which the imitative entries at the *l'aura* figure (bars 72–82) come very close to being a real melodic sequence (although there are none in the piece), to a short passage from 'Qui rise, o Tirsi' from Book VI (Ex. 1.7*a*), which combines the same parallel progressions with a melodic sequence, and finally to the *veloce* figure in 'Mentre vaga Angioletta' (Ex. 1.7*b*). A long-standing improvisational practice thus became fixed through notation and made acceptable, as it were, to society as a conscious compositional technique.

Ex. 1.7*a*.   'Qui rise, o Tirsi'
              (flowers)

Ex. 1.7*b*.   'Mentre vaga Angioletta'
              (and quickly there)

These improvisational practices permeated the compositional style of all early seventeenth-century composers, as can be seen again and again with Monteverdi. The objectionable, unprepared ninth in 'Cruda Amarilli', as Claude V. Palisca has shown, can thus be traced back to an ornamental figure, and the precisely notated embellishments of 'Possente spirto' from *L'Orfeo* already indicate that the coloratura was no longer seen only as a decorative accessory added by the singer, but rather as a constituent element of the composition.

The change in the vocal ornamental practice is also documented by a comparison of Monteverdi's composition with a contemporary setting of 'Mentre vaga Angioletta'. Hieronymus Kapsberger's solo version from his *Arie passeggiate* of 1612 (Ex. 1.8) likewise strives to draw up a catalogue of word-painting embellishments, something to which the Guarini text truly lends itself. At the same time these comparable passages show the gap between Monteverdi's structural

Ex. 1.8.    Hieronymus Kapsberger, 'Mentre vaga Angioletta'
            (and quickly there)
            (twisted)

principles and a monodic style, such as that employed by Kapsberger, which still makes use of older diminution practices, such as ornamental figuration without sequences, embellishments without compositional relevance, and madrigalisms without the instrumental spirit.

One of the secrets of the new vocal style lay in the frequent use of what were originally instrumental practices (and, what is more, were taken from *Gebrauchsmusik*), whose rhythmic drive was until then foreign to the melodic style of songs. It was to achieve this union of song and instrumental organization that Monteverdi drew up a secret plan for 'Mentre vaga Angioletta'—namely, that the first lines are to be sung without accompaniment, and that the instrument may enter only at the words 'musico spirto', exactly at the point when the spirit of music enters the singer's throat.

'Mentre vaga Angioletta' is the most marked exponent of a general trend towards a compositional style that reached its full development in the middle of the century. Book VII contains a number of similar compositions whose origins can be traced directly, avoiding a detour via the chordally accompanied solo song, to elements of the polyphonic style: the two-part madrigals, 'O come sei gentile', 'O viva fiamma', 'Ecco vicine'; the three-part 'Parlo miser' o taccio'; and the four-part 'Al lume delle stelle'. Even the duets and trios of Book VII, apparently written in the style of the Florentine monody, have their roots in Monteverdi's earlier madrigal books. The sonnet 'Interrotte speranze' is, as far as the vocal part is concerned, a return to the experiments of the fourth book of madrigals, which appeared at almost the same time as the first monody prints. It opens with a line which, above a chord that is repeated nine times, begins in unison and glides over a suspension to the third (Ex. 1.9*b*) before returning to the unison at the end of the first quatrain of the sonnet. The melody is dominated by the textual declamation and needs twelve bars to progress stepwise through an octave. All of these features could be perceived as being in the most pure Florentine recitative style, if another similar passage from 'A un giro sol' from Book IV (Ex. 1.9*a*),

Ex. 1.9*a*.   'A un giro sol'
(Certainly when she was born so cruel and wicked)

Ex. 1.9*b*.   'Interrotte speranze'
        (Broken hopes, eternal faith,
          flame and powerful darts in a weak heart)

among others, did not prove once again that the similarities between
the 'old' and the 'new' music around 1600 were just as important as
the differences. Finally, the two-part 'Non vedrò mai le stelle' from
Book VII is based upon the same model. It does not open with a
unison and a suspension, but with another turn typical for Monteverdi's
vocal duets, a solo statement, which is answered by the second voice
while the first continues at the third (Ex. 1.9*c*).

Ex. 1.9*c*.   'Non vedrò mai le stelle'
        (I shall never see the stars)

Monteverdi published only two real monodic compositions bearing the Florentine mark apart from his operas: 'Lettera amorosa' and 'Partenza amorosa' in Book VII. They exemplify Peri's definition of monody as 'something between ordinary speech and a sung melody';[13] here, two decades after the 'invention' of this style, they almost seem like anachronisms. The consequent negation of any formal musical organization is shown primarily in the strict observation of the requirement that the accompanying instrumental chord be altered only when the affect of the text is changed, and culminates with the instruction 'si canta senza battuta' (to be sung without measure). The 'Lettera amorosa' and 'Partenza amorosa', however, were by no means anachronisms; on the contrary they were the most modern of the works Monteverdi had to offer in Book VII. Musical love letters in the declamatory style of opera had become highly fashionable at the beginning of the 1620s in the Venetian salons. It is no wonder that it was just these two pieces, together with the 'Lamento d'Arianna', which Monteverdi reissued four years later. With this publication he juxtaposed 'real' music for theatre with chamber music in the 'theatrical style' (*in genere rappresentativo*). While Arianna only rarely declaims her dramatic lament on a single note, but rather expresses the torments of her soul in broadly dimensioned melodic phrases, the emotional expression in the 'Lettera amorosa' remains more reserved; instead of soaring melodies, the declamation is dominated here by the typical recitation pattern on a single tone, dropping to the lower neighbour tone before the main accent. In the 'Partenza amorosa' this 'reading', 'speaking' character is brought to a level of higher emotional agitation only by the highly charged rests.

The three pieces are not only models for three different levels of emotional intensity; they are also based on different formal principles. Whereas the musical form in the 'Lamento d'Arianna' is generated primarily by the vocal part, the form for the two love letters is carried by the instrumental part. In the continuous declamation of the text in the two love letters the recitation pattern as such is repeated, but not the melodic structure of the whole. Under this declamation, as is particularly clear in the 'Lettera amorosa', Monteverdi repeated certain harmonic progressions section by section and in this way unobtrusively organized the text into corresponding formal parts which had the same tonal framework though not the same length. Monteverdi's idea of shifting the formal structure almost imperceptibly to the instrumental part enabled him to realize Peri's concept of 'spoken song' without sacrificing the music with its own laws. Just how many musical possibilities are concealed in the idea of altering

---

[13] Solerti, *Origini*, pp. 45–6.

only the accompanying chord when the affect of the text changes is shown by a comparison between the simple beginning of the 'Lettera amorosa' (Ex. 1.10*a*) and the fervent one of 'Ardo e scoprir ahi lasso' (Ex. 1.10*b*). The monotony of the 'Lettera amorosa', even when intended, does not have a harmonic basis, but is a result of reserved emotional expression. However, if one considers the two-part madrigal 'Ardo e scoprir ahi lasso', the declamatory possibilities concealed even within this strict harmonic concept become clear. The emotional transport with which this madrigal seems to burst forth is illustrated by four repetitions of the first word, 'Ardo', each one a step higher in a D minor triad. Even the instrumental bass, which remains on one note, participates by following the declamatory rests of the vocal parts. This beginning, with its opening expressive gesture, the increasing tempo of the declamation, the ornamental sighs of the last repetition, leading to a short imitative passage with just as expressive suspensions, dies out with a slow stepwise descent through the octave. This rise and fall is one of the typical characteristics of Monteverdi's compositions for a small number of voices, a dramatic, rather than a rhetoric principle, which was derived from the archetype of scenic music, the 'Lamento d'Arianna'.

'Ardo e scoprir ahi lasso' was first published in the second part of Book VIII; it appeared again in the Book IX edited by Alessandro Vincenti in 1651. It is one of the few madrigals in Book VIII which

Ex. 1.10*a*. 'Lettera amorosa'
  (If my languid looks,
  if the interrupted sighs,
  if the unfinished words)

Ex. 1.10b. 'Ardo e scoprir, ahi lasso'
        (I burn and, alas,
         I do not dare reveal
         that which I carry in my bosom,
         hidden ardour)

may be said without reservation to deserve this name. Many of the compositions for this book are works in honour of certain people, for theatre or entertainments, which could not be associated with any specific genre. What unites them is not the genre but the subject-matter of the texts, and, in the first part, a new stylistic phenomenon.

The very title of the publication announces the heterogeneous nature of its contents: *Madrigali guerrieri, et amorosi con alcuni opuscoli in genere rappresentativo*. Whereas the second part, the *Canti amorosi*, consists primarily of madrigals in the style of the previous decades—although they may vary greatly from one another—the first part, the *Canti guerrieri*, contains an abundance of the most diverse compositions with which Monteverdi richly illustrated his invention, the *concitato genere*.

There has been much ado concerning the concept of the *concitato genere*. At times it was considered to be the invention of the tremolo; at others it was confused with the concept of the *genere da guerra* and was used to characterize any excited mood. The expansion of this concept to *stile concitato*—a formulation never used by Monteverdi—in modern musicology has contributed to this misunderstanding. Monteverdi, however, defined his *genere concitato* precisely:

I reflected how our passions, or emotions, are of three principle kinds, rage [*Ira*], moderation [*Temperanza*], and humility [*Humiltà*] . . . as is affirmed by the best philosophers; and how the nature of our voice itself is at times high, at times low, and at times intermediate; and how the art of music is clearly comprised in the three terms, 'agitated' [*concitato*], 'tender' [*molle*], and 'moderate' [*temperato*]; I have not been able to find an example for the agitated species in any composition of past times . . . and as I know that it is contrasts which deeply move our soul . . . I set myself, with great zeal and toil, to find this species, and I reflected that the martial agitated dances, as is affirmed by the best philosophers, were in the pyrrhic metre, that is, in a fast tempo; and that the opposite [affects] were in the spondaic metre, in a slow tempo. Thus I began to think about the semibreve and, when it was sounded once, perceived it as one foot of the spondaic metre; but when it was divided into sixteen semiquavers, which were all sounded once, and in conjunction with a text of a choleric or wrathful nature, I heard in this small example the similarity of emotional expression which I had been seeking, even when the text in its declamation did not follow the tempo of the instrument.[14]

The *concitato genere* is therefore nothing but an exactly-fixed, rhythmical semiquaver motion on one note and was originally thought of as being only for the accompanying instrument. Monteverdi, however, transferred it to the vocal parts, where the instrumental gesture was adapted accordingly with tongue-twisting speed. It was only together with the elements of the *battaglia*—the popular manner of imitating the tumult of the battle through tone-painting, using *bourdon* techniques, trumpet-like triads, and rhythms reminiscent of drums—that the *concitato genere* joined to form the new *genere guerriero* which Monteverdi introduced with his *madrigal guerrieri*. It is not

[14] In the foreword to Book VIII (1638) (*Lettere*, pp. 416–17).

surprising that among these compositions there are two works of large dimensions in honour of Ferdinand III, to whom the book is dedicated. The bombastic *genere guerriero* is exceptionally suited to extolling an emperor and warlord of the Thirty Years War. 'Ogni amante è guerrier', from which Ex. 1.11 is taken, is one of the works whose generic classification is problematic. Its text is an extremely long succession of unrhymed hendecasyllables. The composition itself is in three parts, consisting of a tenor duet, a bass solo, and a tenor solo; the only unifying element is provided by this martial style. Searching for another name for the genre of this work would only shift the problem. The classical madrigal had dissolved into so many different forms. Monteverdi was definitely partly responsible for this and he himself had difficulties when, in accounting for the plausibility of the arrangement in Book VIII, he attempted to correlate the set of terms, *teatro—camera—ballo* with *guerriera—amorosa—rappresentativa*. Unconsciously the idea of the madrigal of the old school is hidden in this unclear comparison, for only *musica amorosa* is ranked equally with *musica da camera*; this, however, is confounded at least by 'Hor che il ciel e la terra' from the *Canti guerrieri*. Other musicians of his time were clearly more careful with the classification of their works. It was in those very years that a whole series of fantasy names appeared on title-pages; one composer cautiously called his compositions *Fanfalughe* (Whims) or *Capricij composti in diversi modi* (Caprici

Ex. 1.11.  'Ogni amante è guerrier'
(O Grand Fernando Ernesto,
they will bow down to you,
to your unvanquished sword)

Composed in Diverse Styles) or escaped the problem of nomenclature with a literary title such as *Bizzarrie poetiche*. In Monteverdi's eighth madrigal book the word 'madrigal' is merely a collective name for 'secular vocal music'.

# 2

# PASTORAL THEMES

## ARCADIA IN THE MADRIGAL

Monteverdi's madrigals are not only a mirror of the musical situation; they also show the literary taste of their time and of their creator. Monteverdi kept to the current repertoire in his choice of texts. His taste is revealed not so much by the fact that he often chose texts by contemporary poets such as Tasso, Guarini, and Marino, but in that two otherwise extremely popular poets are only seldom represented in his works. These two, Francesco Petrarca and Jacopo Sannazaro, were the patriarchs of the two realms of thought central to sixteenth-century poetry.

To characterize lyric poetry of this century in one word, one would have to speak of 'Petrarchism'. Roughly 130 editions of Petrarch's *Canzoniere* were published between 1501 and the end of the century. The poets practised imitating and transforming the themes, motifs, and metaphors of their paragon: unconsummated love, praise of physical beauty, the interplay between life and death, the tension between worldly and divine love. In hundreds of madrigal compositions Petrarch himself is the author of the text; the settings of texts by his imitators are innumerable.

Jacopo Sannazaro, although also an author of sonnets and canzonas, founded a new literary style with another work. It was to become important for lyric poetry primarily in the second half of the century and was to have far-reaching consequences, particularly for dramatic poetry. With his pastoral romance *Arcadia*, written towards the end of the fifteenth century and published for the first time in 1502, he rediscovered the pastoral idyll of Theocritus and Virgil for Italian literature. *Arcadia* was a mixture of narrative prose chapters and eclogues, in which shepherds and shepherdesses lauded their natural life, dreamed of the Golden Age, and indulged in their memories of the sorrows and joys of love. In the middle of the century Arcadia became the stage for a new theatrical genre, the pastoral drama, for which Torquato Tasso (with *Aminta*) and Giovanni Battista Guarini (with *Il pastor fido*) were to contribute the two most important works.

Then lyric poetry also became peopled with figures bearing the names from Virgil's eclogues, Thyrsis, Chloris, Phyllis, and Amyntas; these names did not stand for individual characters, but only served to conjure up the pastoral idyll.

Two characteristics were the primary source of Arcadia's attractiveness: on the one hand, its idyllic landscape, full of murmuring streams, gentle hills, and luscious meadows, in which spring ruled eternally and where no storm, weed, or vermin burdened the shepherds' lives—a landscape so unreal that a poet could unfold all his dreams of a peaceful world in it; and, on the other hand, its population, the shepherds and nymphs, always young and beautiful, free from social differences, far from day-to-day adversities, always occupied in falling happily or unhappily in love—an equally unreal community, on to which all ideas concerning society and morals could be projected.

Of course Petrarch had also made use of vernal descriptions of nature. He was the author of that famous, truly adventurous enumeration which manages to capture the Arcadian landscape in a single line of a sonnet:

Fior frondi erbe ombre antri onde aure soavi[1]

Flowers, foliage, herbs, shades, grottoes, waves, gentle breezes

But for Petrarch nature always serves either as a simile or as an antithetical framework for the emotional state of the subject. For one of his few settings of Petrarch, Monteverdi chose just this contrast between vernal nature and the lover's sorrow, translating it into a blend between something like a canzonetta and a madrigal. In the quatrains of his sonnet 'Zefiro torna e 'l bel tempo rimena', Petrarch extols the return of spring with its flowers, nightingales, and love; in the tercets he expresses his sorrow about Laura's death, which no other love nor the song of any bird can penetrate. Monteverdi captured the magical atmosphere of spring in an airy, dance-like section in triple time, composed as if for two similar stanzas; at the point where the subject-matter turns, the music suddenly changes to duple time, to another key, to a different kind of melodic line, and to dissonant voice-leading.

The tendency to abandon the often dolorous content of Petrarch's poetry in the second half of the century is revealed by the later preference for Sannazaro's eclogues, with their evocation of a Golden Age, to the shepherds with their lovers' laments, which, although they may have been overcast by tears, were never tragic. Depictions of

[1] Sonnet CCLIX

nature became autonomous in madrigal poetry; spring was described without reference to a poetic subject. Pastoral poetry was different from the pensive, often melancholy texts by the imitators of Petrarch; in addition, its light, playful mood, its stories of flirtatious love which only rarely take a tragic turn, suited the trend towards a lighter, more entertaining tone in music.

Monteverdi, who composed only a single work on a text by Sannazaro 'La pastorella mia spietata e rigida' in the *Scherzi musicali*, also wrote his share of pastoral madrigals. Even within this range of subject-matter they show his preference for a certain kind of text. He only rarely chose texts in which Arcadia was depicted solely as an ideal image of a landscape and a society; an example is the setting in Book VI of the sonnet 'Qui rise, o Tirsi', by Giambattista Marino. It is a shepherd's happy–sad recollection of his love, which ends with the emphatic exclamation 'O memoria felice, o lieto giorno'. Monteverdi took this last line out of its context at the conclusion of the poem and placed it like a ritornello between the individual stanzas. He made use of the schematic disposition of the reminiscent flashes, each of which begins with 'Qui', to change the grouping and number of the voices. The refrain is set as a five-voice homophonic block, which intervenes between the sparkling, virtuoso, descriptive verses, creating order and structure—a madrigal which is typical for the new formal means of organization.

| | |
|---|---|
| Qui rise, o Tirsi, e qui ver me rivolse | |
| le due stelle d'amor la bella Clori. | Canto/Quinto |
| Qui per ornarmi il crin de' più bei fiori | |
| Al suon de le mie canne un grembo colse | Alto/Tenor |
| (O memoria felice, o lieto giorno) | CQATB |
| Qui l'angelica voce e le parole | |
| ch'umiliaro i più superbi tori | Canto |
| Qui di gratie scherzar vidi e gli amori, | Canto/Quinto/Alto |
| quando le chiome d'or sparte raccolse. | Canto/Quinto |
| (O memoria felice, o lieto giorno) | CQATB |
| Qui con meco s'assise, e qui mi cinse | |
| del caro braccio il fianco e dolce intorno | Canto/Alto |
| stringendomi la man l'alma mi strinse. | |
| Qui d'un bacio ferimmi e 'l viso adorno | |
| di bel vermiglio vergognando tinse. | Alto/Tenor/Basso |
| O memoria felice, o lieto giorno. | CQATB |

Here beautiful Clori laughed, Tirsi, and here she turned
her two eyes of love towards me.
Here, to the sound of my flute, she picked to adorn my hair

a lapful of the most beautiful flowers.
    (O happy memory, O joyful day!)

Here one heard her angelical voice and her words,
which tamed the wildest bulls,
here I saw the Graces and the amoretti jesting,
as they bound together her flowing hair of gold.

    (O happy memory, O joyful day!)

Here they sat with me and here she embraced
my side gently with her dear arms
and as she squeezed my hand, she enchained my soul.

Here she gave me a kiss and imbued her decorative face
full of shame with a beautiful vermilion.
O happy memory, O joyful day.

Even in this dreamy, veiled, pastoral world, however, Monteverdi was more interested in dramatic than in lyric texts. Tasso, whom Monteverdi had particularly cherished in his earlier madrigal books, became important to him increasingly as an epic rather than as a lyric poet. Already in Book III the graceful elegance of his pastoral poems had yielded to Armida's and Rinaldo's expressive outbursts of pain and rage from the epic poem *Gerusalemme liberata*. Monteverdi may have taken the ideas of transforming epic poetry into musical madrigals from Giaches de Wert, the director of music at the court of Mantua, who had set long cycles from Ariosto's *Orlando furioso* and Tasso's *Gerusalemme liberata*.

Moreover, in texts from lyric poetry Monteverdi preferred those containing action rather than description. Pastoral poetry proffered him an abundance of texts for this purpose. Dialogues between a shepherd and shepherdess or lonely plaints of the lovelorn were popular subjects for madrigal poetry: farewell or love scenes, short monologues or dialogues, which stood by themselves or were embedded in a description of the situation. At the very beginning of Book I, Monteverdi set such a text, 'Fumia la pastorella'. It was the first of his madrigal cycles, whose three-part disposition paved the way for the subsequent 'Lamento della Ninfa'. In the first part the shepherdess Fumia, singing, passes through meadows populated with amoretti; in the second she praises, in direct speech, the warmth-giving sun; in the third, shepherds and nymphs gather round to listen to her song. Monteverdi's setting, similar to a canzonetta in its lightness with interspersed dance-like sections in triple time, captures the playful character of this charming spring idyll. Although the difference between description and direct speech has not yet been fully developed, one still feels clearly Monteverdi's desire to have the middle section stand in contrast to the others. He begins with an almost solemn homophonic declamation in long note values, with which Fumia hails the sun, and he also ends, after several lines set in a polyphonic style, with a homophonic section, this time dance-like in nature.

Another dramatic scene may be found in Book III (1592)—the first that Monteverdi published at the court of Mantua; ' "Rimanti in pace" a la dolente e bella' exhibits a scenic disposition even more obviously than 'Fumia la pastorella'. Here the direct speech appears to force its way soloistically out of the five-voice context. The text, a sonnet by Livio Celiano, describes a truly heart-breaking farewell scene:

'Rimanti in pace' a la dolente e bella
Fillida Tirsi sospirando disse,
'rimanti, io me ne vo, tal mi prescrisse
legge, empio fato, aspra sorte e rubella.'

Ed ella, hora da l'un e l'altra stella
stilland'amaro humore i lumi affisse
nei lumi del suo Tirsi e gli trafisse
il cor di pietosissime quadrella.

Onde ei di morte la sua faccia impressa
disse: 'Ahi come n'andrò senz'il mio sole
di martir in martir, di doglie in doglie?'

Ed ella da singhiozzi e piant'oppressa
fievolmente formò queste parole:
'Deh cara anima mia, chi mi ti toglie?'

'Farewell', said Tirsi to the sad, beautiful
Fillida, sighing,
'farewell, I must go, the law prescribes this for me,
a wicked fate, a harsh and jealous destiny'.

And she, weeping bitter tears from both eyes,
fixed her gaze
on the eyes of her Tirsi and penetrated
his heart with the most pitiable arrows.

Upon which, he, with death impressed on his face,
said: 'Oh, how I, without my sun, will pass
from torment to torment, from pain to pain!'

And she, overwhelmed by sobs and tears,
feebly formed these words:
'Oh, my dear soul, who takes you from me?'

Striking here—and new, compared to the first two madrigal books—
are the expressive sighing rests at 'sospirando', and the chromatic
voice-leading at 'amaro humore' and 'martir' and 'doglie'. Already
then Monteverdi had gone to the limits of what was allowed with these
means of madrigalistic word-painting. Even more striking, however,
is the formal conception of the piece as evidenced in the quotation
marks and colons, that are, as it were, set to music, and which
Monteverdi used to distinguish the direct speech from the story. This
is most effectively displayed at the beginning of the second section,
where, following the full chord over 'disse', Tirsi's cry of despair,
'Ahi', appears first as a solo, then in three parts (Ex. 2.1*a*). This is also
seen in Fillida's answer, 'Deh cara anima mia', with its seemingly
monodic leap of a sixth in loosely imitative, three-part writing, which
follows upon the almost psalmodic, monotonous murmur of the story
(Ex. 2.1*b*).

Two such dialogues from Book VI, on texts by Giambattista
Marino, translate the alternation between story and direct speech,
already suggested here, to a completely developed alternation between
solo and tutti: 'A Dio, Florida bella', a scene which corresponds to
'Rimanti in pace' in content if not in its painful expression; and
'Presso un fiume tranquillo', in which the solo voices of Filena and
Eurillo stand in contrast to the five-part narrative texture, a scene
which is once again more devoted to the gay flirtatious aspect of the
shepherd's life.

This series of dialogues may be pursued up to the playful two-part
dialogue 'Bel pastor', from the posthumous Book IX, in which the
role of the narrator is eliminated totally. 'Non si levava ancor' from
Book II and 'Al lume delle stelle' from Book VII also belong to this set
of pastoral madrigals in a dramatic setting. The latter reveals its
relationship with a genre which was to develop through the opera: the
lament.

A composer who was already looking for dramatic expression, for
scenic disposition, in lyric poetry must have felt even more strongly
drawn towards poetry for the theatre. The new pastoral plays that had
come into fashion around the middle of the century, particularly in
northern Italy, proved to be true treasure troves for madrigal
composers. It was relatively simple to take individual sections out of
their dramatic context, as the verse forms of the pastoral plays
corresponded to those of the literary madrigal—an irregular succession
of heptasyllabic and hendecasyllabic verses. Battista Guarini's *Il pastor
fido* unlocked a new world for composers. The drama, characterized
by its author as a *tragicommedia pastorale*, was published for the first

time in 1589 and had gone through twenty editions by 1602. The original intention had been to perform it at the Mantuan court in 1591, but it was only in 1598 that the highly regarded performance

Ex. 2.1.    '"Rimanti in pace", a la dolente e bella'
            (He said: 'Oh, how I will pass . . .')
            (formed these words: 'O my dear soul, who . . .')

finally took place. The plot of *Il pastor fido*, in line with the
dramaturgic scheme which had been established since the middle of
the century, consisted of the following: requited and unrequited love,
in which two shepherd couples were involved, Mirtillo and Amarilli
together with Silvio and Dorinda; an intrigue instigated by a satyr and
an evil nymph with almost fatal consequences; and an oracle, which
finally brought about the happy end. Here, in accordance with the
subtitle, Guarini joined the delightful setting of Arcadia with the
dramatic power of tragedy and the cheerfulness of comedy, thus
providing an abundance of highly expressive situations. This was very
suited to Monteverdi's tendency to turn away from descriptions and
towards the emotional outpourings of individuals.

There is a composition on a text from *Il pastor fido* in Book III: 'O
primavera, gioventù dell'anno', Mirtillo's sad evocation of spring,
which always returns, whereas for him only the bitter memory of a lost
love is brought back. It is this antithetical image, taken from Petrarch,
which here, as in 'Zefiro torna e 'l bel tempo rimena', provoked
Monteverdi's use of contrasts in musical expression. In Book IV,
published in 1603, five years after the performance of *Il pastor fido*, the
number of texts from Guarini's pastoral play grew: Mirtillo's farewell
plaint, 'Ah dolente partita'; Amarilli's conflict between duty and love,
'Anima mia, perdona'; and Linco's attempt to persuade Silvio to love,
'Quell'augellin che canta'. Monteverdi, however, altered this last text
to such a degree that one can no longer tell it is from *Il pastor fido*.
Instead it has become one of those idyllic landscapes which Tasso
could describe so inimitably, and which are not necessarily to be
confined to Arcadia:

Quell'augellin che canta
si dolcemente e lascivetto vola
hor da l'abete al faggio,
hor dal faggio al mirto,
s'havesse umano spirto,
direbbe: Ardo d'amore.
Ma ben arde nel core
e chiam'il suo desio
che li risponde: Ardo d'amore anch'io.
Che sii tu benedetto
amoroso gentil vago augelletto.

That bird which sings
so sweetly and flies so wantonly
from the fir to the beech tree,
from the beech to the myrtle,
if it had a human spirit
it would say: I burn with love.
But his heart burns
and calls for its desire
which answers it: I, too, burn with love.
O that you may be happy
you amorous, noble, lovely bird.

Monteverdi's setting creates the same magical world of springlike sonorities as in 'Ecco mormorar l'onde', and conjures up an equally light mood with its playful virtuoso figuration, full of weightless, airy sequences in thirds and sixths (Ex. 2.2). Mirtillo's lament, 'Ah

Ex. 2.2.     'Quell'augellin che canta'
             (lovely bird)

dolente partita', exudes an entirely different spirit. This finale of a scene is rhymed and can therefore no longer be distinguished from a lyric madrigal. Its subject, the relationship between parting and death, was among the most popular motifs of madrigal poetry:

> Ah dolente partita,
> ah fin della mia vita,
> da te parto e non moro? E pur io provo
> la pena della morte,
> e sento nel partire
> un vivace morire
> che da vita al dolore
> per far che moia immortalmente il core.

> O painful parting,
> O end of my life!
> I part from you and do not die?
> And yet I feel
> the pangs of death
> and feel in parting
> a living death
> which gives life to pain
> so that the heart can die immortally.

Monteverdi divided the composition into two sections on the basis of its contents; the second is distinguished from the beginning by means of a lively rhythm which reflects the idea of 'living death'. The first already contains in its core those expressive means which were later to become so important in opera. The beginning is unique. The two sopranos enter in unison and then move to a chain of harsh suspensions, the same technique as seen in 'A un giro sol' from Book III (see Ex. 1.9*a*). Here it appears at the beginning, in the two highest voices, in such an exposed manner that, although there are two parts, something like an intensified solo is suggested. The remaining melodic material is surprisingly simple: diatonically ascending and descending lines, which are set against each other contrapuntally in an ever-varying order. Monteverdi obtains the solemn expression of even these lines by the reiterated repetition of the same turn of phrase at other pitches. The cry of pain, 'Ah fin della mia vita', thus appears three times in the first soprano (Ex. 2.3).

All laments, entreaties, cries of desperation in Monteverdi's operas will later be expressed in a similar way. 'Ah dolente partita' is no longer a simple madrigal; it is a dramatic scene. Finally the entire first *a cappella* portion of Book V is reserved for texts from *Il pastor fido*: Mirtillo's first monologue, 'Cruda Amarilli', and its counterpart as far as the text is concerned, Amarilli's lament 'O Mirtillo', open the

Ex. 2.3.    'Ah dolente partita'
            (O painful parting,
              O end of my life!
            I part from you and do not die?)

collection. Two large cycles dominate the rest of the *a cappella* section: 'Ecco Silvio', the dialogue between Silvio and Dorinda from the fourth act and 'Ch'io t'ami', one of Mirtillo's monologues. The first two madrigals, the main targets of Artusi's criticism, are interesting primarily for technical and stylistic reasons—it is no coincidence that they appear at the beginning of the collection with the declaratory preface. The second cycle is remarkable primarily because it presents a dramatic dialogue. The writing in all of these madrigals is mainly homophonic, the style so declamatory that one senses a recitative spirit. A unified expression of the affect is more important than the interpretation of individual words; the often quite harsh dissonances no longer refer to the text itself, but to the emotions engendered by it.

'O Mirtillo' is the most daring of them. What Artusi called an 'impertinence of a beginning' (*impertinentia d'un principio*) is a seemingly recitative invocation with all the characteristics typical of later opera scenes: the expressive leap of a sixth at the beginning as well as the monotonous afterthought, which conforms with the declamation of the text (Ex. 2.4*a*). Nothing of the contrapuntal style is left here. The madrigal could be performed without difficulty as a solo: the melody is always in the soprano; the other voices could easily be joined together in a chordal accompaniment. When Monteverdi did use counterpoint in this madrigal he employed it in a breath-taking series of dissonances (Ex. 2.4*b*).

Ex. 2.4. 'O Mirtillo'
(O Mirtillo, Mirtillo my soul)

The *a cappella* madrigals of Book V were later characterized by Aquilino Coppini, who published them, with sacred texts, as *musica rappresentativa*. This speaks less for their having been performed dramatically than for the fact that the compositions were already so

Ex. 2.4.b. (who you call most cruel Amarilli)

'dramatic' in themselves that hardly anything separated them from a musical presentation of individual fates on stage. It was no longer any great distance from these monologues and dialogues of Arcadian shepherds and nymphs to the songs of Orpheus and Eurydice.

## ORPHEUS AND EURYDICE: RINUCCINI, STRIGGIO, MONTEVERDI

The beginning of the history of opera is also the history of a dilemma. Something that hardly seemed questionable a few decades later, that was for centuries no longer perceived as a problem, was the most critical point of all for those who initiated this new kind of music theatre: the fact that the dramatic dialogue was not spoken, but sung. None of the efforts concerned with this form of theatre, which was to become a hybrid between recitation and song through musical intensification, got to the essence of the problem, namely that people do not sing when they communicate with one another. An Antigone who defends her disobedience in song? A despotic ruler as a singer? Nobody who reflected on the connection between music and drama at the turn of the seventeenth century would ever have thought of such a thing.

Music in the theatre was restricted to the choruses in tragedies and to the intermedi between the acts of a play, regardless of the genre. It was thus found where there was a lull in the plot and where there was room for a commentary or amazing theatrical effects. The dialogue of a play, however, was not sung. This would have been against the general demand for *verosimiglianza*—for the verisimilitude of what occurred on stage.

There was one place, however, where singing in daily life was nothing unusual, where poetry had its home, and where the shimmering gold veil of a peaceful paradise was drawn over all passions, both good and evil: the distant Arcadia of a previous Golden Age. There was no difference between classes there, where men and gods treated one another as equals, where music was at home, where singing was normal. In his *Trattato della musica scenica*, Giovanni Battista Doni shrewdly answered the question of which genres of drama lend themselves to a musical setting:

As far as the pastoral is concerned, . . . I would say, . . . that one may concede that it has music in all of its parts; . . . in particular because the gods, nymphs, and shepherds there appear in that primeval age, when music was natural and speech was almost poetry . . . [2]

We should not imagine that the shepherds depicted there were the sordid and common ones that tend the livestock today, but those of that older age when the noblest people practised this art. [3]

This distant world could provide a suitable framework for the first dramas set to music in their entirety. Figures who had a more obvious connection to music, however, were transplanted there as protagonists. Apollo, the god of music, and his son Orpheus, whose singing could tame even wild animals, were the main characters in the first opera librettos: Apollo in *Dafne*, first set by Jacopo Peri and Jacopo Corsi in the 1590s and in an expanded version by Marco da Gagliano in 1608; and Orpheus in *Euridice*, composed in 1600 first by Peri and soon thereafter by Caccini. Daphne soon disappeared from the opera stage. The Orpheus myth, however, became, for the first few decades, the most popular subject for an opera, and served as a platform for the change in operatic taste and dramaturgy. The silent dislocation of Orpheus from Thrace to Arcadia is among the manipulations undertaken by the first opera generation on account of *verosimiglianza*. How else could he be brought into contact with the musically talented shepherds and nymphs? Thrace was a rugged region, which had only been taught some manners by his singing and his playing of the lyre; it was therefore unsuited for the setting of a pastoral opera. In order to avoid this calamity, the first librettists made short work of bestowing Thrace with Arcadian qualities.

---

[2] Giovanni Battista Doni, *Trattato della musica, De' trattati di musica . . . tomo secondo*, ed. Anton Francesco Gori (Florence, 1763; repr. Bologna), 15.

[3] Ibid. 16.

The beginning of opera is associated with the name, not of a composer, but of a poet: Ottavio Rinuccini, the author of *Dafne* and *Euridice*. Misled by the supposition that the Greeks and Romans sang their tragedies in entirety and convinced by Peri's stylistic ideas, he wrote two librettos, which, at the beginning, placed their stamp on this young genre. *Dafne* and *Euridice*, however, are not tragedies, something that Rinuccini prudently passed over in silence. They are, on the contrary, direct successors to the pastoral plays and are both modelled on the same scheme: a dramatic development, whose catastrophe is not presented on stage but comes in the form of a messenger's tale, and a happy end; a prologue, and a chorus at the end of every scene; dialogue which takes place in the verse of the pastoral play, and is similar to prose, with a few interpolated strophic lyrics. Society is more important than the fate of the individual; only in this way could an opera whose main character is Apollo be called *Dafne* and one that describes Orpheus's destiny *Euridice*. The catastrophe is turned into a *lieto fine*, a happy ending, even at the risk of having to alter the myth. The fortune of the protagonists finally joins in the dreamy pastoral serenity of Arcadia, where, despite all dangers, the eternal sun of peace shines. For this reason Rinuccini allowed his Plutone to deliver up Euridice without any conditions, thereby relinquishing one of the most dramatic situations of the story of Orpheus. The last scene shows Euridice and Orfeo in a circle of shepherds and nymphs telling of their adventures in the underworld. Rinuccini used the occasion for the performance—the wedding of Maria de' Medici—to justify this truly happy end, instead of eternal loss: 'It could appear to some that it was too daring to alter the end of the Orpheus story, but it seemed to me to be suitable in a time of such gaiety.'[4]

It cannot be denied that Alessandro Striggio's *La favola d'Orfeo* has some similarities to Rinuccini's *Euridice*. Individual scenes are direct paraphrases and its formal organization is modelled on this prototype. The differences, however, are still more important than the similarities and shed light even at this stage on Monteverdi's concept of musical drama, for it is certain that he participated in the shaping of Striggio's libretto.

| **Rinuccini** | **Striggio** |
|---|---|
| Prologue: Tragedia promises a new kind of tragedy, which the world will henceforth follow. It | Prologue: Musica, who is able to soothe every sad heart with sweet sounds, announces the story of |

---

[4] Ottavio Rinuccini, Preface to *L'Euridice*, in Solerti, *Origini*, p. 41.

will no longer be the fate of eminent people, but a story which awakens tender and pleasant feelings.

Orfeo, the demigod, who with her tamed the wild animals and the underworld.

Scene 1: The shepherds and nymphs adorn Euridice with garlands for her impending wedding, while singing songs of joy.

Act I: The shepherds and nymphs prepare the wedding; Orfeo and Euridice assure one another blissfully of their mutual love.

Scene 2: While Orfeo praises his love for Euridice and the shepherds invoke the hymeneal god, the messenger Dafne bursts in with the terrible news that Euridice has been bitten by a snake and has died with Orfeo's name on her lips. Orfeo, inconsolable, wants to follow her to the underworld.

Act II: Together with the shepherds Orfeo praises his Arcadian land and his fortune in love. Silvia bursts in with the news of Euridice's death. Orfeo decides to descend into the underworld and to demand her back from Plutone.

Scene 3: The shepherd Arcetro reports how a goddess appeared before Orfeo, when he, in his sorrow, wanted to despair.

Act III: Led by Speranza, Hope, Orfeo reaches the gates of the underworld. Caronte stands in front of him, but Orfeo lulls him to sleep with his singing.

Scene 4: Led by Venus, Orfeo reaches Plutone and Proserpina. He moves the god of the underworld with his plaints, but only the entreaties of Radamanto, Caronte, and Proserpina serve to persuade Plutone. He delivers up Euridice to Orfeo.

Act IV: Flattered by Proserpina, Plutone returns Euridice to Orfeo on the condition that he does not look at her on the way back into the world. Full of doubt as to whether Euridice is following him, he turns around and loses her once again, this time forever.

Scene 5: The shepherd Aminta tells the shepherds and nymphs of Orfeo's fortune. Orfeo and Euridice appear and describe their

Act V: Having returned alone, Orfeo laments his fate to Echo and renounces all women.

    End of the libretto: He flees the

return to the world. The shepherds and nymphs praise the
power of love.

approaching bacchantes who conclude the opera with a big celebration.

End of the score: Apollo appears
on a cloud and raises Orfeo to the
heavens.

It would certainly be exaggerated to consider the allegories of the two
prologues to be programmatic. They are, however, an indication of
the most important difference between the librettos. Rinuccini's text
is significantly more 'literary' than Striggio's. It offers far fewer
possibilities for the composition of musically closed forms. Apart from
the chorus scenes, there are no 'musical' situations. Whenever there is
a lull in the plot and time for reflection, the text still retains
the declamatory speech of the pastoral drama, not yet showing the
influence of a musical conception. Even Orfeo's lament in the
underworld, although regularized by a refrain, is not much more than
a dramatic recitation. In addition, Rinuccini's libretto lacks exciting
scenes in which the outcome is uncertain; the only *coup de théâtre* is the
appearance of the bringer of bad tidings. All the other scenes are no
more than descriptions of the pastoral world and all its emotional
levels between joy and sorrow.

Where Rinuccini describes, however, Striggio presents; where
Rinuccini's plot glides over the vortex of dramatic development,
Striggio aims right for it; where Rinuccini's scene is the background
for the dialogue, Striggio's dialogue is in itself the scene. Finally,
where the text did not give what the scene could offer, Monteverdi
went one step further and transferred it to the composition.

Monteverdi's predilection for a musical disposition of the plot,
which is characteristic of all his dramatic works, is revealed in his
preference for symmetrically structured scenes in *L'Orfeo*. Even
where there is no symmetry, each act aims towards a musical focal
point. These highpoints are, in part, just those dramatic situations
that are missing with Rinuccini: in Act V it is Orfeo's song in praise of
Euridice, in Act IV it is his passage with Euridice from the
underworld into the world of the living, which ends in catastrophe; in
Act III it is Orfeo's song of entreaty to Caronte, which serves at one
and the same time as the centrepiece for the entire opera; in Act II it is
the turning-point from Arcadian *joie de vivre* to the reception of the
bad tidings. The focal point of Act I is also the centre of the almost
symmetrical disposition of the scene: Orfeo's 'joyful song' (*lieta
canzon*), a declamatory text, which Monteverdi also set as a recitative,
although still managing to endow it with dramatic effect. The song

begins with a homage to the sun, which is omnipresent in this libretto
and symbolizes Orfeo's connection with his father Apollo, the sun
god. It then continues with the question of whether the sun has ever

Ex. 2.5     'Rosa del ciel', *L'Orfeo*, Act I
         (Rose of the Heavens, life of the world and worthy
         offspring of him who steers the universe,
         sun, you, who encircle everything, who see everything
         from the stellar paths, tell me, did you ever see
         a happier and more fortunate lover than me?)

Fig 2.1. *L'Orfeo*, Act I

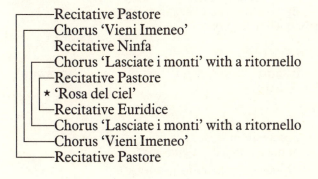

Recitative Pastore
Chorus 'Vieni Imeneo'
Recitative Ninfa
Chorus 'Lasciate i monti' with a ritornello
Recitative Pastore
★ 'Rosa del ciel'
Recitative Euridice
Chorus 'Lasciate i monti' with a ritornello
Chorus 'Vieni Imeneo'
Recitative Pastore

seen a happier person. Monteverdi set the four-line hymn over a single note until Orfeo begins to address the sun directly, at which point the bass takes on some movement and the expressive language of the opening is transformed into a dramatic gesture (Ex. 2.5). This recitative is framed by choruses, instrumental ritornellos, and recitatives in an almost cyclical arrangement (see Fig. 2.1).

The first act, as that of Rinuccini, is less an exposition of the plot than a static image of Arcadian paradise. The second act also opens with the intoxicating *joie de vivre* of that lovely dreamland, which is extolled by the shepherds:

> In questo prato adorno
> ogni selvaggio nume
> sovente ha per costume
> di far lieto soggiorno.
>
> Qui Pan dio dei pastori
> s'udì talhor dolente
> rimembrar dolcemente
> suoi sventurati amori.
>
> Qui le Napee vezzose
> (schiera sempre fiorita)
> con le candide dita
> fur viste a coglier rose.

> In the beautiful meadow
> every god of the woods
> has often, according to custom,
> happily sojourned.
>
> Here one sometimes heard
> Pan, the god of the shepherds,
> sadly, tenderly recall,
> his infelicitous loves.
>
> Here one saw the graceful Napae
> (the company always bedecked in flowers)
> with their white fingers
> pick roses.

This is the same distant, utopic land that Jacopo Sannazaro's shepherds had once praised:

> Allora i sommi dii non si sdegnavano
> menar le pecorelle in selva a pascere
> e, com' or noi facemo, essi cantavano.[5]

[5] Jacopo Sannazaro, *L'Arcadia*, sixth eclogue.

> At that time the highest gods did not disdain
> to lead the flock to the wood to graze
> and in doing so they sang as we do today.

Guarini also had something to tell of it in *Il pastor fido*:

> Allor tra prati e linfe
> gli scherzi e le carole
> di legittimo amor furon le faci.
> Avean pastori e ninfe
> il cor ne le parole
> dava lor Imeneo le gioie e i baci
> più dolcie più tenaci.[6]

> At that time in the meadows and streams
> there were the songs and circle dances,
> the torches of true love.
> Shepherds and nymphs had
> their hearts in their mouths;
> Hymen gave them the sweetest
> and gentlest joys and kisses.

*Scherzi e carole*—this is exactly the image which served as a basis for the beginning of Act II. Here for the first time Monteverdi exceeded the bounds set by the Florentine pastoral plays; the *joie de vivre* of this scene is expressed not only verbally, but also with poetic and musical means which lay outside the possibilities and prerequisites of recitative singing. The text does not consist of recitative verse, but is made up entirely of complete stanzas. Although these may vary metrically, their rhyme scheme is always the same. Orfeo's text is distinguished from that of the shepherds' in more than just the superficial observation that his lines have eight rather than seven syllables:

> Vi ricorda, o boschi ombrosi,
> de' miei lunghi aspri tormenti,
> quando i sassi a' miei lamenti
> rispondean, fatti pietosi?

> Do you remember, O shady woods,
> my long, bitter torments,
> when to my laments the stones
> responded, having turned merciful?

Whereas the heptasyllablic line belonged to spoken poetry and to drama, the octasyllable was from the very beginning tied to a musical presentation because of its regular accentuation; in any case it showed a strong affinity for dance rhythms. It made its way from folk poetry

---

[6] Giovanni Battista Guarini, *Il pastor fido*, final chorus of Act IV.

to literary art and was scorned at first in Florentine circles. It was not suitable for recitative compositions because of its metrical regularity. Rinuccini used it only for the chorus stanzas at the ends of the acts, i.e. outside the plot. Monteverdi and Striggio then made use of exactly that feature of the verse which had hindered its acceptance in the dialogue of the Florentine operas: its dance-like character. Thus the Arcadian *joie de vivre* was not expressed with words and phrases as with Rinuccini, was not told in a recitative, but was placed on view and presented musically. The disposition of the scene is choreographic, and in both the text and the composition moves towards a highpoint (see Fig. 2.2). Dance rhythms predominate in all the songs, the pace intensifies, the instrumentation grows in size, and the scene finally culminates in the exuberant alternating rhythm—already hinted at in Orfeo's opening song, 'Ecco pur ch'a voi ritorno'—of 'Vi ricorda, o boschi ombrosi' (Ex. 2.6).

This extremely regular scenic structure, building as it does towards a climax, could now have returned to the shepherds' songs, had it had

Fig. 2.2. *L'Orfeo*, opening of Act II

| Orfeo | Ecco pur ch'a voi ritorno | |
| ┌─Ritornello 1 | | |
| │ Pastore | Mira ch'a sè n'alletta | (1st stanza) |
| │ Ritornello 1 | | |
| └─Pastore | Su quest' herbose sponde | (2nd stanza) |
| ┌─Ritornello 2 | | |
| │ 2 Pastori | In questo prato adorno | (1st stanza) |
| │ Ritornello 2 | | |
| └─2 Pastori | Qui Pan dio dei pastori | (2nd stanza) |
| ┌─Ritornello 3 | | |
| │ 2 Pastori | Qui le Napee vezzose | (1st stanza) |
| │ Ritornello 3 | | |
| └─Chorus | Dunque fa degno Orfeo | (2nd stanza) |
| ┌─Ritornello 4 | | |
| │ Orfeo | Vi ricorda, o boschi ombrosi | (1st stanza) |
| │ Ritornello 4 | | |
| │ Orfeo | Dite allor non vi sembrai | (2nd stanza) |
| │ Ritornello 4 | | |
| │ Orfeo | Vissi già mesto e dolente | (3rd stanza) |
| │ Ritornello 4 | | |
| └─Orfeo | Sol per te bella Euridice | (4th stanza) |
| Pastore | Mira deh nura Orfeo | |

Ex. 2.6.    'Vi ricorda, o boschi ombrosi', *L'Orfeo*, Act II
            (Do you remember, O shady woods,
            my long, bitter torments?)

a cyclical disposition similar to that of the first act. The turning-point
is even indicated in the text, for the shepherd requests that Orfeo
continue with his music at the end of the scene. Before Orfeo can draw
a breath, however, the mood changes suddenly with the appearance of
the bearer of bad tidings. One can scarcely imagine a stronger contrast
than the one created by this blending of the musical gesture with the
scene: first the *scherzi e carole, joie de vivre*, song and dance; then the
abrupt shift to a highly expressive recitative, 'Ahi caso acerbo', the
outcry that will, like a refrain, dominate the second half of the act
(Ex. 2.7).

Ex. 2.7.    'Ahi caso acerbo', *L'Orfeo*, Act II
            (Ah bitter chance,
            Ah wicked and cruel fate,
            Ah calumnious stars,
            Ah avaricious Heaven!)

From this moment on, the pastoral 'togetherness' is transformed into Orfeo's individual fate. Another outward sign for this is the fact that the chorus appears only at the end of scenes. Even when Orfeo returns to Thrace at the end of Act V, to the place where he had danced and sung with the shepherds, he is alone with the echo. In this, Striggio again has left the confines of the pastoral drama, whereas Rinuccini had obediently stayed within their limits. Herein *La favola d'Orfeo* also approaches a tragedy, not only because there is no happy ending, but also because Orfeo through his own efforts first won his chance and then lost it again.

Whenever the Orpheus story was used as the basis for an opera libretto, one aspect of the myth was always emphasized, regardless of whatever other complications the hero was involved in. This aspect formed its central core and was already predominant in the ancient pictorial representations: the singer was surrounded by a magic aura, a supernatural balm—a true operatic subject. Hardly any composer could resist the opportunity to stage effectively the overwhelming power of Orpheus's song and lyre playing, whether it was used to tame wild beasts or underworld gods. In Striggio's *La favola d'Orfeo* it is the ferryman Caronte whom Orfeo must overcome, a dull, uncouth companion without feelings, on whom Orfeo must exercise all the means at his disposal. Depicting the most powerful music was a stimulating task for every composer; in addition, it indicates what kind of singing was considered to be unrivalled at the time. Orfeo's song of entreaty is an instructive example, but it still poses riddles. The vocal part is notated on two staves; the first presents a simple, recitative declamation, the second a virtuoso, embellished version of the first, bordering on the limits of what is vocally possible. Monteverdi's own instruction here reads: 'Orfeo sings only one of the two versions.' Is it imaginable that Orfeo could have made any impression with as simple notes as those of the unornamented line?

The scene at the banks of the river is a further passage where Striggio and Monteverdi have left the prescribed paths. Here Rinuccini had placed a long recitative in the mouth of Orfeo, which was made up of irregularly grouped lines and interrupted three times by a refrain. Striggio, on the other hand, suggested a closed form in 'Possente spirto' with his six tercets—stanzas comprising three lines apiece. Peri did not place Orfeo's entreaty in contrast to the rest of the recitatives of the opera; only the same setting of the refrain line lends it a musical structure. Monteverdi, however, composed a strophic recitative above a bass, whose pitches were altered only slightly each time. Orfeo always invents new melodies to it and endeavours to soften Caronte with increasingly virtuoso ornaments—an additional point where the scene and the music blend together (Ex. 2.8). The song stanzas are separated from one another by instrumental ritornellos, which are just as demanding as the embellished vocal melody and whose instrumentation varies—two violins, two cornetti, and double harp. They already appear in the interludes of the preceding stanza. The instrumental passages contribute significantly to the impression of the music's overwhelming power. If one were to perform the simple melodic line with them, then the overpowering effect of the music would lie with the instruments—an argument that is not without its merits. The embellished version, however, pushes the virtuoso nature of the instrumental passages far into the background and at the same time clearly shows Monteverdi's idea of extraordinary singing. That is what is so striking in the second line. The ornaments, however extensive they may be, are pressed into the service of dramatic statement. Orfeo flatters and delights Caronte's ear with the truly acrobatic feats of his vocal cords; he also, however, declaims distinctly when he desires to make his intentions clear to Caronte. In writing down these coloraturas Monteverdi undoubtedly wished to avoid a meaningless virtuoso flurry. The double vocal part is therefore an indication of a widespread bad habit on the part of singers, who at that time added as many divisions as possible to every melody, something that Caccini had already condemned in *Le nuove musiche*. It was to prevent just such excesses that Monteverdi demanded that only one of the two lines be sung: if with embellishments, then with those given; if not with those, then preferably

Ex. 2.8.   'Possente spirto', *L'Orfeo*, Act III
(so much beauty)

without any rather than with the wrong ones. It is possible that the ornamented version came about as a result of collaboration with the first man to sing Orfeo—presumably Francesco Rasi, one of the most famous tenors of the time and himself a composer—and that it was then included in the printed score. The utmost that vocal art could offer then was used to illustrate the power of music; for Monteverdi, however, this *non plus ultra* had a function only when it remained within the confines of the dramatic statement.

The fact that the central scene of Act V is the song in praise of Euridice, 'Ma tu anima mia | Tu bella fusti e saggia', and the cursing of the other women just before Apollo's appearance, 'Or l'altre donne son superbe e perfide', rather than the opening echo scene, may seem astonishing at first glance. There are, however, several indications that Monteverdi considered this seemingly recitative monologue to be the primordial Orfeo scene, to be a self-contained unit. To begin with, this monologue, with its supposedly 'open' recitative melodic progress, is divided into stanzas which are clearly distinct from one another. The five-part Sinfonia at the end of the curse is, however, much more important. Up until now all Monteverdi scholars have been unanimous in characterizing this Sinfonia as a recollection of the underworld where it had already been heard twice. In actuality, however, with this Sinfonia Monteverdi was evoking not the underworld, but rather Orfeo's playing of the lyre in the underworld as well as in the world of the living.

In the sixteenth century the lyre was still generally thought to be a bowed instrument rather than a plucked one as believed later; this is substantiated by the pictorial representations of Orfeo with a *lira da braccio* in his hands. It also is striking that Monteverdi required a bowed sound in all of Orfeo's central scenes; this is clearest in the song in praise of the lyre, 'Qual honor di te fia degno', in Act IV (see Ex. 3.4), which is given its structure by a violin ritornello, as well as in the ritornellos of 'Vi ricorda, o boschi ombrosi', where Monteverdi called for a viol consort. The long sustained bass note at the beginning of 'Rosa del ciel' in Act I seems like an evocation of the recitation of epics in the fifteenth and sixteenth centuries in which a singer accompanied himself (chordally) on a *lira da braccio*. 'Possente spirto' in Act III is also embedded in instrumental ritornellos with which Orfeo makes the words more than clear: at the beginning, when he turns to Caronte, and in the last stanza, where he mentions Caronte's name, the string ritornellos are heard; when he speaks of death in the second stanza, cornetti, the classical instruments of the underworld, sound; and when he mentions paradise in the third stanza, the harp, the instrument of the heavens, has its say. Almost always when strings are heard in these passages the lyre is mentioned, as in the much-quoted 'first *accompagnato* recitative in the history of the opera'. In reality it is nothing more than a musical representation of Orfeo, who, while singing and playing the lyre, attempts to appease Caronte with words to the effect that his only weapon is a golden lyre:

> sopra un aurea cetra
> sol di corde soavi armo le dita.

> It is only with sweet chords on a golden lyre
> that I arm my fingers.

Orfeo also speaks of the lyre at the beginning of the song in praise of Euridice: 'A te sacro la mia cetra e 'l canto' (To you I dedicate my lyre and my song); he realizes these words by having the five-part Sinfonia follow. Orfeo's central scenes—the scenes in the opera in which his song and lyre playing are the focal point—refer to a long, specifically Mantuan tradition. It was there at the end of the fifteenth century that the first secular drama of modern times, Angelo Poliziano's *Fabula d'Orfeo*, was performed; Striggio's libretto was based closely on this play. The central scenes of the individual acts also have their prototypes in the *Fabula d'Orfeo*, in which Orfeo actually accompanied himself on a *lira da braccio*.

The echo scene at the beginning of Act V is in another tradition, the one which led from the pastoral drama to the opera. The trick of using the reverberation, so that the landscape becomes an active participant in the plot, fits in splendidly with the image of that dream-like world. Echo had been an Arcadian nymph and, despairing about her unrequited love, had wasted away to an incorporeal voice. A question and answer game soon developed out of the simple pleasure in echoes in poetry; this in turn finally began to influence the plot. The prototype for such dramaturgically important echo scenes is found in Guarini's *Il pastor fido*, where the god of love passes himself off as Echo and prophesies to the unwilling lover, the shepherd Silvio, his union with the nymph Dorinda:

> Quando sarà ch'n questo cor pudico
> amor alloggi?                                    'Oggi'
> Dunque sì tosto s'innamora?                      'Ora'
> E qual sarà colei
> che far potrà ch'oggi l'adori?                   'Dori'[7]

> When in this chaste heart will
> love lodge?                                      'Today'

---

[7] Giovanni Battista Guarini, *Il pastor fido*, IV. viii.

| Will it then fall in love so quickly? | 'Now' |
| And who will it be | |
| who can make me adore her today? | 'Dori' |

There is no doubt that these echo effects were highly suited to musical adaptation. Echoes had already been popular in the madrigals of the sixteenth century; this is most tangible in Orlando di Lasso's 'Ola, o che bon eco'. In Rinuccini's *Euridice* there was no occasion for an echo. *Dafne*, however, has a highly effective scene at the beginning of the first act in which the echo finally reveals itself to be Apollo. From that time on no pastoral opera could do without an echo scene. The availablity of the echo was even employed for the intrigues of later pastoral operas, when a monologue provoked a wrong answer instead of the right one. Orfeo's echo has none of these dramatic qualities. It only strives to console him and dies away after three attempts when this proves to be impossible. Even so, following the underworld scenes, it re-establishes the connection with the first two acts, although none of the Arcadian joy is left.

All Orpheus operas—and many have been written in the course of history—have had their difficulties in finding a plausible ending. The problem was overcoming the discrepancy between Orpheus's unhappy fate and being obliged to provide the opera with a happy ending. The conclusion proffered by Striggio's libretto refers back to the first Orpheus dramatization in Italy, Angelo Poliziano's *Fabula d'Orfeo*. On the other hand, the end, as Monteverdi presented it in the score, based on a celestial motif, is an apotheosis of music and serves as a bridge back to the allegory of the prologue: Apollo, the god of music, raises his son Orpheus, the singer, to the heavens. Striggio's and Monteverdi's solutions, however greatly they may vary from one another, have the advantage over Rinuccini's idea of the triumph of love, in that they did not have to modify the myth. Of course, the occasion was also different. *L'Orfeo* was performed not for a princely wedding, but simply during a carnival season for no special occasion, in the presence of the court and members of the academy, an audience that was proud of its education. A tragic ending, it must be said, would also not have been accepted by this audience at this time. Perhaps the Striggio version was connected with the circumstances concerning the première, for the bacchanalia at the end of Poliziano's *Fabula d'Orfeo* did not only conclude the presentation but was also the opening of the subsequent court ball. Perhaps the bacchanalia in Striggio's libretto had a similar function, the sense of which was lost when Monteverdi published the score. Monteverdi's solution is a brilliant compromise between the unavoidable necessity of having a happy ending and fidelity to the myth.

PASTORAL DRAMA AND COMEDY: *LA FINTA PAZZA LICORI*

It is improbable that the reasons behind Monteverdi's decision to alter the *Orfeo* libretto will ever be brought to light. Was it because there was too little space on the improvised stage in a gallery of the ducal palace for the large dimensions of Striggio's maenad finale; or was the happy ending with the apotheosis closer to Monteverdi's aesthetic perception than the drastic nature of the rather forcefully appended Bacchus festival? The question remains unanswered. It is also impossible to make inferences concerning *L'Orfeo* on the basis of Monteverdi's later music for theatre. Literary taste changed not long after this opera and with it the taste in opera, in such a way that the *favola pastorale* à la Tasso and Guarini died away. Already by the end of the sixteenth century the *commedia dell'arte*, the improvisatory theatre, had taken over the pastoral subject-matter; its figures had begun to amuse themselves in Arcadia. At the beginning of the seventeenth century these figures were already meddling with literary pastoral drama and at the same time the gods lost their immunity. This change began in 1614 with Alessandro Tassoni's epic in verse, *La secchia rapita* (The Stolen Bucket). The Olympic gods, clad according to the Spanish fashion, showed themselves here to be empty-headed and vulgar at a celestial peace conference. In 1618 Francesco Bracciolini published his epic, *Lo scherno degli Dei* (The Mockery of the Gods), in which Vulcan is emasculated after his fellow gods have showered him with scorn and ridicule because he was surprised in a cosy twosome with a female ape. Such *poemi eroicomici* were in part a defensive reaction towards the classical subjects of the Renaissance. Mythology was no longer taken seriously, and pastoral drama was dragged down with it, in particular because the *commedia dell'arte* had already made some headway in this direction. In Ercole Cimilotti's pastoral play, *I falsi dei* (The False Gods) of 1614, the *commedia* figures disguise themselves as gods: Graziano as Priapus, Zanni as Pan, Burattino as Amor, and Pantalone as the winged Genius. This was a very curious image, hardly comprehensible even to the Arcadian shepherds:

Questi dunque soni i numi che dite? Se i celesti spiriti son di sì deforme aspetto quali saran le deità d'Averno?[8]

Those then are the gods, about whom you have spoken? If the celestial spirits already have such a deformed appearance, what will the gods of the underworld be like?

*I falsi dei*, which Cimilotti called a *favola pastorale piacevolissima*, is in yet another way a clear symptom of the change in taste, which

---

[8] Ercole Cimilotti, *I falsi dei* (Milan, 1614), II. i.

would soon affect poetry written for opera. It contains a caricature of
that most popular of pastoral scenes—the echo scene. Instead of
comforting words or important dramatic revelations, the echo here—
naturally in a Venetian or Bolognese dialect—makes suggestions to
Burattino concerning his diet, and Pantalone even offers to thrash the
impertinent voice in the cave:

| | |
|---|---|
| Ti menti razza insia de scanderbecco | Becco |
| Fa te veda fora de quel speco | Eco |
| Ven via, se no te amazzo, e son un beco | Eco[9] |
| | |
| You lie, insidious brood of scandalous beaks | Beak |
| Come out of your cave | Ave |
| Go away, if you don't I'll get you, am I an idiot? | Diot! |

With all due respect for the sentimental world of the shepherds and
nymphs, the poetry for opera began to absorb such burlesque
elements. The first signs exhibit themselves in Stefano Landi's
*tragicommedia pastorale*, *La morte d'Orfeo* (1619). In it Caronte is not
the dull, dark figure of Monteverdi, but a quite lively and mischievous
character with an inclination for brawling. For example, he offers
Orfeo the waters of forgetfulness from the river with a gay drinking
song on his lips. By the middle of the 1620s this transformation from
the pastoral to the more burlesque was complete. The *favola pastorale*
became the playground for grotesque figures. Arcadia lost the aura of
a visionary world which had still surrounded Monteverdi's *L'Orfeo*.
Just as in Tassoni's and Bracciolini's *poemi eroicomici*, the gods in the
opera were delivered up to caricature; the shepherds and nymphs
behaved in ways which no one would have believed possible at the
beginning of the century. The most popular target was the god of the
shepherds, Pan, ugly, hooved, and always falling in love with the most
unsuitable women; it did not matter whether it was chaste Diana or a
lovely nymph, as in *La Flora* (text by Andrea Salvadori, music by
Marco da Gagliano and Jacopo Peri), performed in 1628 in Florence,
or in *Diana schernita* (text by Giovanni Francesco Parisani, music by
Giacinto Cornacchioli), performed in Rome in 1629 and one of the
first musical comedies. Around the same time Monteverdi also showed
how far he had distanced himself from his earlier works. Twenty years
after *L'Orfeo*, the *favola pastorale* no longer seemed an appropriate
vehicle to him. For a commission for an opera for Mantua he
suggested two librettos, both of which were set in Arcadia and
otherwise had nothing in common with one another: Ottavio
Rinuccini's *Narciso* and Giulio Strozzi's *La finta pazza Licori*.
Monteverdi only used the one in order to give emphasis to his

---

[9] Ercole Cimilotti, *I falsi dei* (Milan, 1614), III. iv.

enthusiasm for the other: he did not deem *Narciso*, a text by the very first opera librettist, to be suitable.

I send you the enclosed *Narciso* by Ottavio Rinuccini, which was never printed, nor set to music, nor staged. This gentleman, when he was still alive—I wish with all my heart that he is now in heaven—not only favoured me with a copy, but even invited my approval, for he liked the work very much and hoped that I might set it to music. I have made several attempts and have thought about it quite a bit, and to tell you the truth, in my opinion, I would not be able to give it the force that I would desire because of the many sopranos one would need for the many nymphs involved, and because of the many tenors for the many shepherds, and nothing else for variety; and in addition, because of the tragic and sad ending.[10]

Indeed Monteverdi's verdict is in part justified. The entire first act of *Narciso* contains only female voices, and there is a great preponderance of female roles in the libretto overall. His verdict, however, also reveals a certain amount of rejection of the *favola pastorale* as such. The tragic ending could easily have been expanded to include a joyful, festive final scene, just as in the libretto version of *L'Orfeo*, which also cannot quite be said to have a happy ending. *Narciso* would also have proffered plenty of variety and occasions for music: Narciso's song spurning love, conceived strophically; messengers' tales; chorus and echo scenes, which are nowhere more dramaturgically justified than in this tale, as it deals with the nymph Echo herself. In *L'Orfeo*, moreover, only sopranos and tenors had appeared in the world of the living; only the underworld gods, Caronte and Plutone, were bass roles. Monteverdi's idea of what a drama set to music should be like, however, had changed fundamentally since those days. This becomes clear immediately upon reading his suggestions for Giulio Strozzi's *La finta pazza Licori*, a work which belongs just as much to the genre of pastoral drama as *Narciso*. Monteverdi, however, characterized it as being 'newer, more diverting, and possessing greater variety'.[11]

Among all of Monteverdi's works that no longer survive, *La finta pazza Licori* is the greatest loss. We know neither the text nor the setting. Only Monteverdi's letters give an indication of the importance of this work as a link between his Mantuan and Venetian operas. The fact that the scene was still set in Arcadia may be assumed from the names of the main figures, Licori and Amyntas from Virgil's *Bucolica*. Thematically, however, the fable is already much closer to plays full of intrigue, to the dramaturgy of short, entertaining scenes, to comedy. The plot here does not deal with love's joys and sorrows, but is a lively bit of trickery, by means of which a shepherd is forced into

[10] Letter of 7 May 1627 (*Lettere*, p. 244).
[11] Letter of 22 May 1627 (*Lettere*, p. 248).

matrimony. Licori plays the mad woman in many short scenes until Amyntas has yielded. Monteverdi even got Strozzi to enrich the text with other episodes and additional roles, 'so that the main actress is not as frequently in action'.[12] What may have disturbed Monteverdi about *Narciso* and other pastoral dramas of its ilk already becomes clear here, for there is no longer anything which connects *La finta pazza Licori* with the linear structure of an *Orfeo*, in which the protagonist is almost continuously on stage. Just how 'full of variety' and 'diverting'—concepts which had never played a role in the evaluation of a pastoral opera—*La finta pazza Licori* must have been, is shown in Monteverdi's characterization of the protagonist:

The part of Licori, because of its great variety, must not fall into the hands of a woman who cannot play first a man and then a woman with lively gestures and varied passions; because the imitation of this fictitious madness must be determined only by the present and not by the past or future, and must be based on a [single] word and not on the content of a whole sentence, when she then speaks of war, she must imitate war, when she speaks of peace, peace, when of death, death, etc.; and because the transformations and imitations take place within the shortest time, the woman who plays this most principal of roles, who moves one to laughter and to compassion, must forgo every other imitation other than the present one, which the current word provides her with.[13]

Splitting up the fable into short episodes instead of following a longer dramatic line, light-heartedness instead of deep emotion—the shepherds and nymphs of Arcadia had travelled a long way. For the musical disposition, however, Monteverdi seems to have had a concept similar to that characteristic for *L'Orfeo*, namely of aiming towards a central scene. There were probably so many more in *La finta pazza Licori* that the effect must have been completely different:

It is my aim that she [Licori], with each appearance on stage, should always bring new delight with the new changes; this is certain to be effective in three places: the first in the field, when one hears the sounds and clamour behind the stage in the imitation of her words—this will certainly be very successful [and was evidently an echo parody]; the second, when she feigns death, and the third when she pretends to sleep, whereby at this place music will be used which imitates sleep; at certain other places, however, where the text does not offer any suggestions for gestures or noises or other possibilities for imitation, I fear that the previous and following passages might seem weak; I am waiting, therefore, for Signor Strozzi [to make further improvements on the text].[14]

---

[12] Letter of 22 May 1627 (*Lettere*, p. 248).
[13] Letter of 7 May 1627 (*Lettere*, p. 244).
[14] Letter of 24 May 1627 (*Lettere*, pp. 251–2).

*La finta pazza Licori*, although a play about shepherds and nymphs, is not a *favola pastorale*: it reduces Arcadia to an arbitrary, interchangeable background. The pastoral world, which had dominated the first stage of operatic history, came to an end with the new dramas dealing with thrilling entanglements and intrigues. Only a little later stingy nymphs, sly shepherds, and vulgar gods will appear. A Narcissus who wastes away from loving his own reflection, an Echo who turns to stone because of the sorrows of love, were truly no longer part of this world.

# 3

## OSTINATO AND OTHER BASS MODELS

The use of bass models was one of the fundamental features of seventeenth-century vocal music. They served as a connecting link between the old and the new styles, thus making the break with tradition less radical. After the rules of polyphony and the church modes had gradually lost their constructive influence on composition in the second half of the sixteenth century, new elements of organization had to be found which assumed these functions. The results of such efforts were manifold: they are seen in the use of folkloristic melodies, such as the *bergamasca* or *padovana*, as the lowest part of a polyphonic piece; in the utilization of well-defined rhythmic patterns or even the employment of dance rhythms in vocal music; and in the practice prevalent everywhere of improvising music based on known melodies to sonnets or sections from epics such as Ariosto's *Orlando furioso*. All of these experiments led to a reduction of the number of voices and culminated in monody. At the same time that Monteverdi was searching for new possibilities of textual expression within a polyphonic framework, the instrumentally accompanied solo song was coming to life around him. It was not that Monteverdi did not himself perform madrigals *per cantare et sonare*, that is solo songs with an instrumental accompaniment; his letters repeatedly bear witness to this. It was not until *L'Orfeo*, however, that he devoted himself to the new techniques of composing a solo part above a chordal bass. He let the Florentine composers probe monody's possibilities, not only in the field of the dramatic arts but also in that of chamber music. Caccini's *Le nuove musiche* was published in 1602. This was one of the first printed works in this new compositional style, in which (in addition to several pieces from his opera *Il rapimento di Cefalo*, performed in 1600) three different formal models may be recognized: through-composed madrigals with a virtuoso, embellished vocal part above a supportive chordal bass; strophic songs of a folkloristic nature based on dance-like rhythms; and virtuoso vocal variations over a melodically moving, strophically repeated bass. The structural notes of the vocal part remained unchanged for the most part and were more extensively ornamented with coloraturas from stanza to stanza.

Today the term 'ostinato' is generally associated with a constantly repeated short bass melody, made up of only a few notes, above which a vocal or instrumental part is unfolded. This, however, is already a highly developed, abstract form of the ostinato, which presumes a high degree of formal structure and tonal harmonic conception. 'Ostinato' means, to begin with, nothing more than 'persistent' or 'obstinate', and says nothing about the length of the obstinately repetitive tune, which could be as long as an entire stanza, as in Caccini's vocal variations. The essence of the ostinato, its recognizability, which was later assured *a priori* by the shortness of the figure, was none the less preserved. The origins of the *basso ostinato* lie in a musical practice of improvising above popular melodies, as may first be seen in Spanish instrumental music. From the middle of the sixteenth century on, such improvisations on well-known dances or songs also appeared in print for lute and keyboard instruments. These were melodies that everyone knew and could even make out when altered rhythmically: the *passamezzo*, for example, or the *folia*, the *ruggiero*, or the *romanesca*. Some of these ostinato melodies seem to have been particularly suitable for vocal improvisation; there are a multitude of arias and duets on the *romanesca* and *ruggiero* basses in the early monody prints. The form of the text for such strophic variations was usually an *ottava*—a stanza with eight equally long lines—the most characteristic metre for Italian epic poetry. In this kind of ostinato composition a stanza consisted of a couplet; the bass melody was thus 'obstinately' repeated four times. A direct line may be traced from the improvised performances of epic poetry in the sixteenth century to the strophic basses of early monody, in particular to the fixed patterns such as the *romanesca*.

The meaning of the name *romanesca* as well as the origins of this melody are still not completely clear today. It is equally as likely that it is of Italian as of Spanish derivation. It was commonly known by 1600. Caccini had already written a composition on the *romanesca*, of which, however, only a small section survives. Until late in the 1730s this bass model appeared in music prints throughout Italy. Antonio Cifra of Rome wrote vast quantities of such *romanesche* and even underlaid the melodies with sacred texts. Francesca Caccini of Florence, Giulio's daughter, published no less than four *romanesca-ottave* in her first book of one- and two-part compositions. In Venice, too, the melody was used as a strophic bass. Giovanni Stefani's monody collection, *Affetti amorosi*, published in 1618, contains one

*romanesca*; and last but not least, there is also one in Monteverdi's
seventh madrigal book.

In the case of the *romanesca* and other similar ostinatos, one cannot
avoid speaking of the bass melody, for the melodic progression was
the only thing which was reasonably fixed, and even that could be
altered slightly. The rhythm and tempo, on the other hand, could be
varied and the entire melody expanded to attain the required number
of bars. Ex. 3.1 shows three of the many versions with a clearly
defined rhythm: Antonio Cifra's model, which he used unchanged as a
basis for all his *romanesca* compositions (Ex. 3.1*a*), Stefano Landi's

Ex. 3.1*a*.   Antonio Cifra, *romanesca* melody (1614)

pure *romanesca* melody (Ex. 3.1*b*), and Girolamo Frescobaldi's, which
is lightly ornamented (Ex. 3.1*c*). The metrical ambivalence of all these
models is striking, permitting an interpretation in both duple as well
as triple time. Only the vocal part assures that the metre is reasonably
clearly established either one way or the other.

Ex. 3.1*b*.   Stefano Landi, *romanesca* melody (1620)

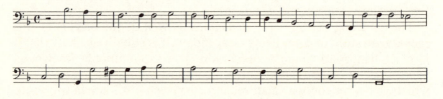

Ex. 3.1*c*.   Girolamo Frescobaldi, *romanesca* melody (1630)

The compositional problems associated with melodic ostinato basses are obvious. The more complex and independent the bass melody proved to be, the more the upper part's possibilities of unfolding freely were limited. Even when 'forbidden' progressions or dissonances were tolerated for the sake of the unity of the vocal part, it always turned out to be more or less a counterpart to the bass. A glance at the melodic structure of the *romanesca* explains the particular popularity of this bass model in vocal music. Apart from several unimportant passing notes, it consists entirely of descending tetrachords and cadence formulas. In the early history of the *basso ostinato* these progressions would show themselves to be particularly versatile in their application; they also suggested, beyond the external agreement in stanzas, caesuras and a possible inner order for the composition. Seen as a chain of tetrachords, the *romanesca* was already an abstract construction, apart from the harmonic mutability of such a simple line of four notes (Ex. 3.2).

Ex. 3.2.    Structure of the *romanesca* melody

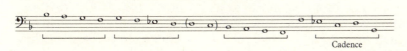

Monteverdi was never very concerned about the fashionable trends in composition. The monodic euphoria of the first decades of the seventeenth century passed him by, hardly leaving its imprint. For him solo songs were dramatic songs; chamber music remained polyphonic music for him, even when the editions of solo chamber arias were sprouting up all around him. It is therefore not surprising that there is only one strophic bass *ottava* by him, a duet on the *romanesca*—'Ohimè dov'è il mio ben'; its structure is such, however, that it can hardly be recognized as a melody any more. It has more or less been reduced to a chordal framework, in which the tetrachords— rather than the lines—are perceived as entities which are denoted as clearly as possible by the caesuras. Bernardo Tasso's poem proffered this possibility because seven of its eight lines are subdivided into two sections according to meaning. Monteverdi could thus effortlessly follow the tetrachordal structure in his composition:

| Ohimè dov'è il mio ben, dov'è il mio core? | (Ist part) |
| --- | --- |
| Ist tetrachord          2nd tetrachord | |

Chi mi asconde il mio ben e chi me 'l toglie?

                       3rd tetrachord (ascending) Cadence Formula

Dunque ha potuto sol desio d'onore　　　　　(2nd part)

darmi fera cagion di tante doglie

Dunque ha potuto in me più che 'l mio amore　　(3rd part)

ambiziose e troppo lievi voglie

Ahi sciocco mondo e cieco, ahi cruda sorte　　(4th part)

che ministro mi fai de la mia morte.

Alas, where is my life, where is my heart?
Who hides my loved one and who takes him from me?
Thus only the desire for honour prevailed
to give me the cruel reason for such pain;
thus ambitious and too frivolous desires
have prevailed in me more than my love.
Ah, stupid and blind world, ah, cruel fate
which makes me the executor of my death.

Instead of the usual sixteen bars or, at the most, twenty bars, the *romanesca* has been expanded to all of thirty bars. Clear rhythmic definition is avoided, the repeated notes of the model are turned into sustained tones. The original melody is reduced to its basic pitches. Instead of forming counterparts to the bass, the upper voices unfold in the imitative style so characteristic of Monteverdi's duets. Its expressive means are taken from the polyphonic madrigal: the harsh dissonance at the beginning, for example, the circular melodic phrases, the falling thirds in a dotted rhythm, and so on. Compared to these parts, the bass melody is insignificant and loses its independence. Although it is an ostinato from a compositional point of view, one can hardly distinguish it from the usual monodic chordal basses by ear (Ex. 3.3).

A completely different concept lay behind another kind of bass model, one which enjoyed great popularity with Monteverdi as well as with his contemporaries. As opposed to the strict ostinato basses, it was characterized only by an unyielding rhythmic motion. The impression made by the rhythmic structure prevails over the free melodic progress. Such 'walking' basses could be used with extreme versatility; they not only could serve as strophic basses, but also could endow a through-composed madrigal with musical coherence. At a time when musical forms were disintegrating and becoming subordinated to the spoken word, resulting of necessity at first in a kind of musical 'formlessness', such possibilities of musical manipulation, which still did not rob the melodic voice of its declamatory flexibility, gained enormous importance. The melodic shape of the 'walking' bass

Ex. 3.3.  'Ohimè dov'è il mio ben'
(Alas, where is my life, where is my heart?)

could as easily consist of indifferent scales as of harmonically binding cadence formulas. Theoretically the *romanesca* model could also have been conceived of as a 'walking' bass. It is characteristic that Monteverdi's first composition over a 'walking' bass appears in a dramatic work, 'Qual honor di te fia degno' in *L'Orfeo* and is a masterful description of a dramatic situation: Orfeo has received Euridice back from Pluto and, turning his head away and seething with inner tension, he makes his way out of Hades. One of the shades of the underworld introduces the scene with the words:

> Ecco il gentile cantore,
> che sua sposa conduce al ciel superno.

> Look at the noble singer,
> who leads his bride to the high heavens.

As Orfeo approaches the earth, he praises his lyre in song while walking in time to 'walking' basses. It is as if he were whistling a harmless tune, step for step, note for note, to distract himself. This, however, is not successful, for by the third stanza he is plagued by the doubts which will seal Euridice's fate. At this point the bass changes to long chords (Ex. 3.4).

A dramatic situation furnished Monteverdi with the idea for a new compositional technique which was soon to reveal its purely musical qualities. Only a little later Monteverdi used it in an entirely different context, in a sacred composition, where again it is without precedent.

Ex. 3.4.    'Qual honor di te fia degno', *L'Orfeo*, Act IV
            (What honour is worthy of you,
             my omnipotent lyre,
             having been able to bend every obdurate mind
             in the infernal kingdom?)

The psalm 'Laetatus sum' from the *Marian Vespers* of 1610 (Ex. 3.5*b*) is composed on four different bass models. The first and most frequent of them is a 'walking' bass, with a clearly defined cadence formula at the beginning, and is interwoven, like a rondo, throughout the whole composition. This bass demonstrates the close relationship between the traditional bass melodies and the 'walking' bass, for it is based on the *ruggiero* model (Ex. 3.5*a*), which was just as popular as the *romanesca* in monody. The reduction of the melody to its basic pitches, presented in equal note values, changed its vocal texture to an instrumental one and established the harmonic framework of regularly

Ex. 3.5*a*.    The *ruggiero* melody

Ex. 3.5*b*.   'Laetatus sum', *Marian Vespers*
(I was glad when they said unto me)

spaced cadences within the bars. Even in 'Laetatus sum', however, Monteverdi connected the 'walking' bass to the situation described at the beginning of the psalm:

> Laetatus sum in his quae dicta sunt mihi
> in domum domini ibimus
> Stantes erant pedes nostri . . .

> I was glad when they said to me,
> Let us go into the house of the Lord.
> Our feet shall stand . . .

'Let us go into the house of the Lord'—as in *L'Orfeo* the basses portray the walking movement. When the feet remain standing in front of Jerusalem then the bass also stops moving, just as in the opera when Orfeo is overcome by doubt and comes to a halt.

In Book VII, the first in which the instruments were included in a major way (for Monteverdi the title, *Concerto*, was nothing more than a reference to the instrumental accompaniment), there are three compositions on 'walking' basses: the two-part strophic canzonetta, 'Chiome d'oro', with an instrumental ritornello, and also 'Vaga su spina ascosa' and 'Augellin', madrigalistic compositions for three voices, whose rhythmic vivacity emphasizes the gay nature of their texts. The through-composed disposition, with its ever-new melodic subjects, is given a rhythmic coherence by the instrumental accompaniment.

'Walking' basses became a thoroughgoing fashion in Venice. There was hardly a collection of arias in the 1620s that did not contain at least one composition on a 'walking' bass, where it usually served as a fundament for strophic songs. It seems possible that Monteverdi stimulated the musicians in his vicinity in this respect, but this is a supposition that would be difficult to prove. The publications of such compositions followed so closely upon one another that it is impossible to decide who deserves the honour of being the 'inventor'. In addition, using publications for dating the compositions is an uncertain means at best. One thing, however, is clear: 'walking' basses were instrumental in nature. It cannot be overlooked that interest in this principle of composition originated in an environment which considered instrumental music more important than that by vocal composers such as Peri or Caccini. With the 'walking' basses it once again proved to be true that vocal music gained added dimensions in being exposed to instrumental influences: it either absorbed instrumental techniques or, as here, was forced to clash with an instrumental principle, thereby winning greater declamatory freedom.

Like Caccini's early 'arias', the compositions on 'walking' basses also became the forerunners of a new genre, the cantata. At first this term meant nothing more than a succession of several through-composed vocal stanzas on a repeated strophic bass. This was thus nothing different from what Caccini understood with the term 'aria' and what appeared in the meantime in innumerable *romanesca* and *ruggiero* compositions. Now, however, the colossal difference between the 'vocal' texture of the ostinato bass melodies and the 'instrumental' character of the 'walking' basses became evident. Whereas the bond between an ostinato-bass melody and its vocal part was usually like an embrace, in which the upper voice could only be a counterpart to the lower, the bond with a completely different kind of support, a coherent, imperturbably regular rhythm, gave the vocal melody a life of its own, without destroying the strophic cohesion. This was also a possibility for formally organizing longer compositions.

Monteverdi's 'Ohimè ch'io cado' on a strophic 'walking' bass appeared in a collection of arias by Carlo Milanuzzi in 1624; in the same year a composition by Giovanni Pietro Berti was published which even bears the title 'Cantata'. Their texts and settings are so similar that they were certainly a result of a mutual exchange of ideas. For example, the first verse of Monteverdi's 'Ohimè ch'io cado' is a quotation from Milanuzzi's composition; the recitation pattern with the lower neighbour note with which Monteverdi concludes each stanza is also taken over from Milanuzzi, where this pattern played a significant role in the shaping of the melody. Monteverdi's composition is distinguished only by its greater dramatic eloquence. This manifests itself primarily at the beginnings of the stanzas, each differing from the others (Ex. 3.6). This alone creates the impression of through-composition, for the second halves of the stanzas are practically all

Ex. 3.6.  'Ohimè ch'io cado'
(1. Alas that I fall,
Alas that I stumble again with my foot just as before
2. Alas, I still know the traces
of the old ardour within my breast
5. O how he knows how to punish,
the tyrant Amor, the boldness of my rebellious soul)

identical. What had originally been furnished by the dramatic situation in *L'Orfeo*—the instrument, the movement—has now been incorporated in a principle of composition, thereby bringing a theatrical emphasis to chamber music.

The bass models that were based on well-known dance melodies, such as the *ciaccona*, were also instrumental, in line with their function. The *ciaccona* probably had its origins in Mexico, making its way to Europe via Spain; like the saraband it was soon decried as a lascivious dance. It was through pieces for lute and guitar that it found its way to Italy, where it was also first put to use in instrumental music until the composers of vocal works noted its qualities. In contrast to all other ostinatos, two things were fixed in the *ciaccona* from the very beginning: strict four-bar periods and triple time. Due to the influence of dance music, the *ciaccona* model was eventually shortened to only four bars, something that was originally not characteristic for the *aria della ciaccona*. It was only around 1625 in Venice that the clearly defined rhythmic and melodic bass pattern, which had evolved from the *ciaccona*, finally brought to the ostinato vocal compositions that feature—already seen in the 'walking' basses—which was to become their main characteristic in the centuries to come: the tension between dependence and free development, between a strict musical form and unlimited declamatory possibilities, between the plain simplicity of the fundament and the melodic exuberance of the vocal line. Monteverdi expressed this polarity inimitably in his duet, 'Zefiro torna'. It is a sonnet on spring by Rinuccini in the style of Petrarch; although the much-belittled expressive powers of the poet do not match those of his paragon, it is exceptionally suited for such a composition. Within its joyful Arcadian setting an abundance of words are found which just cry out for a musical interpretation: the waves, the murmur of the wind, the high mountains and deep valleys, echoing grottoes, singing nymphs, and dancing flowers. Monteverdi flamboyantly presents a succession of continually new musical ideas over the fifty-six repetitions of this two-bar ostinato pattern; the text is split into short fragments, whose musical motifs are either presented in imitation by the voices or tossed back and forth like balls. All of this is not unusual taken by itself, but instead is typical of the duet style found in Book VII. It is only in connection with the ostinato bass that the opposing rhythmical forces which constitute the fascination of this piece come into being. Instead of stabilizing the dance-like rhythm of the ostinato with the upper voices, Monteverdi, by means of syncopations, hemiolas, up-beat and off-beat entrances, keeps it so much in the air that the metric structure of the bass never becomes entirely clear to the listener. The basic principle behind this composition is not the union of an ostinato melody with a vocal part which simply executes a series of variations above it, but the co-ordination of two opposing attitudes: the instrumental strictness of the ostinato and the madrigalistic freedom of declamation. The basic dance-like character, however, which fits exceedingly well with the blithe tone of the poem, is still preserved (Ex. 3.7).

'Zefiro torna' did not appear in a madrigal collection, but in the *Scherzi musicali* of 1632. Monteverdi himself never attached much importance to such light, entertaining compositions. With the exception

Ex. 3.7.    'Zefiro torna'
(Zephir, return and speak sweet sounds)

of two compositions at the end of Book VII, he himself published no other canzonetta or scherzo after his early *Canzonette* of 1584; he was not in charge of the publication of the print of 1607, produced by his brother Giulio Cesare, nor of that of the *Scherzi* of 1632, assembled by the publisher, nor of that of the many compositions found in printed collections, such as 'Ohimè ch'io cado'. It is one of fortune's ironies, however, that it was with just these compositions that Monteverdi influenced posterity; perhaps his own evaluation of such works is an indication that he was more 'the last figure of an older generation' than the 'first of a new one'? Compositions on the *ciaccona* bass were soon rampant; the dance basses became so pervasive in sacred music that Salvator Rosa complained in a satire on music from the 1640s that even the 'Miserere me' was sung everywhere on the *ciaccona*. In this respect, however, Monteverdi was ahead of his contemporaries. He had an unerring sense that such basses should be used only for light, cheerful texts, something that had escaped some of the composers immediately surrounding him. In Giovanni Felice Sances's *Cantade* (1633), for example, the *ciaccona* has to serve as the fundament for a despairing plaint about the coldness of a beautiful woman. Tarquinio Merula, on the other hand, exhibits great sensitivity towards the instrumental character of the dance bass when he makes the lyre, to whose sounds the lyrical ego sings of his new love, the main idea of the composition, as seen in 'Su la cetra amorosa' (Ex. 3.8).

Melodic abstraction and an instrumental character were the particular traits of the dance basses. It was only a little way from them to the shorter ostinatos which even lacked rhythmic definition, and to

Ex. 3.8.    Tarquinio Merula, 'Su la cetra amorosa'
            (On the loving lyre in sweet and joyful style)

complete abstraction. An ostinato, which only comprised a few pitches, without melodically or rhythmically binding the vocal part in any way whatsoever, allowed the greatest possible freedom, not only in the shaping of the melody, but also in the regularity of the phrasing, which was no longer tied either to the lines of the text or to the bass progression. The shorter the ostinato bass, the greater the freedom left to the upper part in determining the placement of the caesuras. The shortest ostinato of those times may well have been the swaying bass in Tarquinio Merula's sacred lullaby of 1638, 'Canzonetta spirituale sopra alla nanna' on the text 'Hor ch'è tempo di dormire', with which the baby Jesus is sung to sleep (Ex. 3.9). Its rocking *ninna-nanna* motif, which is obviously taken from popular music, recurs once again in Monteverdi's setting of the same text in *L'incoronazione di Poppea*, when the nurse Arnalta sings Poppea to sleep.

Ex. 3.9.    Tarquinio Merula, 'Canzonetta spirituale sopra alla nanna:
            Hor ch'è tempo di dormire'
            (Now that it is time to sleep, sleep, sleep)

Normally, however, such short ostinatos consisted of four to, at the most, eight notes, which naturally had to be organized in such a way that the upper voice was assured melodic and declamatory freedom. This seemed, on the one hand, to be offered by the cadence formulas and, on the other, by the descending tetrachords from Spain. We already know the latter from the *romanesca*, where they gave the upper voice such a wealth of possibilities for variation, in their major as well as in their minor forms. Detached from any connection with a complete melody, the tetrachord could then prove its inexhaustible applicability. It became the most popular of all the ostinato basses in the seventeenth century; in comparison, cadential formulas were rare.

Only one composition on a cadential formula by Monteverdi was printed. Again he himself did not publish it; it appeared in the posthumous sacred collection of 1650. It is a setting of the psalm 'Laetatus sum (I)', which uses material from an earlier work, namely the self-same psalm from the *Marian Vespers* of 1610 whose opening was composed on a 'walking' bass model. Monteverdi took the first four notes of this model as an ostinato cadence formula, which he then used as a basis for this imposing composition. It appears 154 times within the piece, mostly in duple time, but sometimes in triple, interrupted only at the beginning of the doxology. Above this framework in the bass appear six vocal parts, usually grouped in pairs, two trombones, a bass curtal (ancestor of the bassoon), and two violins; the vocal and instrumental parts always answer each other with the same motif (Ex. 3.10). In spite of its great size, it is a transparent composition, its seemingly mechanical cadence progression never falling into the ruts of a barrel organ. Above this bass, which holds everything together, Monteverdi instead continually brings new melodic ideas, playing with short motifs, coloraturas, and rhythms until the voices come together for the first time at the doxology. With its beginning in E (as the dominant to the following A) this section is clearly set apart harmonically from the relentless G major of the cadence formula; in addition, it is without the ostinato bass.

Possibly it is just this inescapable harmonic cage which checked the composer's use of such cadence formulas. The descending tetrachords were a more variable structure, even if the version in the major was more tonally fixed than the minor; in the major version a sixth chord is required above the second degree of the scale in order to avoid a

Ex. 3.10. 'Laetatus sum (I)'
(For there are set thrones of judgment)

tritone. Exactly when these short descending fourths became popular may once again only be surmised. As the *romanesca* and the *ciaccona*, they belonged to the general resources of folk and dance music; they appeared only slightly later than the *ciaccona* model in art music. Among the first printed sources are a composition from Giovanni Felice Sances's *Cantade*, 'Usurpator tiranno', on the minor tetrachord, and a 'cantata' from Martino Pesenti's second book of arias, 'Ohimè che veggio', on the major tetrachord. Monteverdi's 'Lamento della Ninfa' from Book VIII also belongs to this group, as do many other compositions by Venetian musicians. In *L'incoronazione di Poppea* we encounter the tetrachord basses several times (in spite of all of the philological problems caused by two of these scenes): in the love scene between the servants, Valletto and Damigella; in the duet between Nero and Lucano after Seneca's death during the vision of Poppea's intoxicating lips; and finally in the famous concluding duet, 'Pur ti miro', which is considered to be the first da capo composition in the history of opera. All three passages are based on the major tetrachord, which tends more strongly towards tonal harmony than the minor one. Whereas the 'bocca, bocca' passage in the Nerone–Lucano duet still vacillates throughout between modal and tonal sonorities, the final duet has completed the step towards tonal harmony (Ex. 3.11).

Ex. 3.11.   'Pur ti miro', *L'incoronazione di Poppea*, Act III, sc. viii
             (I admire only you, I rejoice only in you,
             I embrace you, I bind only you)

The effect of such a succinct framework was similar to that of the cadence formula of 'Laetatus sum (I)'. It allowed Monteverdi continually to introduce new musical motifs, playing with them in such a way as to further the dramatic statement of the love duet. In it, short, almost breathless sentence fragments are tossed back and forth, the flight of the lovers towards one another is represented in the music; this passionate drive, which could scarcely be held in check, could best be given a form by means of the seemingly unaffected ostinato. In the middle section of the final duet, the same sort of short interjections—in this case even presented sequentially—but without an underlying ostinato bass, have a completely different effect; one of teasing playfulness. The return of the da capo, however, intervenes and the breathless ecstacy of the beginning—on the descending tetrachord—is brought back.

It is obvious that the unifying strength of the short ostinatos or of the dance basses was particularly advantageous in compositions with several voices, in which additional variety was offered by the conjoint and disjoint motion of the upper voices and where, conversely, the ostinato bass provided the upper voices with new possibilities in this respect. In solo compositions there was the danger of monotony, if sections on ostinato basses were not sometimes intermingled with other kinds. Although the short ostinatos were highly suited for their use as a basis for lengthy through-composed pieces, which were in this way given musical structure, they only revealed their true importance in conjunction with other compositional techniques. Sances's 'Usurpator tiranno' is typical for the problems associated with a through-composed solo piece on a descending tetrachord. It consists of eight canzona stanzas, each of which unfolds freely above five to seven minor tetrachords and which are separated from one another by instrumental ritornellos, only the second-to-last stanza, set as a recitative, interrupts the flux of the ostinato pattern, which appears in all fifty-one times. The structure of the tetrachord basses is so neutral that it can not only bring about caesuras but also bypass them; one, as well as several tetrachords can be the basis for a complete phrase; a whole tetrachord can even have a function somewhat like that of a suspension (Ex. 3.12a). This structure, whose principles are far from any tonal harmonic constraints and which is based on the free melodic flow of an upper voice above a rigid, unchanging bass framework, tolerates such 'dissonant' turns of phrase as well as hidden octaves (Ex. 3.12b). This composition is already in danger of becoming boring because of its length. Only the alternation of sections diverse in nature made extended compositions possible; the short ostinatos and the 'walking' basses served an important role here as a contrast to the

Ex. 3.12.   Felice Sances, 'Usurpator tiranno'
(Do not ever abandon my soul)
(to his lover's scorn)

chordal basses. The use of strict ostinatos encouraged the alternation between recitatives and arias, the main characteristic of the cantata from the middle of the century onwards. In early works with a strophic disposition there were already 'recitative' and 'arioso' sections, the former more 'textually' and the latter more 'musically' oriented. The textual and musical nexus, as a contrast, is more obvious in the alternating use of basses of diverse structure, as each one conjures up a change in the musical gesture. The importance attached to the bass models is already exhibited in Pesenti's *O Dio che veggio*, a composition of large dimensions, which operates with all the musical means of the time. It changes back and forth several times between a recitative declamation of the text above chordal basses and arioso sections, which are composed above a descending major tetrachord as well as above a 'walking' bass. In this manner, together with an instrumental ritornello, an extended musical work is created with all the qualities of an operatic scene.

Monteverdi's use of ostinato and other bass models, as far as pure chamber music was concerned, came to an end with the *ciaccona* 'Zefiro torna'. The history of the cantata is not—with the exception of 'Ohimè ch'io cado'—indebted to him for anything. He was not so interested in the possibilities for organization and variation possessed by the bass models as in the theatrical components inherent to these basses. His later operas also abound with compositions on such models—descending tetrachords, 'walking' basses, dance basses, and all sorts of other ostinato forms. In his chamber music, however, we encounter an ostinato only one other time: in the 'Lamento della Ninfa', which Monteverdi has notably entitled 'Rapresentativo', in other words, 'in the theatrical style'.

# 4
# THE LAMENT

The chapter about ostinato basses must of necessity be followed by a chapter on the lament. Works on ostinato basses, regardless of whether the plaints are part of a dramatic work or are independent compositions, have a special place in the long history of this genre. Starting in the 1630s and continuing throughout the rest of the seventeenth century, laments were written over descending tetrachords, over chromatic lines with a range of a fourth, and over other short ostinatos. Among these are Monteverdi's 'Lamento della Ninfa' from Book VIII (1638), Cassandra's dirge from Cavalli's *La Didone* (1641), and Dido's farewell from Purcell's *Dido and Aeneas* (1689).

The traditions of the lament, a musical expression of grief or sorrow, extend back into the Middle Ages. Dirges always seem to have been a characteristic of the Italian folk music tradition and were already incorporated in sacred poetry in the thirteenth century. The sequence 'Stabat mater', attributed to, among others, Jacopone da Todi, is nothing more than a description of Mary mourning her Son's death. Laments may be heard everywhere in Dante's *Inferno*, where they often develop into monologues of considerable length, such as the ones held by Guido of Montefeltro, Pier della Vigna, or Count Ugolino. Such laments were also favourite subjects for lyrical poetry in the sixteenth century, expressed in canzonas, sextains, and octaves. The topics for the laments were taken from all fields: private or political fates, general plaints about the wickedness of the world and the hardships of life, and such concrete problems as those enumerated in a lament by one of the most famous Renaissance courtesans after her day was past. Lamentations appear just as frequently in sixteenth-century epic poetry: Erminia's distress concerning Tancredi in Tasso's *Gerusalemme liberata*, Tancredi's dirge for Clorinda, and Olimpia's bewailing on the deserted island in Ariosto's *Orlando furioso* are the most well-known examples. Common to all these laments is the length of the poems and the personal engagement of the narrator, who appears in the first person. These two features do not serve as criteria to distinguish them from other poetic genres; however, it will become clear that these two prerequisites played an extremely important role in the development of the musical genre of the lament. The lament first became a concept, a fashionable style, a genre, with the plaint of Arianna by Monteverdi from Rinuccini's opera *L'Arianna* (first performed in 1608), which moved the entire audience to tears.

In the history of the origins and progress of the solo song, laments stand out as milestones. At turning-points in this musical development, they served as a basis for new trends in compositions. Lamentations were materially involved in the evolution of the solo song. As early as the Florentine intermedi of 1565, Psyche's plaint appears as a solo madrigal, accompanied by four viols, four trombones, and a bass lyre; it is followed by Psyche's descent to hell together with the allegories of envy, jealousy, grief, and shame. In the 1580's Vincenzo Galilei, one of the leading figures in Count Bardi's Camerata, set the lament of Count Ugolino from the *Divina commedia* for tenor with the accompaniment of a viol. Monteverdi's 'Lamento d'Arianna' became a model not only for an opera scene but also for a type of monody. Lastly, Monteverdi's 'Lamento della Ninfa', a lament, was among the earliest compositions over a tetrachord bass. His work and the interest in the latter two types of plaint, both of which bear Monteverdi's imprint, made the lament into one of the most important forerunners of the cantata and finally a frequent subject of this genre. Everything that moved on an operatic stage could raise its voice in lament: women and (more rarely) men; figures from mythology, epic poetry, the Old and New Testament, and history; and later, around the middle of the century, even contemporary historical personalities such as Marinetta, the wife of Masaniello, the leader of the Neapolitan rebels who was murdered in 1647, or Christine of Sweden, who bewails the death of her father Gustav Adolf.

Before the lament had been found to be such a highly suitable subject-matter for monody, this expressive form had also been used in the madrigal. However, it is not yet possible to draw a clear line of demarcation between a genre and every text of a plaintive nature. Not every plaint is a lament in the sense of the genre, and in addition not every lament bears this title. It was only in the seventeenth century that the criteria were developed which then, in retrospect, could also be applied to madrigals. What makes a plaint a lament? In contrast to lyrical poetry and to lyrical reflection, the lament needs a theatrical environment, a narrative framework, in which the actual plaint gains its meaning. In opera the scene was set already; in chamber music—in monodies, ensembles, and cantatas—the setting was either presumed to be known or appeared in the title (as in 'Lamento di Giasone sopra i figlioli morti da Medea' by Sigismondo d'India or 'Lagrime d'amante al sepolcro dell'amata' by Monteverdi), or else it was included in the composition as a narrative framework (as in Monteverdi's 'Lamento della Ninfa', for example, or Saracini's 'Lamento della Madonna', and in almost all later laments from the middle of the century onwards).

This prerequisite, however, had already been met by one of Monteverdi's compositions from Book IV (1603), one which has a special place among his madrigals: Rinuccini's 'Sfogava con le stelle', a short madrigal, which comprises both a narrative framework and a plaint.

> Sfogava con le stelle
> un infermo d'amore
> sotto notturno ciel il suo dolore
> e dicea fisso in loro:
> O imagini belle
> dell'idol mio ch'adoro!
> Sì com'a me mostrate,
> mentre così splendete,
> la sua rara beltade,
> così mostraste a lei
> i vivi ardori miei.
> La fareste col vostr'aureo sembiante
> pietosa, sì come me fate amante.

> A man, sick with love,
> bewailed his sorrows to the stars
> under the nocturnal sky
> and spoke gazing at them:
> O beautiful images
> of my idol, whom I adore!
> Just as you show me
> through your splendour
> her rare beauty
> you should show her
> my passionate ardour
> You would make her with your golden lustre
> merciful, just as you cause me to love.

Unique in this composition are the psalmodic passages in a style similar to that of *falsobordone*, in which the voices recite the text only in accordance with the demands of the spoken metre, without a musically fixed rhythm. The contrast between the, as it were, 'spoken' and 'sung' sections is thus created, an anticipation of the antithetical pairing of the recitative and aria. The entire narrative framework alternates between psalmody and homophonic declamation; the beginning of the direct speech is clearly set off from this by its polyphonic structure (Ex. 4.1). The psalmody interrupts the loose,

Ex. 4.1.     'Sfogave con le stelle'
             (and spoke gazing at them: O)

madrigalistic style four more times: at the repetition of 'O imagini belle' and at the beginning of the final couplet, which is repeated three times. These are all points which demand increased attention and greater comprehensibility of the text. Although 'Sfogava con le stelle' is not a lament in the generic sense, its textual and musical characteristics already place it in the vicinity of the monodic plaints which would later make use of such texts which had previously been set innumerable times as madrigals.

One of Monteverdi's two lament–madrigal cycles, written in 1610 and published in 1614 in the sixth madrigal book, not only has a title 'Lagrime d'amante al sepolcro dell'amata' (The Tears of a Lover at the Beloved's Sepulchre) but also a history. After the sudden death at a very early age of Caterina Martinelli, who was supposed to have sung the role of Arianna in 1608, Duke Vincenzo drew up a series of events designed to immortalize this newest of his fancies and, at the same time, to celebrate his sorrow. In addition to daily requiem masses and the construction of a mausoleum in the Chiesa del Carmine, he commissioned the young Count Scipione Agnelli to write a poem on Caterina's death, in which the shepherd Glauco (i.e. Vincenzo) bewails his dead nymph (i.e. Caterina). Two years later Vincenzo had Monteverdi set this text to music. Agnelli availed himself of an antiquated poetic form of Dante's and Petrarch's, rarely used any more in the sixteenth and seventeenth centuries because of its formal strictness, the sestina. It consists of six stanzas of six lines, whose end words do not rhyme, but reappear throughout the stanzas, each time in a different order in accordance with some complex scheme. The conclusion is formed by a three-lined envoy employing all six end words. Because of this strict structure, in the hands of an untrained poet, the personal involvement of the lyrical ego inherent in the lament was turned into mere rhetoric. As a result Monteverdi had his problems in setting it. He fulfilled this obligation by having extended passages of the text declaimed homophonically, only shifting to a full polyphonic style at a few places (Ex. 4.2). Even the word-painting characteristic for the madrigal remained stereotypic; the word 'tomba' (tomb), for example, is represented by a descending melody and a trio of lower voices. The few really interesting passages, however, bear such a striking resemblance to another madrigal, presumably earlier in date, that it appears that Monteverdi transferred them as makeshift

Ex. 4.2.    'Lagrime d'amante al sepolcro dell'amata', third part
            (Night will give the only light on earth,
            Cintia will light up the day)

elements to this ill-favoured lament. Then, as if he wanted to make this relationship clear to everyone, he placed this composition directly after the sestina in Book VI; it is, namely, the setting of Petrarch's sonnet 'Ohimè il bel viso'. The similarity exhibits itself not only in the technique, characteristic of Monteverdi, of having a descending line in long note values in one voice while a lively melody appears sequentially in the others, something we have already seen in 'Ecco mormorar l'onde', 'Qui rise, o Tirsi', and other earlier madrigals; it manifests itself primarily in the direct quotation of the despairing 'Ohimè', with which the Petrarch setting opens (Ex. 4.3*a*) and which Monteverdi transferred to the fifth section of the sestina (Ex. 4.3*b*). The same technique also makes the only really direct outburst, 'Ahi Corinna Corinna, ahi morte, ahi tomba', into the dramatic highpoint of the cycle; its plaint, petering out to a unison, is also similar to 'Ohimè il bel viso'.

Monteverdi took the basic structure of this composition—the gradual emotional intensification, the sudden turn towards hopelessness, and the re-attainment of self-control at the end—from the work in which he had created the archetype for the genre of the lament, the 'Lamento d'Arianna'. It was a piece of music of almost legendary fame, one which outshone the entire performance of the opera, overshadowing everything else. Everywhere where Monteverdi's name was mentioned afterwards, Arianna's lament was mentioned in the same breath; according to a report from Florence, there was no house in that city with a harpsichord which did not have the music for the lament. Copies also circulated elsewhere; all of Italy seemed to be stirred by the craze for the lament. In the memorial for Monteverdi in *Fiori poetici* the 'Lamento d'Arianna' is still the only work mentioned by name: 'Who has the strength to hold back the tears when he hears the just lament of the unfortunate Arianna?'[1] Luigi Rossi, to whom music history is indebted for the large number of lament compositions he wrote, made a copy of it himself, and Giovanni Battista Doni thought it was 'perhaps the most beautiful composition of that genre of our time'.[2] For Monteverdi himself the lament was 'the most essential part of the opera' (*la più essential parte dell'opera*).[3] Nevertheless it only appeared in print for the first time in 1623, together with the two monodic compositions from the seventh madrigal book. Although the opera itself is no longer extant, its loss is perhaps not all that serious; its chronological vicinity to *L'Orfeo*

---

[1] *Fiori poetici raccolti nel funerale del molto illustre e molto reverendo signor Claudio Monteverdi . . . consecrati da D. Gio. Battista Marinoni . . .* (Venice, 1644), 7.

[2] Doni, *Trattato*, p. 25.

[3] Letter of 20 Mar. 1620 (*Lettere*, p. 157).

Ex. 4.3*a*. 'Ohimè il bel viso'
(Alas, the beautiful face,
Alas the sweet glance,
Alas)

suggests a similarity of styles and, as the opera was written under great
time pressure, injurious to polished creativity, its quality probably did
not meet the standard of Monteverdi's other compositions. Throughout his entire life this opera remained his child of sorrow, one he
always fussed over, but with which he was never entirely happy,

Ex. 4.3*b*.  'Lagrime d'amante al sepolcro dell'amata', fifth part
(Alas, poor earth,
Alas, flower of all beauty,
Alas)

always remembering the traumatic torments which accompanied its
birth.

What, however, was so special about this composition, what
aroused the enthusiasm? What distinguishes the 'Lamento d'Arianna'
from the various plaints from previous Orpheus operas? Why did the
fame of this particular composition spread so quickly? First of all,
non-musical aspects played a not insignificant role here. Scarcely any
opera had been performed for such a large audience before. Virginia
Andreini's dramatic skill contributed to the great effect that the
lament made on the spectators. Primarily, however, it was because
plot, staging, and music had never before been fused together in such
unity in presenting the fate of an individual as in this complete
picture, even without its choreographic disposition. It can at the most
be compared to Orfeo's entreaty on the banks of the river, a
comparison which Monteverdi himself made: 'Arianna moved the
heart because she was a woman, and Orfeo likewise because he was a
man . . . the story of Arianna led me to a fitting lament, that of Orfeo
to a fitting entreaty'.[4]

Monteverdi's music blends all levels of Arianna's fate—the
situation, her reaction, and her state of mind—in a way that goes far

[4] Letter of 9 Dec. 1616 (*Lettere*, p. 87).

beyond the type of presentation typical of early operas. Peri characterized this in the foreword of his *L'Euridice* as 'surpassing ordinary speech, falling so short, however, of the melody of song as to take on an intermediate form'.[5] Monteverdi had not restricted himself in such a manner in *Orfeo*, and even less so in the 'Lamento d'Arianna'. The music of his compositions always remained independent, did not subjugate itself to the text; to the contrary, it revealed what could only be felt between the lines. Rinuccini's endeavour to write a true tragedy, in which the fate of the individual transcends the Arcadian community, found its master in Monteverdi's setting. Arianna is not a porcelain nymph, she is of flesh and blood and does not exhaust herself with veiled lyrical plaints; she rebels and reproaches Theseus, who has left her to marry in splendour in Athens; she summons all the horrors of the seas—violent storms, sharks, and whales—to revenge her; she gives tongue to the whole gamut of her despair, from resignation to hysteria, before, horrified at her own lack of restraint, she begs Theseus for forgiveness, and tries to temper her torment in rhetoric. Monteverdi's setting of the despairing resignation of the first line, 'Lasciatemi morire', became a paradigm for all laments for the next few decades: the ascending chromatic progression, the large descending leap with the following upward motion (Ex. 4.4*a*). This laborious, dragging declamation is so much more

Ex. 4.4*a*  'Lamento d'Arianna', first part
(Let me die)

expressive than, for example, the hectic opening of Severo Bonini's setting of the same text from 1613 (Ex. 4.4*b*). In addition Monteverdi's version allows an intensification of the pace, a swelling and subsiding, which may also be observed in the first four sections of the composition and is a structural principle of the lament.

The beginning of the second section, the sigh 'O Teseo, o Teseo mio', becomes the motto of the entire lament; Arianna repeatedly calls herself to order with this motif, which appears with and without

---

[5] J. Peri, *L'Euridice* (1600), in Solerti, *Origini*, pp. 45–6.

Ex. 4.4*b*    Severo Bonini, 'Lamento d'Arianna'
               (Let me die)

modifications; in several places it brings the swelling and falling of the
melody and of the declamatory tempo to a close. This may be seen in
the reproaches of the third section, which clearly demonstrate
Monteverdi's extraordinary sensitivity towards the text. The 'material' recriminations are hurled with the same motif, which appears four
times, as if counted on her fingers; the most drastic reproach,
however, comes to a climax on the highest note of the passage before
making its way down through an entire octave and coming to a close
(Ex. 4.5).

The outburst of fury in the fourth section proceeds similarly: a slow
build-up, until Arianna's dammed-up feelings overflow with a torrent
of the shortest declamatory note values, forced out in a tempo that can

Ex. 4.5.    'Lamento d'Arianna', third part
             (Are those the crowns
              with which you adorn my hair?
              Are those the sceptres?
              Are those the gems and gold?
              To leave me unprotected
              to be tormented and devoured by wild beasts)

hardly be understood. This is the place in the lament which comes closest to the aesthetics of *Sprechgesang*. In other passages musical structures predominate—the antithetical statements, for example, in which Arianna compares her bleak future with his lustrous one:

> Ma con l'aure serene
> tu te ne vai felice, et io qui piango;
> a te prepara Atene
> liete pompe superbe, et io rimango
> cibo di fere in solitarie arene;
> te l'uno e l'altro tuo vecchio parente
> stringerai lieto, et io
> più non vedrovvi, o madre, o padre mio.

> With favourable winds
> you sail happily forth, and I weep here;
> for you Athena prepares
> joyful and superb fêtes, and I remain here
> as food for wild beasts in a solitary clime;
> and one and then the other
> you will joyfully embrace your elderly parents and I
> will see you no more, O mother, O father mine.

Monteverdi delimits these antitheses by juxtaposing a cadential bass with one which moves with stepwise motion and, more importantly, by smuggling a hidden triple metre into the vision of happiness and festivity (Ex. 4.6).

Not much occurred to Monteverdi in the last, the rhetorical stanza, lacking as it does the immediacy of the first four sections. Devoid of expression, it never advanced beyond sterotyped monodic formulas; even these were not consciously employed to illustrate the text. It is just this, however, that is otherwise one of the secrets of Monteverdi's music, not the 'invention' of new musical elements, but the use of existing possibilities at exactly the right place in order to interpret the text. Thus one of the characteristic features of the Arianna lament is

Ex. 4.6.    'Lamento d'Arianna', second part
            (With favourable winds
            you sail happily forth, and I weep here)

neither an invention of Monteverdi's nor an achievement of monody, but was already a popular plaintive figure in madrigals. This figure consisted of falling melodic phrases which opened with a large descending leap—like the beginning of this lament—and often landed on the leading tone of the following key. Interjections, such as 'Ohimè, O Dio', and similar, were thus turned into musical sobs. None the less, it was just this kind of interjection which was copied in almost all other laments, even those by Monteverdi himself.

The basically 'musical' conception of the 'Lamento d'Arianna' and, in particular, the use of madrigalistic elements of style in a solo song enabled Monteverdi to make, without difficulty, a five-part arrangement of this composition. This was a rare occurrence in an era in which one generally rewrote polyphonic pieces for a solo voice, but was by no means unique. Despite being one of the most fervent of Monteverdi's admirers, Giovanni Battista Doni criticized this arrangement severely;

I have never been able to induce myself to believe that the most beautiful and most perfect music is madrigalistic; for the imperfection brought to it by the mutilation of the poetry, the confusion of meaning, the surfeit of repetitions, and the perturbation of the rhythm is too great . . . it would be nice if one could write a kind of music which had all the perfections of the madrigal and much more, without the imperfections; and this would be the case if a single or several singers always were to sing the same melody, while other diverse parts, let us assume four, were played and not sung; it would be best done by *viole*, or similar instruments, which can sustain notes . . . with which one could execute all of the artifices such as fugues, imitations, repetitions, etc. which the singers would otherwise make; and then the text would not be so unintelligible as it is in our madrigals and in our motets . . . It should not be silently overlooked that all music could then progress with a beautiful flow and gracious movement and that, as one does today, it is not necessary to give many voices separate, uncomfortable, and not very graceful movement, because it is impossible for all voices to have a nice progression. And as proof of this, one should consider the progressions, the movements of the solo version of the 'Lamento d'Arianna' and that of the same piece set by Monteverdi polyphonically at the request of a noble Venetian—and one will see that the solo voice always sings well and with a beautiful flow, but in the polyphonic version one often hears certain less attractive progressions, which are little suited to the text . . .[6]

Thus Doni's objections were concerned not so much with the madrigal version of the 'Lamento d'Arianna' in particular, as with the general superiority of the solo song over polyphony. This composition suggested itself as an example, not only because Doni presented it as a

---

[6] Doni, *Trattato*, p. 98.

paragon for dramatic music, but because it exists in both versions and therefore allows direct comparison. The question of whether such an expression of an individual's emotions must of necessity suffer in a polyphonic arrangement was not of primary significance; what was more important was Doni's central premiss, based on late-sixteenth-century neoclassical aspirations. The problem still remains, however, of whether the polyphonic version lacks intensity of expression in comparison with the solo, or whether it seems artificial, instead of speaking directly to the heart.

Even a quick glance reveals the essence of the arrangement and shows—apart from its polyphonic nature—Monteverdi's idea of what the dramatic disposition of a lament should be: the madrigal comprises only the first four sections of the complete form of Rinuccini's lament, as it appears in the solo song. These four sections not only form the main bulk of the lament, but also actually contain everything that is necessary to understand Arianna's emotional state— a beginning, a climax, and a conclusion, which can easily do without Rinuccini's final, monumental maxims. Limiting the lament to the first four sections allows it to become more concise without losing any of the story or intensity. It was not a stopgap measure, to be justified in any way possible, but a conscious revision, for even the sacred *contrafactum* ends at the same place as the madrigal.

The individuality of the inner emotions is undoubtedly lost in the five-part madrigal. On the other hand, Monteverdi used just this polyphony to intensify the emotions exhibited. Personal, individual plaints were nothing special for the madrigal; such passages from Guarini's *Il pastor fido* were popular not only with Monteverdi. The change from theatre to chamber music opened up new possibilities. By means of the madrigalistic style the extravagant theatrical gesture was transformed into an equally dramatic description of an emotional state, one, however, which was determined more by the music—two different approaches which led to the same result. In addition to the monodic techniques of representing emotional climaxes by means of larger melodic leaps or quick declamatory rhythms, the five-part writing offered other possibilities as well: the juxtaposition of sections with few voices and those with many, of homophonic and polyphonic passages, of high and low ranges, as well as the possibility of repeating entire sections or single lines of the text. It is a result of this last feature, for example, that the first section is given a new form, in which the memorable opening line appears not only at the beginning and the end, as required by the text, but one additional time in the middle. The antithetical visions at the conclusion of the second section, in which Arianna compares her tragic fate with Teseo's happy future, gain musical force through the juxtaposition of all voices with just a few (Ex. 4.7).

Arianna's outburst, probably the passage in the lament which is the most personal, the most dramatic, and least suited for a polyphonic adaptation, loses only a little of its emotional intensity in the five-part version. Monteverdi replaces the semiquaver *parlando* section of the solo version with one declaimed in crisply dotted homophonic

Ex. 4.7.   Five-part setting of 'Lamento d'Arianna', second part
           (for you Athena prepares
           joyful and superb fêtes, and I remain here
           as food for wild beasts)

rhythms, first with only three voices, then repeated with five. The abrupt stop, the horror caused by her own words, depicted by a general silence in the solo version, is represented here by an exposed tenor entry. The dramatic content of the lamentation scene is just as clear in the madrigal, although the difference in the genres necessitated the use of different means.

With this dramatic structure of building to a climax and then subsiding, the 'Lamento d'Arianna' became the model for a large number of similar laments in the next two decades. For example, Claudio Saracini wrote two sacred laments. One of them was based textually on the 'Stabat mater'; the other, 'Cristo smarrito in stile recitativo. Lamento della Madonna' (1620), imitated Monteverdi closely several times, without, however, losing its independence as a

Ex. 4.8*a*.   Claudio Saracini, 'Cristo smarrito in stile recitativo.
　　　　　　　Lamento della Madonna'
　　　　　　　(Gasping and weeping,
　　　　　　　　she turned her beautiful eyes to Heaven, saying:)

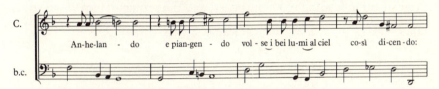

Ex. 4.8*b*.   'Lamento d'Arianna', third part
　　　　　　　(Weeping in vain,
　　　　　　　　shouting in vain for help,
　　　　　　　　the wretched Arianna)

Ex. 4.8*c*.   Claudio Saracini, 'Cristo smarrito in stile recitativo. Lamento
　　　　　　　della Madonna'
　　　　　　　(O God, O God)

Ex. 4.8*d*.  'Lamento d'Arianna', second part
(O God, turn around)

composition (Ex. 4.8). At the end of the 1620s Jacopo Peri also set a
lament scene for an opera, *Iole ed Ercole*; but this project foundered in
the tangle of intrigues at the Florentine court. The most zealous
imitator of such effective lament scenes, however, proved to be
Sigismondo d'India. His monodic collections contain no less than five
laments, three of them in a single print. The same dramatic principle
which served as a basis for the 'Lamento d'Arianna' is observed, both
musically and textually, in all of these: a quiet beginning, an
intensification leading to an outburst, and the return to hopelessness.

| | |
|---|---|
| ARIANNA: | Lasciatemi morire |
| | Let me die |
| IOLE (Peri): | Uccidimi dolore |
| | Kill me, pain |
| GIASONE (d'India): | Ancidetemi pur dogliosi affanni |
| | Just kill me, sorrowful pangs |
| ARIANNA: | O Teseo, o Teseo mio |
| | O Theseus, O my Theseus |
| GIASONE: | O figli, o cari figli |
| | O my sons, O my dear sons |
| IOLE: | Alcide, Alcide ingrato |
| | Hercules, ungrateful Hercules |
| DIDONE (d'India): | Enea, mia vita |
| | Aeneas, my life |
| ARIANNA: | Son queste le corone |
| | onde m'adorni il crine |
| | questi gli scettri sono |
| | queste le gemme e gl'ori? |

Are those the crowns
with which you adorn my hair?
Are those the sceptres?
Are those the gems and gold?

DIDONE:

Quest'è l'onor
quest'è la fé
son queste le promesse?

Is that the honour,
is that the faith,
are those the promises?

ARIANNA:

O nembi o turbi o venti
sommergetelo voi dentro a quell'onde,
correte orchi e balene
e delle membra immonde
empiete le voragini profonde!

O clouds, O storms, O winds,
let him be sunk in the waves;
hurry nautical beasts and whales,
fill the deep watery abyss
with your filthy bodies!

DIDONE:

Su su spirti d'Averno
venite o furie ultrici a mille a mille,
venite meco a vendicar oltraggio!

Come come,
you spirits of hell,
come you revenging furies in thousands,
come with me to avenge the outrage!

GIASONE:

Squarcia il ricco manto, a terra cada
la gemmata corona, seggio e scettro!

Tear the rich cloak, may the jewelled crown,
throne, and sceptre fall to the earth!

Such shared linguistic traits could be ennumerated indefinitely; it is therefore logical that the settings also follow in the footsteps of the 'Lamento d'Arianna'.

With all of these more or less successful imitations of Arianna's plaint, the lament reached an impasse and froze into a stereotype which could, at the very most, have some effect in the dramatic context of an opera. It was only when Monteverdi combined the technique of the short ostinato bass models with the content of the lament in the 'Lamento della Ninfa' from the eighth madrigal book that a new realm with new possibilities for the composition of such pieces revealed itself. This work, which Monteverdi himself characterized as 'Rapresentativo', resists all comparison with other compositions of the time. It is the plaint of a nymph who has been abandoned by her lover. Three men comment on it sympathetically, at times joining together to accompany her song, at times doing so individually. A ten-stanza poem with a refrain by Rinuccini served Monteverdi as a basis for this piece. It contained all of the elements of a lament scene; a narrative framework at the beginning and the end, and, in between, a lament six stanzas in length.

1.   Non havea Febo ancora
    recato al mondo il dì,
    ch'una donzella fuora
    del proprio albergo uscì,
    Miserella ahi più no, no
    tanto giel soffrir non può.

4.   Amor, diceva, e 'l piè
    mirando il ciel fermò:
    Dov'è, dov'è la fe
    che 'l traditor giurò?
    Miserella ahi più no, no
    tanto giel soffrir non può.

5.   Fa che ritorni mio
    amor com'ei pur fu,
    o tu m'ancidi ch'io
    non mi tormenti più.
    Miserella ahi più no, no
    tanto giel soffrir non può.

1.   Phoebus had not yet
    brought the day to the earth,
    when a damsel
    left her dwelling.
    O the poor thing,
    she can no longer bear such pain.

4.   Amor, she said, and stood
    still looking heavenwards,
    where is the fidelity
    which was sworn by the traitor?
    O the poor thing,
    she can no longer bear such pain.

5.   Make my love return,
    as it once was,
    or kill me,

so that I need no longer torment myself.
O the poor thing,
she can no longer bear such pain.

It was only by relaxing the poetic structure, however, that Monteverdi was able to create that incomparable scene whose magic no analysis can penetrate. He turned the refrain into the commentary and eliminated it from the stanzas of the narrative framework. In order to remove any memory of the strict strophic structure from the remaining plaint, he relaxed the refrain to such an extent that it is no longer recognizable as a 'refrain'. The lamentation of the nymph is framed by two three-part ensembles and is over a descending minor tetrachord. The musical structure is surprisingly simple, the melodic material remarkably limited. Nevertheless, the floating quality of the concord of the voices creates that ethereal sadness which leaves one dumbfounded. In an astonishingly small range, extending mainly from $e''$ to $a'$ (in connection with the leading tone $g\sharp'$) and only rarely down to the lower octave, the same melodic segments are repeated over and over in an irregular order: an ascending line, the recitation on a single note, the falling fifth, and the falling tritone typical for the lament since Arianna's plaint (Ex. 4.9). The upper voice unfolds the plaint above the rigid construct of the descending tetrachord bass and is concerned neither with harmonic rules nor with the tempo. Monteverdi, in the preface to the piece, expressly demands that the latter be varied in accordance with the mood:

The three voices [i.e. the narrative framework] . . . are printed thus in part-books because they should be sung in a tempo beaten with the hand; the other three voices, which sympathize softly with the nymph, are notated in the score, so that they may follow her plaint, which should be sung in the tempo of her emotional state [*tempo dell'affetto dell'amino*] and not in a tempo beaten with the hand.

By means of such an ingenious negation of any structural plan, the tension between the inexorable scheme of the ostinato and the freedom of the upper part is made clear in the 'Lamento della Ninfa'. The ostinato bass is turned into a mere stage for a musical drama, which on the other hand would fall apart without that part's cohesive force. The title 'Rapresentativo' therefore does not so much suggest a dramatic performance as serve as a characterization of what takes place in the music. The 'Lamento della Ninfa' is much more 'dramatic' in its musical disposition than many pieces which were written purely for the stage. Apart from the ostinato, it is primarily the 'asides' which endow it with its dramatic character; they first invaded opera music in the eighteenth century and then in the

Ex. 4.9.    'Lamento della Ninfa'
          (Never will you have such sweet kisses
          from this mouth, poor thing,
          never any gentler, ah, be silent, poor thing,
          for he knows too much.)

nineteenth became one of the most popular tricks for structuring a musical scene.

In contrast to Arianna's lamentation, the 'Lamento della Ninfa' was not imitated directly. The short ostinato motifs based on a descending tetrachord, however, became a specific feature of lament compositions. Nicolò Fontei's solo 'Pianto d'Erinna' (1639) is based on such a tetrachord bass (Ex. 4.10*a*), as is Barbara Strozzi's political lament

Ex. 4.10*a*. Nicolò Fontei, 'Pianto d'Erinna'
(Where, where do you go, my heart,
let me come too,
stop)

about the French conspirator, Henri Cinq Mars, who was hanged in 1642, 'Mentre al devoto collo' (Ex. 4.10*b*).

Both compositions already combine the lament form (narrative framework and plaint) with the main characteristic of the cantata (the recognizable distinction between recitative and aria). The lament also continued to survive, however, in its old, recitative form, whether in chamber music or in its original function as an operatic scene. An opportunity for a lament could be found in essentially any operatic material, even after the mythological subjects began to yield to the historical ones. Ottavia's departure from Rome in *L'incoronazione di Poppea* is the last of Monteverdi's laments. It is effectively placed between Arnalta's comic vision of social advance and the beginning of the final apotheosis. It is, to be sure, a recitative, and bears all the features of Arianna's plaint, which have, however, been clearly enhanced by the mature expressiveness of the last two madrigal books. One can scarcely think of any music more 'dramatic' than that which

Ex. 4.10*b*. Barbara Strozzi, 'Il lamento. Sul Rodano severo'
(While you extended around my devout neck that kind arm, then you gave me)

Monteverdi extracted—by means of Ottavia's weeping stammering which obscures any coherent statement—from the simple text 'A Dio Roma, a Dio patria, amici a Dio' (Ex.4.11).

Ex. 4.11. 'A Dio Roma', *L'incoronazione di Poppea*, Act III, sc. vii
(Farewell Rome, farewell my country, my friends farewell)

In comparison, Penelope's entrance scene in *Il ritorno d'Ulisse in Patria*, which shares some common traits with the 'Lamento d'Arianna', is much more conventional. This opera does, however, contain a parody of a lament: the lamentation of the greedy parasite Iro about the slain suitors, whence he lost the hands that fed him. He does not so much lament their death, as the fact that his stomach would henceforth be empty. In this connection it is hilarious when Iro, in the exalted language of lament poems, reflects on food and drink rather than upon the crown and sceptre when he is abandoned not by Theseus or Heracles, but by his provender:

> Chi soccore il digiun, chi lo consola?
> Infausto giorno a me ruine armato:
> poco dianzi mi vinse un vecchio ardito,
> hor m'abbatte la fame, dal cibo abbandonato.

> Who succours the hungry man, who consoles him?
> Ill-starred day, armed for my ruin:
> just a little while ago a bold man vanquished me,
> now hunger fells me, who has been abandoned by food.

This parodic scene may be an indication of the degree of public recognition (or saturation?) that the genre of the lament had attained. Iro's lament may have been progressive in this: it is one of the first parodies of a serious genre, something that was so popular later in the *opera buffa* of the eighteenth century, whose butt was the *opera seria*.

# 5

# CHURCH MUSIC

It is a feature of all periods of change that the old and the new coexist for a while, more or less harmoniously. The dispute about the *seconda pratica*, the fight against counterpoint, and the propaganda for monody all clearly document the struggle for priority. But even the chordally accompanied solo song, so rapid in its ascent, only managed to displace the polyphonic madrigal and the sociable custom of singing around a table after a time. In the middle of the seventeenth century collections of five-part madrigals still appeared in print, unopposed and passed over in silence.

Things were more complex with sacred music. Here the general musical development of the times was also joined by ecclesiastical constraints. These stipulations, based on an ideal conception of liturgical music, led to a stylistic schism which still holds sway today between the 'old' and the 'new' styles. The old style has always remained the same while the new style has followed the current taste in secular music. The Council of Trent (1545–63) had concerned itself with—among other things—the reform of church music and had recommended a musical style which was free from secular influences and in which the text was comprehensible. As a consequence, at the beginning of the seventeenth century Palestrina's works were declared to represent the ideal style for sacred music, at least for liturgical compositions. Thus it is not only because a stylistic change always needs a generation or so to take effect that the old and the new have coexisted in sacred music since the end of the sixteenth century, but also because the old was prescribed and began to live a life of its own at the side of the new.

There was only one place though where this old style—pure *a cappella* music, vocal polyphony in the style of Palestrina—was cultivated exclusively, and that was in the Sistine Chapel. Already in the other churches of the Vatican City, in the oratories, in the Jesuit seminaries of Rome, new music was performed as well. Outside the Papal State, particularly in Venice, local traditions continued to be

I.   Frontispiece to the *Fiori Poetici* (1644)

## STVDIOSI LETTORI.

Onvi marauigliate ch'io dia alle stampe questi Madrigali senza prima rispondere alle oppositioni, che fece l'Artusi contro alcune minime particelle d'essi, perche sendo io al seruigio di questa Serenissima Altezza di Mantoa non son patrone di quel tempo che tal'hora mi bisognarebbe. hò nondimeno scritta la risposta per far conoscere ch'io non faccio le mie cose à caso, & tosto che sia rescritta vscirà in luce portando in fronte il nome di Seconda Pratica, ouero Perfettione Della Moderna Mvsica, delche forse alcuni s'ammireranno non credendo che vi sia altra pratica che l'insegnata dal Zerlino; ma siano sicuri, che intorno alle consonanze, & dissonanze, vi è anco vn'altra consideratione differente dalla determinata, la qual con quietanza della ragione, & del senso diffende il moderno comporre, & questo hò voluto dirui si perche questa voce Seconda Pratica tal'hora non fosse occupata da altri, si perche anco gli ingegnosi possino fra tanto considerare altre seconde cose intorno all'armonia, & credere che il moderno Compositore fabrica sopra li fondamenti della verità. Viuete felici.

II. Foreword to the Fifth Book of Madrigals (1605)

III.   Battista Guarini, *Il pastor fido*: engraving of the beginning of Act III from the
1602 edition

# LA
# FAVOLA D'ORFEO
## RAPPRESENTATA IN MVSICA
Il Carneuale dell'Anno MDCVII.

*Nell' Accademia de gl'* INVAGHITI *di* MANTOVA;

Sotto i felici auspizij del Sereniſſimo Sig. DVCA
benigniſſimo lor protettore.

In MANTOVA, per Franceſco Oſanna Stampator Ducale
Con licenza de' Superiori. 1607.

IV.   Title-page of Alessandro Striggio's libretto of *Orfeo* (1607)

# L'ORFEO

## FAVOLA IN MVSICA

### DA CLAVDIO MONTEVERDI

RAPPRESENTATA IN MANTOVA

Anno 1607 & nouamente data in luce

## AL SERENISSIMO SIGNOR

D. FRANCESCO GONZAGA

Prencipe di Mantoua, & di Monferato, &c

In Venetia Appresso Ricciardo Amadino.

M D C I X.

V.   Title-page of the 1609 printed score of *Orfeo*

VI.    Beginning of 'Possente spirto' from *Orfeo*

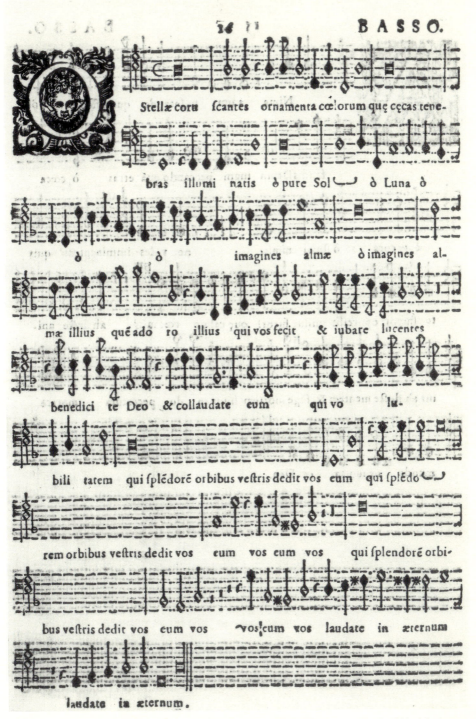

VII. Sacred contrafactum of 'Sfogava con le stelle' from the Fourth Book of Madrigals
(bass partbook)

## Modo di rappresentare il presente canto.

LE tre parti, che canteno fuori del pianto dela Ninfa; si sono così separatamente poste, perche si cantano al tempo dela mano ; le altre tre parti, che vanno cnmmiserando in debole voce la Ninfa, si sono poste in partitura, acciò seguitano il pianto di essa, qual ua cantato a tempo del'affetto del animo, & non a quello dela mano.

VIII.   Beginning of the *Lamento della ninfa* (Eighth Book of Madrigals), printed in
score

cultivated. The Cathedral of S. Marco was the only place which could compare musically in importance with the Sistine Chapel. The directors of music at S. Marco—among others, the famous musicians Willaert, Zarlino, and de Rore—had already in the middle of the sixteenth century begun to place choirs in various locations within the church, having them sing both together and in alternation. This polychoral style, whose effect is based on blocks of sound rather than on ingenious polyphonic balance, was expanded considerably by Andrea Gabrieli and later by his nephew Giovanni Gabrieli at the turn of the century. Instrumental blocks were contrasted with vocal ones; the number of voices rose to as many as twenty; the sonority of the individual blocks was differentiated by the use of varied instruments. This music certainly did not represent austere piety. The wealth of the metropolis also displayed itself in the splendour of its church music.

Around 1600, together with the first prints of secular solo songs, the first sacred monodies appeared. Lodovico da Viadana's *Cento concerti ecclesiastici*, however, are not copies of the chordally accompanied song associated with Florence. On the contrary, they exhibit regular contrapuntal writing between the vocal part and the instrumental bass. In the first two decades of the new century the new monodic style began to make itself felt in sacred music as well, at first sporadically, but after 1610 with increasing frequency. Numerous collections of solo motets, polyphonic *concerti ecclesiatici* on liturgical and non-liturgical texts, appeared in print. The musical means were those found in secular compositions: echo effects could be used for answers from heaven, just as in operas; the Bible texts lent themselves equally well to madrigalistic word-painting; and nothing spoke against transferring the virtuoso duets and trios developed in madrigals to sacred texts. Sacred music, as long as it was not written in the old style, was a secular art. Monteverdi's sacred compositions are always exceptionally vivid where he makes use of the expressive means of the madrigal and, in particular, of the opera. The fact that he was a dramatist at heart, although employed longest as a director of music at a church, is especially reflected in his sacred music. The fact that he was chosen unanimously by the Venetian procurators as the director of music at S. Marco, although as a court musician he had only a few sacred compositions to his name and instead was a well-known opera composer, shows on the one hand that there was no question of his mastery of the old style and, on the other, that the difference between the sacred and the secular *métier* was considered to be of little importance.

Monteverdi's sacred output—apart from the compositional exercises written when he was fifteen or sixteen and a few compositions found in various collections—comes down to us in three large publications: the publication of 1610 comprising the *Missa 'In illo tempore'* and the *Marian Vespers*; the *Selva morale e spirituale* of 1641; and the posthumous collection edited in 1650 by the publisher Vincenti containing a mass and some compositions on psalms. The latter two are completely different from the publication of 1610 in one respect. They contain works long in use, polished by time and practice, chosen from the immense number of sacred compositions as being worthy of publication: a colourful mixture of monodic, polyphonic, polychoral, and instrumentally accompanied vocal pieces. *Selva morale e spirituale* is a compilation of various musical settings of individual sacred texts: there are, for example, three versions of 'Confitebor', two of 'Beatus vir', three of 'Salve Regina'. The existent possibility of interchanging a 'Gloria' and a 'Crucifixus' in a preceding mass also would seem to imply that practical considerations had been taken into account. These compositions for liturgical use are framed by four pious Italian compositions and two non-liturgical sacred *contrafacta*, the last of which is based on the 'Lamento d'Arianna'.

Monteverdi had something else in mind with the publication of 1610. Nothing in it had already suffered the wear and tear of daily use. The collection, in honour of the Virgin Mary, was designed to recommend the composer as being well-versed in both the old and the new styles, an intention which reveals itself in the title: *Sanctissimae Virgini Missa senis vocibus ad Ecclesiarum Choros ac Vespere pluribus decantandae cum nonnullis sacris concentibus ad Sacella sive Principum cubicula accommodata* (The Six-voice Mass Suitable for Church Choirs Dedicated to the Virgin Mary as well as the Vespers for Several Voices with some Sacred Songs Suitable for Chapels and Princely Chambers). The collection is dedicated to Pope Paul V, one of the most important popes of the Counter-Reformation. Monteverdi probably hoped to obtain a job from him at one of the numerous Roman churches. It has more of an academic than a practical character; beyond the superficial distinction between the old and the new styles, the second part was organized, as Helmut Hucke has demonstrated recently, in accordance with a theological scheme reflecting the spirit of the Counter-Reformation.

The *Marian Vespers* exhibit the intention of ordering, of codifying, all the multifarious ideas concerning musical style that had begun to shoot up all over Italy around 1600; of realizing them in an exemplary fashion; and finally of presenting them as almost 'classical' compositions like the older vocal polyphony. The publication of 1610 is at one and the same time a manifest and a retrospective, a tutor on sacred music and on the possibilities available for sacred compositions. Together with *L'Orfeo*, published the year before, it is a kind of musical legacy, written at a time in Monteverdi's life when he was intensely frustrated with the development of his career in Mantua and, at forty-three years of age, facing the fact of his getting older and as a result beginning to sum up his past activity and to take new bearings.

The question of whether the *Marian Vespers* is a musical entity or a loose collection of individual compositions still provokes Monteverdi scholars today. It is closely connected with the uncertainty about which liturgy this work should be associated with. In place of the antiphons which normally frame the five vesper psalms, there are *concerti* for one, two, or three voices, whose texts were frequently used for motets in the sixteenth century (and are designated as such in the following table):

| Title | Liturgical genre | Instrumentation as it appears in publication of 1610 |
|---|---|---|
| 'Domine ad adiuvandum' | Introit | sex vocibus et sex instrumentis, si placet |
| 'Dixit Dominus' | Psalm | à sei voci e sei instrumenti |
| 'Nigra sum' | Motet | ad una voce |
| 'Laudate pueri Dominum' | Psalm | à 8 voci sole nel Organo |
| 'Pulchra es' | Motet | a due voci |
| 'Laetatus sum' | Psalm | à sei voci |
| 'Duo Seraphim' | Motet | Tribus vocibus |
| 'Nisi Dominus' | Psalm | a dieci voci |
| 'Audi coelum' | Motet | prima ad una voce sola, poi nella fine a 6 |
| 'Lauda Jerusalem' | Psalm | A sette voci |
| 'Sonata sopra Sancta Maria, ora pro nobis' | Litany | Sonata à 8 sopra santa Maria; Parte che canta sopra la sonata |
| 'Ave maris stella' | Hymn | à 8 |
| 'Magnificat I' | Hymn | à Sette voci, e sei instrumenti |
| 'Magnificat II' | Hymn | à 6 voci |

Are the *concerti* substitutes for the antiphons? Were they inserted freely within the context of the vespers? Or were they merely inserted by the publisher as supplementary material with no connection to the vesper liturgy? These questions have been extensively discussed by Stephen Bonta, Jeffrey Kurtzman, and James Moore. The study of other *Marian Vespers* between 1600 and 1620 has shown that it was not uncommon to substitute the polyphonic motets for antiphons. In addition, the recommendation in the title that the work be performed in princely chambers demonstrates that it was not even intended for strict liturgical usage. Lastly, the selection of the texts for the *concerti* reveals a theological concept which allows the *Vespers* to stand as a whole, at least as far as its contents are concerned. Because the entire publication was not designed for a performance but as a present for Pope Paul V, the question of whether it was intended for complete and unabridged performance is not of great significance. It is far more important to recognize that it has, as do all of the later madrigal books, an underlying unifying concept.

No matter how the question concerning its liturgical connections is answered, the musical essence of the *Marian Vespers* is secular. This is exemplified by Monteverdi's appropriation of an entire instrumental section from *L'Orfeo* (performed three years previously): the Toccata which sounds in the opening movement, 'Domine ad adiuvandum me festina'. The motets with only a few voices and analogous passages in the psalms, in particular, are permeated by madrigalistic word-painting and theatrical gestures. They are at times so similar to the madrigals in Book VII that the musical style, whether sacred or secular, appears to be interchangeable. The melody to the words 'Surge amica mea' (Arise, my friend) in the solo motet 'Nigra sum', for example, ascends in stepwise motion, something that could be found in any madrigal (Ex. 5.1).

'Duo Seraphim' is not only the theological core but also the centre of virtuosity in the *Marian Vespers*. It, along with the two-part 'Pulchra es', is among the first extant vocal *concerti* by Monteverdi. It contains all the elements of his duo and trio techniques and joins word-painting and text interpretation with a virtuosity that borders on the limits of what is possible.

Ex. 5.1.    'Nigra sum', *Marian Vespers*
            (Arise)

Duo Seraphim clamabant alter ad alterum: Sanctus Dominus Deus Sabaoth. Plena est omnis terra gloria eius. Tres sunt, qui testimonium dant in caelo: Pater, verbum et Spiritus sanctus. Et hi tres unum sunt. Sanctus Dominus Deus Sabaoth. Plena est omnis terra gloria eius.

Two seraphim called to one another: Holy is the Lord God of hosts. The whole earth is full of his glory. There are three who bear testimony in heaven: the Father, the Word, and the Holy Spirit. And these three are one. Holy is the Lord God of hosts. The whole earth is full of his glory.

To begin with, the numerical symbolism of the composition is striking: two seraphim sing in two parts; the three that bear testimony in three; the unity of God the Father, the Word, and the Holy Spirit is expressed by a unison passage. The enumeration of 'Pater verbum et Spiritus Sanctus' is, as it were, counted out by the composition: the same coloratura appears three times in a row, once in each of the three voices, before they are brought together at 'Et hi tres unum sunt' (Ex. 5.2). Monteverdi takes advantage of the scene of the two seraphim

Ex. 5.2.    'Duo Seraphim', *Marian Vespers*
(the Father, the Word, and the Holy Spirit. And these three are one)

calling to one another for an expressive chain of suspensions and alternating coloraturas, a style typical for his duets: going from a unison via a suspension to homophonic thirds; a motif is then tossed back and forth and is followed by an increasingly dense and virtuoso passage. The essence of Monteverdi's duet technique is revealed in these few tightly constructed opening bars as well as the secret of his dramatic conception of intensification and relaxation (Ex. 5.3).

'Audi coelum', the last of the motets inserted between the psalms, transfers the dramatic–musical artifice of the echo from the pastoral drama to sacred music. In fact this idea did not originate with Monteverdi; Emilio de' Cavalieri had already had Anima's questions concerning the meaning of worldly joys answered by Heaven in his sacred opera, *La rappresentatione di anima, et di corpo* (1600). Monteverdi, however, was the first to use it away from the operatic stage. The text of the motet lends itself to a setting with an echo:

> Audi, coelum, verba mea,
> plena desiderio,

Ex. 5.3.    'Duo Seraphim', *Marian Vespers*
            (Two seraphim called to one another)

et perfusa gaudio.                                    Echo: audio.
Dic, quaeso, mihi:
Quae est ista, quae consurgens
ut aurora rutilat
ut benedicam?                                         Echo: Dicam.
Dic nam ista pulchra
ut luna, electa
ut sol, replet laetitia
terras caelos, maria                                  Echo: Maria.
Maria virgo illa dulcis,
praedicata de propheta Ezechiel
porta orientalis.                                     Echo: talis.

Hear, Heaven, my words,
full of desire
and suffused with joy.                                Echo: I hear
Tell me, I beg:
who is she who rises
and glows like the dawn,
that I may praise her?                                Echo: I will say.
Say if this one,
beautiful as the moon
and chosen as the sun
fills with joy the earth, the heavens, the seas.      Echo: Mary.
Mary, that sweet Virgin,
foretold by the Prophet Ezekiel
to be the portal to the East.                         Echo: as such.

Usually Monteverdi simply repeats the final coloratura associated with
the respective echo words. The name Maria, however, is hailed several
times, and the voices are linked together here by short, almost
overlapping figuration (Ex. 5.4). Monteverdi published a second
setting of the same text in the *Selva morale e spirituale*, in a
composition that is somewhat misleadingly entitled 'Salve Regina' (I).

Ex. 5.4.     'Audi coelum', *Marian Vespers*
             (the seas. Mary. Mary)

In it, the first half of the 'Audi coelem' text is fused with that of 'Salve Regina'. This setting of the piece also uses an echo device. In addition to the usual echoes of the final coloraturas there is a passage in which short echo motifs appear with increasing frequency, developing into an imitation, only to fall back to an echo at the end (Ex. 5.5).

Each of the psalms of the *Marian Vespers*, as well as the hymn 'Ave maris stella' and the Magnificat, are based on a cantus firmus. In spite of this, all the psalms are composed so differently from one another that they appear to be a catalogue of their composer's talents.

Ex. 5.5.　'Salve Regina' (I)
　　　　　(salvation for sins)

Polyphonic techniques are joined with *falsobordone* and concerted sections (in 'Dixit Dominus' and in 'Laudate pueri'); ostinato basses are incorporated (in 'Laetatus sum'); the psalms for two choirs, 'Nisi Dominus' and 'Lauda Jerusalem', document Monteverdi's sureness in the Venetian style.

The first psalm, 'Dixit Dominus', contains instrumental ritornellos, which draw on the motifs from the preceding vocal sections; this idea was inspired by *L'Orfeo*, and was without precedent in sacred music. In addition, 'Dixit Dominus' once again shows Monteverdi's obvious predilection for symmetric forms. The composition is based on four different styles, which are ordered and employed according to a well-thought-out plan. Monteverdi combined the simplest and most traditional kinds of psalm setting—cantus firmus and *falsobordone*—with the most modern techniques of composition in a structure that had been tried and proven in madrigals and operatic scenes, but which was totally new for sacred music (see Fig. 5.1).

Fig. 5.1. 'Dixit Dominus', *Marian Vespers*

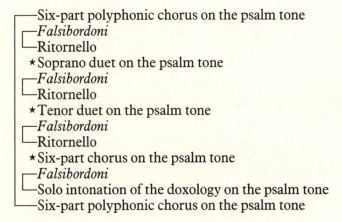

Except for the *falsobordone* sections, which all end with a final polyphonic melisma, the chant melody is present at all times, although its form undergoes many changes. At the beginning, following a solo intonation, a rhythmicized version of it serves as thematic material for a contrapuntal section with a countersubject. In the six-part section, 'iudicabit in nationibus', the psalm tone is in the choral bass part. In both of the vocal duets, however, Monteverdi combines the old cantus firmus technique with the new chordal accompaniment of monody; the instrumental bass for the vocal parts is nothing more than the pitches of the chant melody.

The beginning of 'Laudate pueri' is shaped according to the same principle as that of 'Dixit Dominus': following a solo intonation, a rhythmicized version of the chant melody with a countersubject is used as a basis for a two-choir polyphonic section. Here, too, the psalm tone is present at all times. In the sections with only a few voices, it does not appear as an instrumental bass, but moves from voice to voice in the choir. 'Laudate pueri' would have to be characterized as the most traditional composition of the *Marian Vespers* if it were not for two passages which suddenly disrupt the polyphonic structure. Both are in a dance-like triple metre, display a theatrically exaggerated ascending movement, and reflect the words, 'suscitans in terra' and 'erigens' (Ex. 5.6).

The two Magnificat compositions at the end of the publication are linked by one and the same psalm tone. The second of these works

Ex. 5.6.　'Laudate pueri', *Marian Vespers*
　　　　　(raising)

turns out to be a reduction of the first 'large' one to a six-part choir and organ continuo. As is usual for the Magnificat settings of his time, Monteverdi divided the text into individual sections with varying instrumentation and number of voices. In the twelve sections of the first Magnificat the variation of the instrumentation is particularly striking. Monteverdi prescribed cornetti, recorders, trombones, and string instruments; in addition he made explicit recommendations for the organ registration. The psalm tone moves to a different vocal part in each section, where it is joined by virtuoso solo parts, pairs of instruments, two choirs, or the full orchestra:

| Title | Instrumentation |
| --- | --- |
| 'Magnificat' | 7 vocal parts, 2 violins, 3 cornetti, *viola da braccio* |
| 'Et exultavit' | Cantus firmus in bass, 2 tenors |
| 'Quia respexit' | Cantus firmus in tenor, 2 violins, 3 cornetti, *viola da braccio*; 2 *fifari*, 2 trombones, 2 recorders |
| 'Quia fecit' | Cantus firmus in alto, 2 basses, 2 violins |
| 'Et misericordia' | Two three-part ensembles; cantus firmus in their respective upper voices |
| 'Fecit potentiam' | Cantus firmus in alto, 2 violins, *viola da braccio* |
| 'Deposuit' | Cantus firmus in tenor, 2 cornetti, 2 violins |
| 'Esurientes' | Cantus firmus in thirds in the two sopranos, 3 cornetti, *viola da braccio* |
| 'Suscepit Israel' | Cantus firmus in tenor, 2 sopranos |
| 'Sicut locutus est' | Cantus firmus in alto, 2 violins, 2 cornetti, 2 trombones, *viola da braccio* |
| 'Gloria' | Cantus firmus in soprano, 2 tenors |
| 'Sicut erat' | Tutti |

Monteverdi also makes use of ideas from his first operas and his madrigals in the Magnificat. 'Et exultavit', 'Quia fecit', and 'Suscepit Israel' display his typical imitative duet style. The accompaniment of the two violins in 'Quia fecit' is already reminiscent of the underworld scene in *L'Orfeo*. This relationship becomes completely clear in 'Deposuit'. In the opera, the echo-like writing for the pairs of cornetti and of violins punctuated Orfeo's entreaty to Caronte. In 'Deposuit' they accompany the chant melody with quite similar coloraturas and at the same time interpret the text. The cornetti (the underworld instruments in *L'Orfeo*) accompany the fall of the mighty, the violins the rise of the humble; the compositional style, however, remains the same throughout.

The echo effect is heightened once again to operatic exaltation in the 'Gloria'. Before the chant melody begins, the solo tenor displays great virtuosity in a single, long coloratura over a pedal point. The echo tenor repeats the concluding melisma. After the entrance of the chant melody, the echo always answers with complete, although quite short motifs, up to and including the extended concluding phrase, in which these short figures appear in rapid succession. Although the echo passages are in essence theatrical, the pure chant melody, which is sung here for the first time by the sopranos, appears ethereally angelical in contrast to the tenor duet. The mixture of transcendence and theatrical exaggeration is characteristic for the *Marian Vespers*, and also for many compositions from *Selva morale e spirituale* and the posthumous collection. It documents the sensuous, luxurious piety which represented one aspect of the Counter-Reformation and which corresponded much more with the new style of church music than with the aloof, old style, which had been purged of wordly 'frivolities'.

The hymn 'Ave maris stella' is, like the 'Sonata sopra Sancta Maria', a complete composition in and of itself. The cantus firmus, a medieval hymn melody, is treated here in yet another way. In the first and last stanzas it appears in the traditional manner as the top part of a polyphonic composition, in this case in eight parts divided into two choirs. In the second to sixth stanzas it is placed in triple time, and presented at times in homophonic choral writing and at others as solos. These intermediary stanzas are, in addition, separated from one another by a ritornello, also in triple time. Using the essence of the hymn melody, Monteverdi again constructed an almost cyclical complex, in which the old and new styles are juxtaposed harmoniously.

Even the 'Sonata', although instrumental, is based on a cantus firmus, the invocation from 'Sancta Maria ora pro nobis'. This figure appears eleven times in the composition, each time in a different rhythmic form. Stylistically the 'Sonata' shows the influence of Venice. It is similar to instrumental canzonas by composers such as Giovanni Gabrieli in its ternary form, its frequent metric changes, its rhythm and instrumentation. The technique of including an ostinato cantus-firmus phrase within an instrumental movement was already in use long before the publication of the *Marian Vespers* and is typical for northern Italy. It is true for the 'Sonata' as well as for almost all other sections of the *Marian Vespers* that they are not 'inventions' of Monteverdi's but are embedded within long-standing traditions. They are, none the less, new and distinct from these in the balanced conjuncton of old and new techniques, in the perfect amalgamation of religiosity and theatricality, in the awareness of the musical possibilities and of the limits in interpreting the text, in the well-thought-out

construction of larger entities on the basis of a single given element.
What is true for the individual compositions is also true for the entire
*Marian Vespers*. It is a catalogue of the regional styles in Italy, an
exemplary collection for the application of the cantus-firmus technique, a series of texts that do not appear to belong together.
Nevertheless, from these Monteverdi managed to put together a
musical aggregrate which is a complete entity.

The tendency to 'secularize' sacred music becomes even more
evident in the later publications. It is not only that Monteverdi also
uses stylistic models from his madrigals for sacred texts. The parallel
chains of thirds and sixths above a bass descending with stepwise
motion, which first appeared at the end of 'Ecco mormorar l'onde' and
were so important in the development of his duet style, cannot be
dispensed with for the words 'Cantate et exultate' in 'Cantate Domino'
(1620; Ex. 5.7). It is not only that all catchwords that just cry out for
word-painting in the typical madrigalistic fashion—*sagitta, fugge,
currit, spargit, fluent*, and whatever other words describing movement
may be found in the psalms—are treated with particular care. Beyond
these limits of madrigalistic word-painting, however, the text was
presented with theatrical, dramatic interest. The word 'Surgite' from
the psalm 'Nisi Dominus' can be interpreted, to be sure, with a simple

Ex. 5.7.    'Cantate Domino'
            (Sing and rejoice)

leap of a fifth as in the *Marian Vespers*; it can also be clearly emphasized, as in the second 'Nisi Dominus' from the posthumous collection, by moving up the steps of a triad (Ex. 5.8*a*); one can also, however, derive a soaring gesture from this single word, as in the first version of the psalm in the posthumous collection, in which the ascending movement, reinforced by a declamatory rhythm taken from speech, seems almost to want never to end (Ex. 5.8*b*).

Ex. 5.8*a*. 'Nisi Dominus (II)'
(Arise)

Ex. 5.8*b*. 'Nisi Dominus (I)'
(Arise)

On occasion the music venerating Jesus and Mary displays undisguised erotic traits, as do the texts themselves. An effort is required to reconcile the almost exaggerated naturalism of the languishing sighs 'o dulcis virgo Maria', at the end of all three settings of 'Salve Regina' in the *Selva morale e spirituale* with the concept of church music which has been purged of all frivolity. It cannot truly be said that the ascetic approach is the foremost trait in this veneration, as is particularly evident in the panting sighs in the second 'Salve Regina', uttered by the two tenors over a chromatically rising bass as if fighting for self-control (Ex. 5.9). The second 'Salve Regina' is a further example of Monteverdi's art of creating music of great impact whilst using the simplest of compositional techniques. The piece consists of little more than the answering of one voice by another: as an echo, as an imitation with a different continuation, as a canon; intensification is achieved by the change from solo to two-part writing in thirds. The melody of the canonic passages is split up into segments, all equally short, causing an obstruction of the musical flow which is abetted by the basso continuo. As a result these passages at times actually appear to be homophonic with interspersed rests (Ex. 5.10).

Ex. 5.9.    'Salve Regina (II)'
             (O sweet Virgin, O Mary)

Ex. 5.10.  'Salve Regina (II)'
(rejoice, O son of Eve)

Sacred music seen through the eyes of the art of madrigal-writing, and what is more, garnished with operatic quotations! It is enough to make an advocate of 'pure' church music shudder. Such purism, however, was foreign to those times. The appeal for autonomous church music was more of a helpless cry than a decree. Otherwise Monteverdi could scarcely have placed what is perhaps his most 'secular' composition at the end of the *Selva morale e spirituale*.

### CONTRAFACTA AND PARODIES

Contemporaries were unanimous in declaring 'Lasciatemi morire'—the plaint of the abandoned Arianna, whose fate had moved entire audiences to tears—to be the best and most genuine dramatic music. It seems, therefore, even more astonishing to encounter just this most successful of Monteverdi's compositions in the *Selva morale e spirituale* as the 'Pianto della Madonna'. In it, in place of Arianna on the cliffs, Mary laments at the foot of the cross. The archetype of dramatic music as a sacred lament? Not—as with Claudio Saracini—a newly composed, sacred lament scene in a secular monody collection, but Monteverdi's best-known composition in a sacred collection 'sold' as a Latin setting in the tradition of the 'Stabat mater'?

From the Middle Ages on, compositions which were originally secular were commonly underlaid with sacred texts, a practice which was often observed even in Monteverdi's time. Such *contrafacta* in no way disturbed religious sensibilities. With the beginning of the Counter-Reformation, whose aims included the utilization of the arts as a means of Catholic propaganda, a great demand had risen for sacred pieces which could be played outside the church services, in monasteries, in academies, at court, or in the houses of patricians. At the end of the sixteenth century entire collections of *madrigali spirituali* appeared; Monteverdi himself published just such a print in 1583. In addition, at the end of many collections of secular madrigals or solo songs, one or several sacred Latin or Italian compositions were included. Tarquinio Merula's lullaby for the Baby Jesus (see Ex. 3.9) belongs in this category, as does Claudio Saracini's 'Stabat mater', entitled 'Pianto della Beata Vergine Maria', at the end of his third book of arias.

Devotional adaptations of well-known compositions, however, were particularly popular. In 1607 Aquilino Coppini, professor of rhetoric at the university of Padua and a friend of Vincenzo Gonzaga and Monteverdi, published a collection of secular madrigals, by Monteverdi and a number of other famous composers, underlaid with sacred Latin texts. The great success of this publication induced him to underlay two further collections with new texts and publish them in 1608 and 1609. In his adaptations Coppini let himself be inspired primarily by the content of the madrigals; 'Una donna fra l'altre' was turned into 'Una es', 'Ah dolente partita' into 'O infelix recessus', 'Anima dolorosa' into 'Anima miseranda'. At times, however, he let himself be guided merely by the sonorities of the words, as when 'Quell'augellin' was converted into 'Qui laudes'. The music remained untouched in these *contrafacta*; only the rhythm had to be changed a little here and there when the Latin text's metre was different from the Italian one. Even what is probably the most suggestive of Monteverdi's madrigals, 'Sì ch'io vorrei morire', with a setting as audacious as the content of the text, full of breathless sighs, pressing suspensions, and surprising turns toward the minor, under the title of 'O Jesu mea vita' could assume a sacred mantle in the veneration of Jesus:

> Sì ch'io vorrei morire,
> hora ch'io bacio amore
> la bella bocca del mio amato core!
> Ahi car'e dolce lingua!
> Datemi tant'humore
> che di dolcezza in questo sen m'estingua
> Ahi vita mia! A questo bianco seno,
> deh, stringetemi sin ch'io venga meno!
> Ahi bocca, ahi baci, ahi lingua io torno a dire:
> Sì ch'io vorrei morire.

> Yes, I wish to die,
> now whilst I, full of love, kiss
> the beautiful mouth of my beloved!
> O, dear and sweet tongue!
> Give me so much of your humours

that I may die of sweetness on this breast.
O, my life! On this white breast,
O, press me until I perish!
O mouth, O kisses, O tongue, I say once again:
Yes, I wish to die.

O Jesu mea vita
in quo est vera salus,
o lumen gloriae amate Jesu,
o cara pulchritudo
tribue mihi tuam
dulcedinem mellifluam gustandam.
O vita mea, o gloria coelorum,
ah restringe me tibi in aeternum
O Jesu, lux mea, spes mea, cor meum, do me tibi
O Jesu mea vita.

O Jesus, my life,
in whom there is true salvation,
O light of glory, beloved Jesus,
O blessed beauty,
give me your
mellifluous sweetness to taste.
O my life, O glory of the heavens,
ah, bind me to you eternally.
O Jesus, my light, my hope, my heart, I give you myself,
O Jesus, my life.

It was thus nothing out of the ordinary for Arianna's lamentation to be transformed into Mary's. The author of the Latin text is unknown. He remained close to the original opera text and avoided all direct references to people or places with admirable adroitness. The appearance of a literal translation was none the less maintained:

ARIANNA:  et io rimango cibo di fere in solitarie arene

          and I remain here as food for wild beasts in a solitary clime

MARIA:  et ego relinquor preda doloris solitaria et mesta

          and I remain here, prey to sorrow, alone and sad

In particular, the Latin poet profited from the similarity in sound between the names Teseo and Jesu; the frequently recurring exclamations, such as 'Ahi Teseo mio', could thus easily be turned into 'Ah Jesu mi'. He also managed gracefully to circumvent Arianna's curse in the fourth section of the lament, that the waters and storms might overwhelm Theseus, by having Mary implore the earth that it might swallow her up. The rest of the text can, without difficulty, be translated literally. Monteverdi left the musical substance of the 'Lamento d'Arianna' largely untouched. Only the rhythmic treatment of the basso continuo shows the greater independence acquired by the instrumental accompaniment since the early days of the solo song: for example, in passages of increased agitation Monteverdi broke up the long chords, having them articulated several times. He was thus also able to take the harmonic progression of the vocal part into account, something which he had passed over in the 'Lamento d'Arianna' with the harmonic nonchalance typical of the time (Ex. 5.11).

Ex. 5.11*a*. 'Lamento d'Arianna'
            (Are those the crowns
            with which you adorn my hair?)

Ex. 5.11*b*. 'O Jesu mea vita'
            (Are those royal insignia
            which crown your hair?)

The 'Lamento d'Arianna' was not only the most famous of Monteverdi's compositions; it was also the piece with which he most strongly identified himself. A certain measure of self-conceit is thus revealed by its location at the end of the only collection of sacred works which he himself published in Venice.

The 'Pianto della Madonna' is not the only transformation of a secular into a sacred composition in the *Selva morale e spirituale*. It is, however, the only true *contrafactum* in the sense that only the text has been changed. The other adaptations, based on material from the *Scherzi musicali* of 1632, and Books VII and VIII of the madrigals, are none the less all new compositions, even when they appropriate entire sections as structural elements. Economy of labour played a not insignificant role in this kind of adaptation, commonly referred to as parody. It is known that Monteverdi composed very slowly; there is reason to believe that such parodies of his own works helped him to cope with the immense workload in Venice. It is still surprising, however, that he chose just these works, which were known as secular compositions, for a publication which can represent only a fraction of his sacred music.

The solo psalm 150, 'Laudate Dominum in sanctis eius', is based on musical material from 'Armato il cor' and 'Zefiro torna e di soavi accenti', the two tenor duets which first appeared in the *Scherzi musicali* of 1632. Monteverdi himself included 'Armato il cor' in Book VIII among the *madrigali guerrieri*. Just how popular these pieces were, 'Armato il cor' with its typical *guerra* triads and a bass similar in style to the *concitato genere* and 'Zefiro torna' with its *ciaccona* bass, is shown by the fact that both of them were reprinted in the posthumous ninth book of madrigals. To begin with, Monteverdi borrowed the triadic melody from 'Armato il cor'. This he first coupled with a bass that is strongly reminiscent of the *ciaccona* and then, at the words 'sona tubae' and 'Tympano', with a *concitato* bass. Later the *ciaccona* 'Zefiro torna', is unmistakably quoted in both the bass and vocal part (Ex. 5.12; see Ex. 3.7).

The 'Confitebor terzo alla francese' from the *Selva morale e spirituale* is based upon two compositions from the *madrigali amorosi* from Book VIII: 'Chi vol haver felice' and 'Dolcissimo uscignolo'. One of the many controversies about terminology in the research on Monteverdi

Ex. 5.12. 'Laudate Dominum'
(Praise him with cymbals)

centres on the meaning of *alla francese*. The question of whether *canto alla francese* designates a style of singing, a specific grouping of the singers, or a type of composition has been answered differently time and time again. Monteverdi, as is almost always the case, has contributed to this confusion. In the foreword to the *Scherzi musicali* of 1607, Giulio Cesare Monteverdi refers to *canto alla francese* as a style of composition which his brother brought back from his trip to Flanders and introduced in Italy. The titles of 'Dolcissimo uscignolo' and 'Chi vol haver felice', however, bear the following two in-structions: 'Canto a voce piena [full], alla francese' and 'Canto a voce piana [soft], alla francese', which are opposite in meaning; it cannot be decided which of the two instructions is plagued by the printer's error. The confusion is not lessened by a letter from Francesco Rasi to Duke Vincenzo in which he complains about a style of singing, the *canto alla francese*. Characteristic for all of Monteverdi's *alla francese* composi-tions is the formal disposition with an alternation between a soloist and a chorus; in addition, one syllable of the text often appears over two quavers and there is a tendency towards a regular periodic structure. These are all features shared by the compositions in the *Scherzi musicali*, which are, to be sure, not entitled *alla francese*; the term is none the less referred to for the first time in the foreword. *Alla francese* surely indicates a type of composition as well as a character-istic grouping of the voices performing it. The manner of singing, which is of necessity always related to the style of composition, must have contributed to a 'French' impression.

There seems to have been a particularly pronounced interest in French music and French culture in Mantua around 1607/8. Not only had Ottavio Rinuccini brought the French genre of the *ballet de cour* to Mantua with the *Il ballo delle ingrate*. It is also during this period that the two settings of a French pastoral dialogue were written: *Bel pastor, dal cui bel guardo*, set by Marco da Gagliano (published in 1611) and Monteverdi (published posthumously in 1650), is an Italian trans-lation of the dialogue *Pâtoureau, m'aime tu bien* by Jean Passerat. The two *alla francese* madrigals are probably also from this period.

'Confitebor (III) alla francese' displays all of the features of these *alla francese* compositions: short passages with two quavers per syllable in the melodic progressions, alternation between a chorus and soloist, and a regular periodic structure. The two madrigals from the *madrigali amorosi* are joined together seamlessly, by the shift of 'Dolcissimo uscignolo' from minor to major (Ex. 5.13). Finally, the first 'Beatus vir' from the *Selva morale e spirituale* appropriates the instrumental ritornello and the 'walking' bass from the lively canzonetta 'Chiome d'oro' from Book VII of the madrigals. The psalm verses, which are

Ex. 5.13*a*. 'Confitebor (III) alla francese' and 'Chi vol haver felice'
(I will praise the Lord)
(He who wants to have [the heart] happy)

Con - fi - te - bor ti - bi__ Do - mi - ne

Chi vol__ ha - ver__ fe - li - ce

Ex. 5.13*b*. 'Confitebor (III) alla francese' and 'Dolcissimo uscignolo'
(he sent redemption to his people)
(Sweetest nightingale)

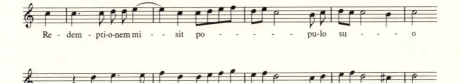

Re - dem - pti-o-nem mi - - sit po - - - - - pu-lo su - - - o

Dol - cis - si - mo usci - gno - - - - - - - lo

presented by various groupings of the voices, are joined together structurally by the bass.

Monteverdi never displayed as much interest in sacred music as in secular. He never expressed himself theoretically on the subject; even the letters in which he refers to his church music suggest half-heartedness as opposed to the enthusiasm he was capable of bringing to discussions concerning opera. Saving time is therefore certain to have been one of the reasons why he made parodies of some secular works. It is striking, however, which of the parodied works Monteverdi published. He did not choose any of the highly expressive works of the seventh and eighth madrigal books, only light, entertaining, 'modern' compositions; the 'Lamento d'Arianna' must be excepted, of course, but it has a special place in his work in any case. The fact that Monteverdi also knew how to integrate the text with the musical form in these compositions and did not 'sing the "Miserere" on the *ciaccona*' bears tribute to the school of madrigal writing in which he received his training. The parodies in the *Selva morale e spirituale* are most certainly a concession to the tastes of the time. They are, however, more than that: *genere guerriero, concitato genere, ciaccona* bass, *canto alla francese,* 'walking' bass—they are a catalogue of all the new types of composition which Monteverdi had conceived or 'invented', and which later came into style, so that it was forgotten who had suggested them first. The 'Lamento d'Arianna' fits into this constellation. A secret pointer towards their creator's innovations is concealed in the parodies of the *Selva morale e spirituale*—as well as a modicum of inventor's pride.

### THE MASSES

No domain of Monteverdi's sacred works could remain untouched by the new style. For every work in the old style there is a corresponding setting in the *Selva morale e spirituale* in the new style. Monteverdi presumably composed an equal amount in both styles; the post-humous collection and a collection of motets printed in 1620, in which four of Monteverdi's compositions are found, rectify somewhat the image of himself as a 'modern' composer which Monteverdi presents in the *Selva morale e spirituale*. The only place where the old style predominated was the mass. Three complete mass cycles survive today: the *Missa 'In illo tempore'* from the collection of 1610, a four-part *a cappella* mass from the *Selva morale e spirituale*, and a four-part *a cappella* mass from the posthumous collection. The fact that all three appear with an organ part has nothing to do with the musical structure; the organ parts are musically superfluous, fashionable appendices.

Even the masses, however, do not remain entirely free from the new style. Among the oddities of the *Selva morale e spirituale* are several, isolated sections of the ordinary of the mass, which come after the *a cappella* mass. According to the instructions, these movements can be substituted for the corresponding ones of the mass. The suggestion seems strange, almost as if it were an excuse for publishing these unrelated movements. Even if the keys were to fit together, the instrumentation is so different that the substitution would create a breach in style: a seven-part Gloria with two violins and four *viole da braccio* or four trombones; a four-part *a cappella* 'Crucifixus'; a two-part 'Et resurrexit' with two violins; a three-part 'Et iterum venturus est' with four trombones or *viole da braccio*. These sections from the ordinary of the mass are associated again and again with the mass of thanksgiving for deliverance from the plague. A chronicler reported that loud brass instruments accompanied the voices in the Gloria and Credo. The contents and the disposition of the *Selva morale e spirituale* suggest that Monteverdi wanted to make the best and most expressive parts of his masses available to a larger audience, as he did with the lament from his opera *L'Arianna*. Artistic considerations under the guise of the suggested substitutions thus predominated over liturgical ones.

Indeed these compositions are among the most polished of Monteverdi's sacred works. There is, for example, the four-part polyphonic 'Crucifixus' based on the chromatically descending lament fourth, which seems to anticipate Bach's 'Crucifixus' from the B Minor Mass. It is an austere, ascetic movement, but none the less full of deep sorrow (Ex. 5.14). And then there is the sumptuous Gloria, which simply has everything: a seven-part homophonic chorus, a seven-part chorus in *concerto* style, vocal duets answered by the violins, two- and three-part imitations, ostinato basses, dance-like sections in triple time. Even without the trombones, whose parts have

Ex. 5.14. 'Crucifixus'
(And was crucified also for us, under Pontius Pilate)

not survived, the opulence of this music can hardly be matched (Ex. 5.15).

The complete masses are all works in the old style, but none the less differ from each other entirely. The simplest turns out to be the one from the *Selva morale e spirituale*. It is strictly polyphonic with homophonic sections at 'Et incarnatus est', 'Qui locutus est', and 'Et expecto resurrectionem mortuorum', and others in triple time at 'Gratias agimus' and 'Et resurrexit'. It is a work clearly composed with its function in mind: easily sung melodies, a small range in the individual voices, no rhythmic difficulties. In contrast to this cleverly constructed but uncomplicated and transparent composition, there is something artificial, studied, about the *Missa 'In illo tempore'*. One cannot avoid seeing that a performance of this work was of secondary importance to the composer; the composition itself reveals his intention of presenting an academic example of his capabilities in the old style in this parody mass.

Underlaying secular compositions with sacred texts and transforming one's own secular works into sacred ones were not the only possible ways to utilize pre-existent musical material. Selecting thematic material from other compositions for use as constructive elements in a new one was also popular. In liturgical music, works of this nature—'super . . .' or 'ad imitationem . . .'—were particularly common. In contrast to *contrafacta* such as the 'Pianto della Madonna', in which only the text was exchanged, parodies of this kind were new compositions. Their motifs could be taken from sacred as well as from secular works. Saving time was not a consideration here; to the contrary, if one chose *soggetti* from a well-known composition, one had first to free oneself from the model in order to create a new work. According to a colleague, the great work and effort (*studio et fatica grande*)[1] that Monteverdi expended on the *Missa 'In illo tempore'* may be felt in the composition. If the result is still an impressive piece of music, it is primarily because Monteverdi, despite the constrictions imposed by the requirements of stylistic purity, could not even here disavow his musical nature. The mass is composed on *soggetti* from a motet by the Netherlander, Nicolas Gombert, who died around 1560. Indeed the unusual circumstance of Monteverdi publishing the *soggetti* indicates that he wanted this composition to be understood in an exemplary fashion.

Monteverdi's intention is clearly obvious from the very first. The mass is written in a strict polyphonic style. It has the flowing, non-stopping, long-breathed melodic phrases of the Netherlanders, which

[1] Letter from Bernardo Cassola to Cardinal Gonzaga of 26 July 1610 (Vogel, 'Monteverdi', p. 430).

Ex. 5.15.  Gloria
(Glory be to God on high)

he has created from Gombert's ten *soggetti* and intertwined with all of the artifices at his disposal. Only the 'Et incarnatus est'—also in accordance with tradition—is homophonic and clearly set off by its tonality. The fact that a passage from 'Et in spiritum Sanctum' is found once again in the 'Amen' of the psalm 'Laudate pueri' from the *Marian Vespers* is less a proof of the modernity of the Gombert mass than an indication that the origins of some of the new techniques lay in the old style. Even within the strict style, however, Monteverdi still manages to seek out the possibilities inherent in Gombert's *soggetti* for utilizing his preferred techniques of composition, the sequence and the ostinato. Both of these stylistic features were abhorred by the Palestrina School, but were none the less very popular in the generations preceding Palestrina, as is exemplified in the works of Gombert himself and his teacher Josquin. The choice of the second *soggetto* proved to be particularly felicitous, as its first four notes already constitute a sequence and could be extended through repetition; the second part is then treated in a similar manner and used as a sequential countersubject (Ex. 5.16). This double sequence is

Ex. 5.16.   Second *soggetto* from the *Missa 'In illo tempore'*

found for the first time in the second Kyrie. The second *soggetto* first appears in its entire length at the beginning of the movement; this opening is then followed by a long section in which the two sequential motifs shift continually from voice to voice. This movement appears a second time with slight melodic modifications of the countersubject at the end of the Credo. The inversion also works as a sequence. Monteverdi takes advantage of this at the words 'et expecto resurrectionem mortuorum'; in this form the ascending motion of both melodic sequences can even symbolize the resurrection. At the end of this lengthy section, the bassus and cantus come together for a long progression of parallel tenths, although the texts are out of phase by several syllables; the countersubject appears sequentially in the sextus (Ex. 5.17). The effect is unmistakable: even if no strict contrapuntal rule has been infringed upon, the end result is something completely different from the floating style of Palestrina and his School. Passages of this sort are much more pervaded by an instrumental spirit than by one of vocal polyphony. In addition, it

Ex. 5.17. Credo, *Missa 'In illo tempore'*
(And I look for the resurrection of the dead)

becomes increasingly clear that there is a tendency for the bass to become the most important voice of the composition. This is even more obvious in the Sanctus, where the beginning of the section on the words 'pleni sunt coeli et terra' is composed over a real ostinato bass. This bass consists of a succession of four notes (g–c–g–c') which appears two times in semibreves and two times in values which are twice as long. It would certainly be going too far to see a functional tonal relationship in this progression; at the same time it is striking that the notes just happen to be the first and fifth degrees of an Ionian scale in C, the main key. This four-note succession has also been gleaned from the second *soggetto*, which has already demonstrated its versatility, particularly in the Sanctus (Ex. 5.18). Here, however, Monteverdi turned the tempo relationships around; the two-note sequence appears in shorter note values than the descending scale. The latter, now a series of long notes, motivated the presence of the cherished parallel sonorities within the strict polyphonic style. Monteverdi even chose the same coloratura as the one found in 'Ecco mormorar l'onde', in 'Cantate Dominum' from 1620, and in the 'Dixit Dominus' from the *Marian Vespers*. The choice of places where Monteverdi makes use of techniques, such as the sequence and the

Ex. 5.18. Sanctus, *Missa 'In illo tempore'*
(thy glory, Hosanna in the highest)

ostinato which were originally instrumental, is striking: the end of the Kyrie, the end of the Credo, at 'pleni sunt coeli', and at 'Osanna'. The intention is obvious; these stylistic features lend themselves to the representation of increased emotion, splendour, joy. They appear at places of particular emphasis.

The four-part posthumous mass is full of personal traits of this nature, although once again in an apparently impersonal, strictly polyphonic style. Here Monteverdi went even further; the stylistic features which almost seem foreign in the *Missa 'In illo tempore'*, as if they had crept in without his being aware of it, are now employed consciously and without stylistic restraints, in the same manner as in the new style he himself had helped to establish: long, artfully interwoven coloraturas, sequences, madrigalistic constructions, and other similar artifices. In the 'Osanna', with its long chains of sequences over the descending tetrachord, the ideas latent in the *Missa 'In illo tempore'* seem to have been developed to their utmost.

It would be fruitless to speculate why Monteverdi himself published only the plain four-part mass, and not this one. In addition, too much has been lost for one to conclude that a qualitative judgement lay behind this choice. Monteverdi, like all other composers of his time, was a master of both styles; he nevertheless remained true to what for him was the heart of every composition: the inseparable connection between the music and the contents of the text.

# 6

# THE MUSICIAN IN SOCIETY

## MANTUA AND VENICE

For many years during his stay in Mantua, Monteverdi was prized, at most, by a few select members of the musical world; he was not generally known, let alone famous, and was one of many at the splendid Mantuan court. Colleagues such as Giaches de Wert, who stimulated Monteverdi in his first years there, Giovanni Gastoldi, who had immortalized himself with his light *balletti*, although he was a director of church music, and the prolific madrigalist Benedetto Pallavicino were better known than he was. By 1605, after fifteen years of service to the duke, he had only five madrigal books and a couple of early works to his name. This picture changed with the performances of his two operas, the *L'Orfeo favola in musica*, and *L'Arianna*. His fame as an operatic composer spread through Italy with the speed of lightning. Federico Follino, the court chaplain, in ordering Monteverdi back to court from Cremona where he was residing after the death of his wife, remarked that the time had come for him to attain the greatest glory that man can have on earth. Undoubtedly his comment was intended as an incentive. Follino could not guess that Monteverdi really would become an international star with the 'Lamento d'Arianna'.

In fact, Monteverdi did not profit from his fame, either financially or in his situation at court. Although the duke valued him highly, he paid more attention to the famous musicians who were invited to the Mantuan court from elsewhere than he did to his own director of music, who in any case had always to be available and subject to the duke's wishes. Monteverdi's fame was that of the duke. In the social hierarchy of the court, musicians did not stand much higher than artisans. They were used when they were needed; after they had fulfilled their obligations they were ignored. It should not surprise us that Monteverdi did not rebel against this subordinate position. He had no choice but to accept the situation, which would have been no different at any other court. He composed whatever he was commissioned to write, primarily occasional music for tourneys, ballets, and theatrical works, hardly any of which survives. He played *viola da braccio* whenever he was ordered to, and he did his best to enhance even the most inconsequential poetry of his noble patron in his musical settings.

His utter dissatisfaction with this existence is revealed by a letter from Cremona to the ducal secretary Chieppio. It is an astonishing document, which could only have been written in a state of extreme indignation; it is one of those letters which it would have been better to throw away rather than send. Monteverdi must have had great confidence in the secretary, for he risked a dishonourable discharge. As he wanted to quit his job at the Mantuan court anyway, this risk obviously did not bother him very much. The letter throws light on the burden of daily life at court and reveals vividly something of Monteverdi's personality, which was not often displayed so openly:

Today, the last day of November, I received a letter from Your Lordship, in which I learnt of His Highness's command to return to Mantua immediately. Thus the illustrious Signor Chieppio commands me to come and slave away anew. I say, however, that if I do not recuperate from the exertions of the theatre music, my life will undoubtedly be short; because of the great toil of the past [months], I have acquired a headache and such a severe, itching rash around the waist that I have not been able to eliminate it more than partially, neither with cauteries, nor with oral purgatives, nor with blood-lettings and other powerful means. My father attributes the headache to the fatiguing studies and the itch to the Mantuan climate which is bad for me, and fears that the air alone would be my death within a short time. Your Lordship should now consider what then the addition of the studies would do, if I were to come in order to receive the thanks and favours from the goodness and benevolence of His Highness, as he commands. I say to you that the fortune I have experienced in nineteen consecutive years in Mantua has given me more occasion to call it misfortune, and inimical to me, not friendly. For, if it granted me the favour of being able to serve His Highness the Duke in Hungary, then it also granted me the disfavour of necessitating me to make additional expenditures for this trip, for which my poor household almost still has to suffer today. If it ordered me to serve His Highness in Flanders, it once again crossed me on that occasion by making Claudia, living at Cremona, bring expense to our household with her maid and servant, for at that time she did not receive more than 47 lire a month from His Highness, except for the money received from my father. If fortune caused the duke to raise my wages from twelve and a half to twenty-five Mantuan scudi per month, then it also went against me by having the duke resolve to send me word by Signor Federico Follino that with this raise he intended that I should take care of Signor Campagnolo, then a choirboy, and, because I didn't want this vexation, I had to forgo five scudi for those expenses, and so I remained with the twenty scudi that I still receive today. If fortune favoured me in the past year in having the duke commission compositions for the wedding from me, then it also once again brought misfortune in that it presented me with an almost insurmountable task, and in addition it caused me to suffer from cold, lack of clothes, servitude, and almost from hunger by the loss of Claudia's wages, and from severe illness, without the merest public sign of esteem on the part of His Highness, for Your Lorship knows that the favours of princes bring their servants honour and are of use to them, particularly on an occasion when there are foreigners. If fortune granted me a garment from His Highness, to be suitably attired at the wedding, then it also harmed me, because this garment was made of silk and floss-silk and was without an undergarment, without stockings and a belt and without a lining for the coat, so that I had to spend another twenty Mantuan scudi of my own. If it has favoured me with so many opportunities for being spoken to by the duke, then it has also brought harm in that the duke has only spoken to me of work, and has never shown his pleasure of profit. And if, finally (in order not to be too lengthy), it has granted me the favour of letting me believe that I received a pension from His Highness of one hundred Mantuan scudi from the captaincy of the piazza, then it also has ensured that after the wedding it was no longer a hundred but only seventy . . . Whence, My Lord, I must draw the conclusion from what has been said; I will say that I will never receive goodwill and favours in Mantua, but rather (having returned) can only expect an ultimate downfall from my misfortune. I know very well that His Highness the Duke has the best intentions towards me, and I know that he is a very generous prince, but I have so much bad luck in Mantua, and Your Lordship can see it from the following case: I know that His Highness had decided after Claudia's death to continue paying me her wages. But as soon as I arrived in Mantua he changed his mind and, to my misfortune, did not pass on this order, so that I have up to now lost more than two hundred scudi and lose more with every day. He also decided, as I have said before, to give me the twenty-five scudi a month, but lo, he suddenly changed his mind, and to my misfortune, five scudi were deducted, whereby Your Lordship can clearly see what bad luck I have in Mantua. What more should I write to Your Lordship! To give two hundred scudi to Messer Marco de Galiani, who did, so to speak, nothing, and to give me, who did what I did, nothing! I therefore, by the love of God, implore the most illustrious Signor Chieppio, as he knows that I am ill and unlucky in Mantua, that he may arrange an honourable dismissal from His Highness, for I know that only good will come from this for me. Signor Federico Follino promised me, when he invited me by letter last year to Mantua from Cremona for the work for the wedding, I say he promised me what Your Lordship can see for yourself in his letter, which I enclose, but in the end it came to nothing, or if I got something, then it was 1500 lines to set to music. Dear Sir, help me get an honourable dismissal, which appears better to me than anything else, because I shall have a change in air, work, and fortune and who knows—if worst comes to worst—what else can I do but remain as poor as I am.[1]

---

[1] Letter of 2 Dec. 1608 (*Lettere*, pp. 33–7).

At first glance this letter seems to be about money—a perennial subject in Monteverdi's correspondence, primarily because he had continually to send out reminders about sums that should have been made over to him regularly. The letter is, however, concerned with more than this: it is about the almost unbearable dependence; about the iniquities resulting from princely unreliability; and about the disregard for him as an artist as well as a person. The fact that Monteverdi, in spite of everything, let himself be persuaded to return to court, only shows how dependent he still was on the duke's goodwill. Although he was more than forty years old and a respected musician, he had no other professional alternative.

In spite of all the humiliations he suffered and all the vexations, Monteverdi none the less remained linked with the Gonzagas until his death. With the exception of Book IV and Book VI of his madrigals, all his publications which appeared after he went to Mantua were dedicated to members of this family; this also means that he often received some contribution towards the publishing costs or some recompense. Books III and V of his madrigals are dedicated to Duke Vincenzo, the *Scherzi musicali* of 1607 and *L'Orfeo* to Vincenzo's eldest son Francesco, Book VII to the wife of his second son Ferdinando, Book VIII to the Austrian emperor, stepson of Vincenzo's youngest daughter Eleonora; the *Selva morale e spirituale* is dedicated to Eleonora herself. Of Monteverdi's own publications, Book VI of the madrigals is the only one without a dedication. Having been in Venice for two years, he could hope that the edition would sell well and justly so: the book was reprinted twice within a short time period. At the same time new editions of his earlier madrigal books began appearing; after Books IV and V had been reissued repeatedly in Venice, editions of Books III, IV, and V even appeared in Antwerp in 1615.

How different everything was in Venice! A republican wind blew there. Venice maintained diplomatic contacts with all European countries and endeavoured to remain as neutral as possible politically. Trading connections with the entire world gave the city an international air and its population a healthy sense of pride. Money was spent there that had been earned; the skilled merchants knew the relationship between quality and price. Venice was the centre of the publishing business, including that of music. The works printed with care by Amadino, Magni, or Vincenti made their way out into the wide world. The choir of S. Marco had been famous throughout Europe since the middle of the sixteenth century; the procurators spent a lot of money to bring the best Italian musicians to Venice. Any European who wanted to study music in Italy went to Venice and then brought the name of his teacher back home with him. The organist at S. Marco, Giovanni Gabrieli, had a flock of German and Danish students. Heinrich Schütz studied with Gabrieli at S. Marco from 1609 to 1612 and not with Monteverdi, whom he was later to hold in such high regard, in Mantua. When Monteverdi himself had become the director of music at S. Marco, a whole series of students from the north came to him—musicians, attending their princes, who used the opportunity of being in Venice to take a few lessons from the famous master.

The move from Mantua to Venice must have seemed to Monteverdi like going from a cage to a banqueting hall. The fact that the climate of the port on the Adriatic was lighter and healthier than the oppressive Mantuan air is almost a symbol for the general transformation of his life. He was finally free of financial worries. More importantly however, this position, although it demanded much of him, at last brought him what he had most lacked at the Mantuan court: recognition, respect, prestige, and authority. Having once breathed in this air, he would not have been willing, at any price, to go back to the Mantuan or any other court. He gave vent to his relief at finally being respected as a person in a letter to Striggio in March 1620, in which he turned down an invitation to return to Mantua. Superficially the letter again is concerned with money; but the contrast between his Mantuan and his Venetian situation speaks even more clearly than the comparison of his financial prospects. Procurator Landi's proud statement, referred to at the end of the letter, must have had the effect of a slap in the face in Mantua:

The procurators . . . have never regretted their decision, but instead have honoured me and still honour me in this manner, that no singer is accepted in the choir without the opinion of the Maestro di Capella [sic] having first been consulted, nor do they want any report about the affairs of singers other than that of the Maestro di Capella; nor do they take on organists, nor an assistant director of music, without having heard the opinion and report of the Maestro di Capella; nor is there any gentleman who does not esteem and honour me, and when I perform some music, either chamber or church music, then I swear to Your Lordship that the whole city comes running. Then the service is very pleasant, because all of the choir, with the exception of the Maestro di Capella, is subject to a work schedule; he even makes the schedule himself, and can give the singers liberty to be absent or not, and when he himself does not come to a service, no one says anything about it. And his income is assured unto death, and cannot be disturbed by the death of procurators or princes, and if he faithfully and respectfully fulfils his duty, then he can expect a raise, and not the other way around; and his wages, if for once he does not go to fetch them, are brought to his house . . . Then there is occasional income . . . because those who can get the Maestro di Capella for their performances, do not hesitate to engage and pay him thirty, forty, or even fifty ducats for two vespers and a mass and also express their thanks afterwards with choice words. Now let Your Lordship weigh on the scales of your very refined judgement the amount which you have offered me in His Highness's name and see whether, on good and solid grounds, I could make the change or not . . . And therefore Your Lordship may see that the world would surely have much to say against me, and, if the others did not do it, then what would Basile and her brother, Campagnolo, and Bassano [singers at the Mantuan court] say, who up until now have been much more highly regarded and paid! And how ashamed I would be in front of them, if I saw them rewarded more than myself! And then what would the city of Venice say! I leave it to Your Lordship to consider that His Highness made me a better offer through Campagnolo [1619] than now . . . and when I said that I did not want anything more to do with the treasury, he offered me [still more] . . . God save me from having to go daily to the treasurer and having to beg him to give me what is mine. I never suffered more emotional anguish in my life as when I had to go and demand, almost for the love of God, what was mine from the treasurer. I would rather take to the road than return to such impertinences . . . When His Excellency, the procurator Signor Landi, together with the other Excellencies raised my salary by another 100 ducats, he spoke the well-considered words: 'My noble colleagues, he who wishes to have a servant worthy of his task, must treat him commensurately'; thus, if the duke has in mind that I should live honourably, then he should also treat me that way, even when I do not ask it of him, in order not to bring me into trouble, for here I am treated honourably, as Your Lordship can verify.[2]

In spite of the respect they had for their famous director of music, the procurators made sure that the quality of the choir did not suffer from his absence. Although they accepted Monteverdi's work on the side, his excursions into the world of chamber and theatre music, they did insist, however, that he participate wholeheartedly in the highest church festivals—Easter, Christmas, and the annual wedding of the doge with the sea. When Monteverdi, because of preparations for wedding festivities in Parma, requested an extension of his leave into December, the procurators ordered him politely, but unmistakably, to return. His presence at the Christmas preparations at S. Marco had precedence over tourneys and intermedi at foreign courts. Even the procurators' liberality had its limits when it came to the question of the quality of the church music entrusted to them.

### THEATRE MUSIC

'Theatre music' is not necessarily to be equated with 'opera'. There were many and varied occasions on which it was felt that their festive

[2] Letter of 13 Mar. 1620 (*Lettere*, pp. 148–53).

character would be enhanced by stately performances; and there were just as many forms of musical entertainment. The opera, a complete drama set to music, was only one of them. There were also ballets, horse ballets, tourneys, intermedi, musical settings for prologues to spoken dramas, and all kinds of shorter dramatic scenes with and without ballet. There was no lack of opportunity to display splendour, thereby demonstrating magnificence, wealth, and power: princes' weddings and birthdays, victories which needed celebration, coronations and enthronements, high feast days, state visits, and just simply court festivals. The importance of the festivity corresponded with the expense; the stage sets, stage machinery, gorgeousness of the costumes, and performances full of special effects were just as important, if not more so, than the music. The more impressive the spectacle, the more extensive the performances, the more luxurious the execution, the greater then the effect on the prince's reputation, as spread by the tales of the invited guests and by the reports of the legates present.

In contrast to *L'Orfeo*, *L'Arianna* was a festival opera *par excellence*. It is only from this viewpoint that it does not seem surprising that the Duchess Eleonora Gonzaga, upon seeing the work at one of the rehearsals, thought that the libretto was too 'dry'[3] and ordered Rinuccini to make the plot more entertaining—a demand that in no way corresponded with the concept of a *favola per musica*, not to mention a *tragedia* as Rinuccini called his work. *L'Arianna*, however, was supposed to fulfil a function different from that of *L'Orfeo*, which owes its existence to a burst of enthusiasm for a new musical genre: *L'Arianna* was to be the high point of the wedding festivities for the successor to the throne. The duke had several good reasons, apart from his love for the arts, for making the festivities as splendid as possible. There was, first of all, the diplomatic success implied by this wedding: it would connect his small principality with one of Italy's most powerful and expansive families, the house of Savoy, whose ruler, Carlo Emanuele, had always had an eye on Monferrato, a rich Mantuan possession on his border. The danger of an invasion seemed to have been avoided by the marriage of Margherita of Savoy with Francesco Gonzaga. The festivities were intended to demonstrate palpably the grandeur and importance of Mantua to the Savoyard princes. In the background, however, there was also the desire to outshine the Medici family, whose wedding festivities in 1589 and 1600 had surpassed everything of the sort until then. Although Vincenzo had outstanding musicians, poets, and actors at his disposal

---

[3] Solerti, *Albori*, i. 92.

at his own court, he also invited the best Florentine artists, such as Marco da Gagliano and Ottavio Rinuccini, to Mantua. He then flattered them in a way such that Monteverdi felt cruelly slighted. The festivities, however, did not fulfil their main purpose. Carlo Emanuele shunned this demonstration, thus showing the duke of Mantua whom he considered to be more important: after Vincenzo had accompanied his son to Turin for the nuptials, Carlo Emanuele decided to stay away from the Mantuan part of the wedding and instead sent his two, no less arrogant sons, who then disrupted the Mantuan protocol. This was a clear affront on the part of the mighty Savoyard towards the less powerful Gonzaga.

The chronicler of the events, Federico Follino, recorded everything that Carlo Emanuele missed. From 24 May to 8 June the wedding guests were kept on the move. Court balls, plays, fireworks, and other grandiose entertainments followed hard upon each other's heels: on 28 May *L'Arianna*, in the morning of 29 May a hunting excursion, in the evening a comedy, on 30 May outings, on 31 May a nocturnal fête on the lake, on 1 June a court ball, on 2 June Guarini's comedy *L'Idropica* with a prologue and intermedi by Gabriello Chiabrera, for which Monteverdi and four other composers wrote the music, on 3 June a tourney entitled *Il trionfo dell'onore*, on 4 June Rinuccini's *Il ballo delle ingrate*, and on 5 June a *Balletto d'Ifigenia*. Monteverdi was surely not the only one who was brought to the brink of total exhaustion by the preparations for this spectacle.

Monteverdi was well acquainted with the genre of the ballet, as represented by *Il ballo delle ingrate*. It was a kind of aristocractic entertainment from France in which pantomime, dance, and vocal and instrumental music were blended together to form a single genre. One cannot even guess just how many ballets of this sort were written at the Mantuan court. They were ephemeral works, flung together hastily for amusement, and only in exceptional cases worthy of being included in printed collections. Giulio Cesare Monteverdi wrote in the foreword to the *Scherzi musicali* of 1607 that Claudio was occupied most of the time with tourneys, ballets, and comedies. There is a letter from 1604 in which Monteverdi reflects upon the scenic realization of a ballet dealing with allegorical and mythological topics in which Endymion as well as dancing shepherds and stars are mentioned. The *Scherzi musicali* concludes with a *balletto* in homage to beauty, *De la bellezza le dovute lodi*, a three-voice vocal and instrumental composition with alternating rhythms.

The characters of *Il ballo delle ingrate* are taken from ancient mythology: Venus, Amor, and Pluto. The subject-matter of this short, frivolous play, however, is court society itself. In front of the entrance to hell, Amor asks his mother Venus to convince Pluto to allow those women who remained deaf to the pleas of their lovers to return to earth, so that these haughty women might see what hellish torments such cruelty leads to. Pluto agrees and, after these prudish ladies have danced a sad ballet, turns to the women in the audience and threatens them with a similar fate if they deny their lovers their favour. After a still more dismal dance Pluto sends them back to hell. One of them turns around once more and adjures the ladies present to have pity on their lovers, a warning that was certainly superfluous at Vincenzo's merry court.

The largest portion of *Il ballo delle ingrate* is recitative dialogue. Even so it serves only as a framework for the high point, the dance of the ungrateful women. This is the dramatic and musical climax of the play, involving a large instrumental ensemble and displaying a wealth of various rhythmic models. If, none the less, the lament of the unthankful spirit at the end appears more impressive to us today, then it is because the ballet's effectiveness depended mainly on the choreography and the costumes, and also because the emotional power of this short passage does not fall short of that of the 'Lamento d'Arianna'. The simplest and most moving expression of its language, whose declamation alternates between recitative and arioso, is found in the long refrain (Ex. 6.1). The dance of the prudish women,

Ex. 6.1.    *Il ballo delle ingrate*
            (Serene and pure air,
             farewell forever,
             farewell O heaven, O sun,
             farewell bright stars)

however, was the high point of the ballet performance primarily because the duke and his son took part in it. Only the singers and the instrumentalists were professional musicians. Foremost of them all was Virginia Andreini, the highly active star of the wedding festivities, who had to sing the lament of the ungrateful spirit in addition to the role of Arianna and to her parts in the dramas. The ballet itself was danced by eight ladies of the court and six noblemen, as well as by Francesco and Vincenzo Gonzaga. They were all enveloped, as Follino reported, in costly, bizarre garments which appeared to consist of ashes and embers. The participation of princes in such a performance was a novelty for the pleasure-loving Mantuan court, but had been customary at the French court for more than twenty years and was soon to become fashionable in Italy as well. Rinuccini had taken this idea from Paris where he had often been a visitor since 1600, when Maria de' Medici had become the queen of France. The stage action and the court society were blended together above and beyond the traditional homage to the princes in *Il ballo delle ingrate*; the demarcation between fantasy and reality was blurred. Instead of dancing on stage, the sixteen aristocratic dancers progressed to the main floor of the theatre so that they could dance surrounded by their peers; the seventeenth, Virginia Andreini, remained on stage.

For Monteverdi the move from Mantua to Venice also implied a change in his compositional duties. While ballets and intermedi were part of the director of music's daily fare at court, at a church the director of music was required primarily to supply masses and motets. All were forms of occasional music which were not suitable for publication. Not one of the many intermedi and tourneys for which Monteverdi wrote the music is extant; and, apart from *De la bellezza le dovute lodi*, only three ballets have survived: *Tirsi e Clori* at the end of Book VII of his madrigals, and the *Ballo, Movete al mio bel suon*, and *Il ballo delle ingrate* in Book VIII. This selection is not fortuitous. Monteverdi wrote *Tirsi e Clori*, a light-hearted pastoral work for two solo voices and five-part chorus, for Duke Ferdinando Gonzaga, to be used at a court festivity; later he placed it, as if a homage, at the end of the book of madrigals dedicated to Caterina de' Medici, Ferdinando's wife. *Movete al mio bel suon* is in honour of the imperial dedicatee of Book VIII. Rinuccini's *Il ballo delle ingrate* was presumably performed once again twenty years after the Mantuan production, at Ferdinand's court in Graz. In every case there is a direct link between the work and the person to whom the publication is dedicated. There are other, artistic reasons why the profusion of intermedi, ballets, and tourneys were not published. Although Monteverdi, even in Venice, also carried out commissions for Mantua and Parma, he himself did not value this form of musical production very highly. It was the portrayal of human passions, the revelation of human traits, and not the musical accompaniment of stage effects, that interested him in theatre. Monteverdi's musical imagination was kindled by the fate of an individual and not by theatrical extravagance, for which a completely different kind of music was required. Even with the opera *L'Arianna* only the lament survived, the central scene, which drew its forcefulness solely from Arianna's mental state. Intermedi fulfilled a different purpose from operas; they were subject to a different kind of dramaturgy and required another type of musical expression. A text which would have been impossible for an opera could none the less be suitable for intermedi. A work which, for example, did not include a homage to the princes might be acceptable for an opera, but was insufficient for courtly theatre music. Monteverdi, in connection with a commission from Mantua, reduced the difference between music for intermedi and that for operas to a simple but compelling formula: opera music for him was 'sung speech' (*parlar cantando*), and theatre music was 'spoken song' (*cantar parlando*).[4]

For Ferdinando Gonzaga's wedding Monteverdi received the commission in 1616 to set a *favola marittima* by Scipione Agnelli, the author of the lament sestina in the sixth madrigal book. For several reasons Monteverdi did not like this text, *Le nozze di Tetide*, at all. Primarily he felt that the fable lacked power of expression, a purpose, and a moving denouement. Instead of a commanding character, he could see only romping godheads and sirens. These were not active, but representative figures; in addition there were also winds, which were completely devoid of individual personality:

Moreover I have seen that the interlocutors are the winds, amoretti, zephyrs, and sirens, and that therefore many sopranos would be required, and in addition that the winds should sing, namely the zephyrs and the boreals. How, dear Lord, can I imitate the speech of the winds if they do not speak? And how can I by their means move the passions? Arianna moved them because she was a woman, and similarly Orfeo moved them because he was a man and not a wind. Music can imitate their sound, but without speech; [it can imitate,] for example, the noise of the winds, the bleating of sheep, the neighing of horses, etc., but not the speech of the winds, because it does not exist . . . The fable also, as far as my no little ignorance is concerned, does not move me at all, and it is only with difficulty that I understand it; nor do I feel that it carries me in a natural manner to an end that moves me. Arianna

---

[4] Letter of 9 Dec. 1616 (*Lettere*, p. 88). (See also Nino Pirrotta's discussion of the terms *recitar cantando* and *cantar recitando* in his book, *Music and Theatre from Poliziano to Monteverdi* (Cambridge, 1982), 241–5, as well as Frederick W. Sternfeld's discussion of the terms *recitare, favellare, parlare*, etc., in 'A Note on Stile recitativo', *PRMA* 110 (1984), 41–4).

inspired me to a true lament and Orfeo to a true song of entreaty, but with this text I do not know to what end [it inspires me], so that I would like to know from your Lordship what the music in this fable should achieve?[5]

Thus only an individual human fate could be expressed in the musical language which Monteverdi called *parlar cantando*—as an imitation of human feelings, clarification of the text, and characterization of an emotional state. Everything else, the self-personification of a siren or a sea godhead, required song, required what Monteverdi called *cantar parlando*; here the text provided a basis, a stimulation for the music— as musical decoration. When Monteverdi heard that Agnelli's text was not for an opera but for a series of intermedi, his problems with the libretto were solved instantly. The fate of an individual was in any case unsuitable subject-matter for intermedi; the winds, however, as allegorical figures, did indeed have their place there. The fable had to contain everything that would make a court festivity more splendid. Such music was easier and faster to compose than the expression of a human being. Monteverdi then demanded more ballet, more instrumental sinfonias, and an extended homage to the princely nuptial pair as the conclusion. He knew exactly what the social circumstances required and let himself be guided by them in his realization of theatre music. His works for the princely wedding in Parma, for example, were drawn up specifically for the room in which the performances were to take place; in addition they were fashioned with the variety and splendour demanded by an occasion of this nature.

The scenario of the tourney *Mercurio e Marte*, which completely exhausted the technical capabilities of the large theatre in the ducal Palazzo della Pillotta, reads like a description of a magical forest:

First Aurora appears with the Months and the Golden Age in the heavens. Discord ascends from the underworld with an entourage of Furies and goads Mercury into hindering the planned tourney. Mercury, in a celestial chariot, casts a spell on the knights on stage, leaving them unable to move: the challenger, the duke, on a rock in the ocean, the first body of knights amidst stones, the second in an infernal marsh, the third under Mt Etna, and the fourth in the stomachs of some sea monsters. Then Mars appears in the heavens, vows revenge on Mercury, and asks the gods to free the knights. Venus descends from the heavens with a multitude of amoretti, frees the challenger, and causes a city to rise in front of his eyes. Apollo calls Orpheus, who sings so entreatingly as to dissolve the stones which were holding the first body of knights fast. The Muses watch the drama from Parnassus. Then the fight begins. Juno appears in the heavens with a costly chariot and requests Berecyntia to request Proserpina to request Pluto to free the second body of knights. The series of requests, which is executed immediately

---

[5] Ibid. 87.

afterwards, is successful: Pluto appears in a flaming chariot and orders the infernal monsters to lead the knights to the battlefield. Again battle is joined. Then Amor appears on the coat of arms of the Medici (the family of the bride) in the heavens, praises the bride, and scolds the goddess of war, Bellona, because she has not yet freed the third body of knights. Bellona hurries to do this; in the side entrance of the theatre a magnificent carriage appears with the knights, who also immediately begin to fight. Then Saturn peeps out from the highest part of the heavens and asks Neptune to free the last group of knights. Neptune, however, does even more: surrounded by Tritons he orders the ocean to spread out so that the fighting can take place in the water. And indeed the floor of the theatre is suddenly flooded with water, in which Galatea causes two islands to rise, so that the tourney may be brought to a close. Jupiter, together with all the other gods, then hurls Discord from the heavens and thus bestows eternal marital peace on the bride and bridegroom.

What can the music have been like, able as it was to hold its own against this abundance of dramatic effects and choreographic events to such a degree that its fame outshone the enthusiasm for the spectacle? Apparently it was not evident that Monteverdi had his difficulties with Achillini's text. More than a thousand lines in length, it was more rhetorical than musical and offered him few expressive possibilities or situations suited for music. Perhaps his music made an impression just because he was able to confer individual expression upon certain passages within the required musical decoration; and this despite the fact that it dealt not with individual fates but with the representation of quite diverse gods, epic heroes, and allegories. Once again Monteverdi also employed techniques which had made the composition of *Le nozze di Tetide* so much easier—the *cantar parlando* and a great variety in instrumentation: 'And where I could not find diversity in the affects I have attempted to vary the instrumentation.'[6]

The transitoriness of such productions, tailor-made for specific occasions, did not prevent Monteverdi from devoting careful thought to their performance. He did, certainly, confer more interest and enthusiasm on *La finta pazza Licori* than on any other dramatic composition—as a through-composed opera with a predominant protagonist it corresponded with his ideal of theatre music. It is characteristic that his considerations in this case are concerned exclusively with Licori's role. Here, as whenever possible, he wrote the parts to match exactly the voices of the people who were to sing them, adjusted the size of the orchestra to fit that of the room, and gave much attention to choosing an instrumentation suitable to the subject-matter. From his deliberations it becomes obvious again and

[6] Letter of 4 Feb. 1628 (*Lettere*, p. 305).

again that Monteverdi preferred small ensembles because they allowed the vocal parts more artistic freedom. The large size of the Teatro Farnese in Parma made him somewhat sceptical about the solo parts; apart from all other more fundamental objections, his rejection of *Le nozze di Tetide* was also based on such practical theatrical problems:

Firstly music wants to be mistress of the air and not only of the water; by that I mean to say that the events for the musical ensemble described in the fable all take place in the depths and near the earth, which is a great drawback for a beautiful sound, because the instrumental accompaniment would have to be composed for the lowest and largest wind instruments, which would be heard by all and would have to be played backstage [*poichè le armonie saranno poste ne fiati più grossi del aria della terra fatti così da essere da tutti uditi et dentro alla sena da essere concertati*][7], for which reason Your Lordship can easily judge with your highly refined and educated taste that because of that defect, [as far as string instruments are concerned], instead of one chitarrone one would need three; instead of one harp, three, and so on; and, instead of a delicate voice, one would need a forced one. Moreover, if one wants to imitate the text properly, it would have to be supported, in my opinion, by wind instruments instead of by delicate string instruments, because the music of the Tritons and other seagods should, I believe, be accompanied by trombones and cornetti and not by citterns or harpsichords and harps, as the plot takes place in the ocean and as a result far from civilization; and Plato teaches [in *The Republic*] that the cithara is suitable for the city and the tibia for the country; so that either the delicate sounds would be improper or the proper ones would not be delicate.[8]

It is for this reason that Monteverdi much preferred to fulfil commissions whose librettos centred on a person or an episode, works whose dramatic content surpassed their need for extravagance. This preference met with favour in the social structure of the republican city. The patrons there did not spend money with the unrestrained joy of princes who feel compelled to glorify themselves. The self-assurance of the patrician families in Venice had other roots. Although one might be rich, educated, and interested in the arts, one did not suffer from megalomania and prodigality. It does not mean that splendid parties and stately plays were not also staged there. Such spectacles, however, were organized primarily by the academies, which began to proliferate at the beginning of the seventeenth century. In private houses, assuming there was no wedding to be celebrated in a spectacular manner, one indulged in more select pleasures. Especially popular were cultivated evening entertainments

---

[7] This passage of the letter is so unclear that it can only be interpreted. Other versions speak of 'large wind instruments' (Fortune and Arnold) and 'wind machines' (Schrade).

[8] Letter of 9 Dec. 1616 (*Lettere*, p. 86).

in which first some music was heard and then a shorter dramatic work with music performed. Alessandro Striggio's dramatic poem 'Lamento di Apollo' was so appropriate for such evenings that Monteverdi was asked to perform it at one of the patrician homes when it became known that he was setting it for his friend. The following is from a letter he wrote to his friend Striggio:

Certain gentlemen have heard the 'Lamento di Apollo' and they were so pleased with the manner of its invention, of its text, and of its music that they think—after an hour of music which at the moment is customarily presented at the house of a certain member of the Benbi [Bembo?] family for an audience of the noblest ladies and gentlemen—they think, I say, of having it performed on a small stage.[9]

In productions of this sort, in which the staging is reduced to a minimum and, as it were, only suggests the action, the quality of the text was much more important than in other more elaborate theatrical events. Such a work also had to be shorter, more concise, and more complete. Italian literature, particularly its epic poetry, offered a profusion of stories which were dramatic although not theatrical. Foremost here were Ariosto's *Orlando furioso* and Tasso's *Gerusalemme liberata*, which soon became sources also for operatic texts. Monteverdi set two such episodes in collaboration with his friend and patron, the patrician Girolamo Mocenigo. Whether this collaboration meant merely that Mocenigo provided the rooms and occasions, or whether the suggestion came from him, is not clear, but it is also unimportant. Here Monteverdi could realize his ideas on his own, without being dependent on the occasion's demands and the patron's requirements. Here the audience came to listen to his music, not because of the spectacle. One of the two works which we know about from his letters is lost: *Armida*, the scene from *Gerusalemme liberata* in which Rinaldo abandons Armida. It is a series of stanzas from Canto 16, for the most part in direct speech. Armida's plaint is clearly reminiscent of those of Arianna and Olimpia: the same build-up, the same outburst of rage, the same collapse—and presumably a similar musical setting. The other work, performed in 1624 in Mocenigo's house, is based on a completely different kind of dramaturgy: the *Combattimento di Tancredi e Clorinda*, the battle between the crusaders and the Saracens from Canto 12 of *Gerusalemme liberata*. Here the direct speech is limited to a few linguistic duels. The rest of the sixteen stanzas presents a description of the battle: Clorinda loves Tancredi; she, disguised as a man, encounters him encased in armour and combats him vigorously, disregarding all rules of battle, until she is so

[9] Letter of 1 Feb. 1620 (*Lettere*, pp. 129–30).

near death that she begs to be baptized; when he takes off her helmet to sprinkle her with water, he recognizes the woman he loves; he almost despairs, but she dies in blessed peace as a Christian.

The *Combattimento di Tancredi e Clorinda* is the only theatrical composition which Monteverdi produced during the time between the Mantuan and the Venetian operas and which he later also published, and is thus the only one which has survived until today. For several reasons it would be unwise to make assumptions about the other lost works on the basis of this piece. First of all, as it took into account the place where it was originally performed, it required only a very small number of musicians: the three singers, Clorinda (soprano), Tancredi (tenor), and Testo, the narrator (tenor); five string players; and a harpsichordist. Secondly, the *Combattimento* has far too little dialogue to enable one to draw conclusions from it concerning, for example, *La finta pazza Licori*. The dramatic action is carried not by discourse, but by the narrative, which is treated melodically in a highly reserved manner. This music is not inspired by the specific words of the text, but instead provides a programmatic instrumental accompaniment, which, as it were, describes the battle while the two singers present it in pantomime. In the foreword to the *Combattimento* Monteverdi explains his ideas concerning this union of music with pantomime:

After some madrigals have been sung without gestures, suddenly from the part of the room where the music is to be played, Clorinda enters, armour-clad and on foot, followed by Tancredi, armour-clad and on a horse, upon which Testo [the narrator] begins to sing. They should make their steps and gestures in accordance with the text, no more nor less, whereby they must observe the tempi, the beats, and steps carefully, and the instrumentalists the excited and soft sonorities, and the narrator must watch out that the words are spoken at the right time, in such a manner that everything is united into a homogeneous whole in the imitation . . . The instruments, that is four *viole da braccio*, soprano, alto, tenor, and bass, and a contrabass, which plays along with the harpsichord, must imitate with their bow strokes the passions of the text, which the voice of the Testo must sing clearly and firmly and with good diction, as his words deviate quite a bit in time from the instrumental accompaniment, so that one understands the text well. He is not allowed to make any ornaments or trills other than in the stanza which begins with 'Notte'. Otherwise the pronunciation should be in accordance with the passions of the text.

The small number of musicians involved was not only appropriate for the room but also dramaturgically well-founded: the requisite unity of instrumental sonorities, song, and gesticulation could hardly have been accomplished with more. The strings take over, even replace the action; all kinds of motion, of fighting, happen in the instrumental accompaniment. Even the beginning is a dramatic scene in music (Ex. 6.2): Clorinda paces back and forth in front of the city gates (Ex. 6.2*a*); Tancredi on his horse blocks her path; he gallops faster and faster after her (Ex. 6.2*b*).

Tasso's description of the vicious battle, in which 'rage causes every knightly art to be forgotten', inspired Monteverdi to technical and

Ex. 6.2.    *Combattimento di Tancredi e Clorinda*
            (She traverses the crest of the hill)

stylistic innovations in the instrumental accompaniment. Again it was a theatrical, a dramatic idea which led to these innovations, the pizzicato and the decrescendo. The clanging of the swords, the muffled blows of the sword pommels, the crashing-together of the helmets and armour is all depicted in descriptive music which is worlds apart from the traditional madrigalistic text interpretation. The text itself is declaimed as monotonously as possible; it only provides the independent instrumental accompaniment with cues; it does not share in its motifs.

The string accompaniment, however, describes not only external events, but also states of being. The *Combattimento* is a paradigm for the *concitato genere*, one of the two extremes of human emotional expression. Not only do the instruments illustrate the rage of the combatants—even the narrator declaims in the same tongue-twisting manner (Ex. 6.3).

Ex. 6.3.    *Combattimento di Tancredi e Clorinda*
(Affront provokes anger to revenge)

*Preghiera e morte* (prayer and death)—the other end of the span of human emotions—were represented by Monteverdi by means of quite different instrumental sonorities. For Clorinda's collapse, for her short, fragmented phrases, uttered with her last strength, he transferred to the string accompaniment an effect that until that time was used only for voice, the decrescendo. Clorinda's ecstasy after her baptism is linked by her voice with quiet chords in the strings and dies with them in a long concluding tone. Although it is a conciliatory ending, it remains unusual (Ex. 6.4).

Normally even this type of cultivated entertainment required a happy ending. Indeed for the 'Lamento di Apollo' Monteverdi

Ex. 6.4  *Combattimento di Tancredi e Clorinda*
(Heaven is opening, I depart in peace)

composed, in addition, a concluding ballet. It is no wonder that the society present at this sad ending almost wept and were enraptured by this 'new style, never heard of or seen before'.[10] The *Combattimento di Tancredi e Clorinda*—which musicologists have such difficulties in classifying—is also, in the broadest sense, theatre music, fashioned for an audience from which one could exact more than one could from court society. It is a Janus-headed work, for in his choice of text and instruments Monteverdi evoked the recitation of epics in the sixteenth century in which a singer musically presented texts from the great epic poems and accompanied himself (chordally) on the *lira da braccio*. With the means of the time-honoured recitation of epics, Monteverdi created a work which in some of its details is among the most innovative of his compositions. If this type of musical production none the less had no future, then it was because it was based on an extremely individual cultural interest, one which was bound to a certain degree to forms of social intercourse currently fashionable.

## PUBLIC OPERA

Here it is carnival time, which entices all foreigners and even keeps the citizens in suspense, even though they are accustomed to enjoy it each year after a year's work in public or private business. The opera theatres inaugurate it with unbelievable pomp and circumstance; it is no less than what in various places is brought about by princely splendour—with the sole difference that the pleasure that the princes offer with liberality is a business in Venice, and cannot be carried out with the same magnificence as the

[10] Foreword to *Combattimento* (*Lettere*, p. 419).

festivities with which the princes often celebrate births and marriages, so that they may better display their own glory.[11]

Nothing could more aptly describe the revolutionary change that took place in the history of the opera in 1637 than this description from Cristoforo Ivanovich's history of theatre in Venice, which was published in 1681 in *Minerva al tavolino*, a collection of his works. The history of opera as a commercial institution was ushered in by the performance of *L'Andromeda* in the Teatro San Cassiano. For the first time those who wished to watch an operatic performance had to pay an admission fee. For the first time the takings had to cover the expenses of the performance. The prerequisites for the production of an opera thus underwent a complete change. The court opera was a special event and was designed to endow some specific occasion with festive splendour. It was tailored for the occasion and was intended to glorify whosesoever honour was being celebrated. The public opera was independent from such special events; it was one of the many festivities in which the Venetians plunged themselves in the carnival season. Whereas the special character of a court opera was in part due to its lack of repetition, repetition was a matter of absolute necessity for a commercial opera. In contrast to court operas, which were performed at most a couple of times, the commercial ones were given throughout the entire carnival season. A prince's primary desire, leading him to indulge in great extravagance, was to display his wealth by parading the high costs of the production before the audience. A commercial theatre, on the other hand, tried to keep the costs as low as possible and still present a magnificent show. This also meant that sets, machines, and costumes had to be used for several operas. The success of a court opera was measured in the glory reaped by the prince; that of the public opera in the number of performances and the money that came in. And finally, the make-up of the audience differed: a court opera was watched by invited aristocractic and clerical guests, while distinguished citizens of the town came, if at all, to the second or third performance; in the public opera theatre, members of the patrician families regularly rented boxes, and anybody was allowed in the gallery and stalls who could pay the admission fee of four lire. This was truly without respect for rank, for, as Ivanovich reported, the custom of wearing a mask during the carnival season expunged the social barriers.

It is obvious that all of these factors had to have an effect on the dramaturgy and the music. Despite all the innovations, the old maxim that money rules still held true. The audience's taste was as strong a

---

[11] Cristoforo Ivanovich, *Minerva al tavolino* 2nd edn. (Venice, 1688), 377–8.

moving force in the public opera houses as that of the noble producer in court operas. Its effect in Venice can be seen in the tendency towards comic scenes with servants and nurses, towards rapid successions of self-contained scenes, and towards odd entanglements and increasingly bizzare mechanical stage effects; in the second half of the century there was hardly an opera in which at least a sea monster, a bear, or a live elephant did not play a leading role. The more expensive a machine was, the more often it had to be employed. The plots then, of necessity, became schematized. The enthusiasm of the first few years, when musicians and poets from Rome performed operas in Venice which were comparable to the magnificant affairs financed by the papal family, was not financially viable in the long run. Cuts had to be made where they would least bother the paying public. The chorus, which had still appeared here and there in the first few years, was the first victim of these economic measures; the second was the instrumentation of the orchestra. Although the instrumentation of sacred works, particularly for high feast days, was opulent in Venice, the opera orchestra was rather meagre: single strings, no winds, and a variety of continuo instruments—two or three keyboard instruments and two theorbos. Only the scenery and, more importantly, the singers were exempt from these measures; they determined whether or not an opera was a success.

The gap between Monteverdi's early and late operas is not only a matter of the thirty years' difference in time. It is also a result of the differing conditions under which he composed them. In addition, many changes had occurred elsewhere during the 1620s and 1630s; the centre of opera composition had moved from Florence to Rome, where beginning in the late 1620s, the Barberini family had continually commissioned new works. Monteverdi certainly knew those which had appeared in print; those which had not would have been described to him by members of the Roman opera company. The new challenge in theatre music apparently fascinated Monteverdi so much after so many years of 'abstinence' that, with an almost unbelievable creative drive, particularly in a man of more than seventy years of age, he composed three operas in four years: *Il ritorno d'Ulisse in patria* in 1640, *Le nozze d'Enea con Lavinia* in 1641, whose music is lost, and *L'incoronazione di Poppea* in 1642.

The authenticity of the score of *Il ritorno d'Ulisse* in the Viennese Nationalbibliothek has been affirmed just as often as it has been cast in doubt. One of the main reasons for the doubts lay in the major deviation of the text in the score from the libretto: five acts in the latter, three in the former, and in addition a completely different prologue and conclusion. Wolfgang Osthoff later found no less than seven variant versions of the libretto. This weakened the only solid argument, and the discussion concerning authenticity got pushed out on to an aesthetic limb. The confused situation of the sources also reveals, however, the kind of alterations this sort of public theatre piece was subject to. As opposed to the madrigals and *L'Orfeo*, where there exist no other prints than those edited by Monteverdi himself, an 'official last version' for his later operas for the commercial stage cannot be identified. Moreover, to insist on searching for an authentic version would only demonstrate a lack of understanding of the nature of such 'consumer art'.

The change in circumstances, however, did not prevent Monteverdi from devoting the same musical care that he had given to all his other works to the individual, undoubtedly interchangeable scenes of the new kind of opera. Quotations from his late madrigals appear over and over again in *Il ritorno d'Ulisse* as well as in *L'incoronazione di Poppea*. This reveals once again, on the one hand, the close connections between the two groups of music and, on the other, the ephemeral character of such music, which was not intended to be saved for the world in a superb print. Even with these quotations, however, Monteverdi made quite sure that the musical image corresponded with the text. It makes no difference for the musical interpretation of the text whether it reads 'è breve sogno' (a short dream), from the conclusion of 'Voi ch'ascoltate', a madrigal from the *Selva morale e spirituale*, or 'è cosa vana' (a vain thing), the final words of 'Humana fragiltà' in a recitative from the prologue in *Il ritorno d'Ulisse*. The disjointed end of the madrigal 'Ardo e scoprir ahi lasso' from Book VIII fits just as well with the words 'si tronca sulle labbra le parole' (Ex. 6.5*a*) as with Tempo's remark from the same prologue 'che se ben zoppo ho l'ali' (Ex. 6.6*b*).

The elan which the pioneers brought to public opera is still clear in *Il ritorno d'Ulisse*. The opera contains a number of choruses, ranging from three voices to an eight-voice chorus of gods in the heavens and ocean. Even under the assumption that *coro* at that time meant 'ensemble', i.e. that a maximum of eight chorus singers appeared on stage, this meant a considerable expenditure. It could be financed only with the help of unstinting efforts by the opera theatre's initiators, in whom Ivanovich found so much to praise. The orchestral writing here continues to be in five parts. The scenery does not fall short of the music: the sets changed from Penelope's palace to a forest, from a beach to the high seas. A ship was turned into stone; an eagle flew over the stage; the earth opened up to swallow Ulisse only to release him shortly thereafter. The structure of the plot exemplifies the new kind of dramaturgy, in which a larger dramatic line is sacrificed for a

Ex. 6.5*a*.   'Ardo e scoprir ahi lasso'
             (the words die on the lips)

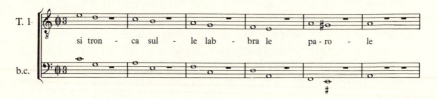

Ex. 6.5*b*.   *Il ritorno d'Ulisse*, prologue
             (even though I limp, I have wings)

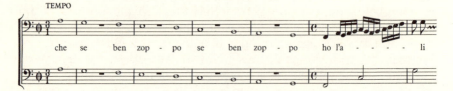

colourful succession of very diverse scenes. Instead of a few select
characters, a multitude of multifarious actors romps on stage: the
gods, Minerva, Juno, Jupiter, and Neptune; the protagonists, Ulisse,
Penelope, and Telemaco; the suitors, Antinoos, Pisandros, and
Amphinomos, together with their attendants, Iros and Eurymachos;
the young servant, Melantho, the old nurse, Euryklea, and the
swineherd, Eumetes. Several interwoven threads of action guarantee
variety and entertainment. First of all, there is the gods' quarrel about
Ulisse: Nettuno, who seeks revenge; Giove, who attempts to pacify
him; Minerva, who guides Ulisse's footsteps, at times as a shepherd,
at times as a mentor; and Giunone, who begs mercy from Giove for
Ulisse's family. Secondly comes Ulisse's return home in stages: he
appears in front of the swineherd in the guise of an old beggar and
announces the return of his master; he makes himself known to his
son Telemaco, who has been brought home from Sparta by Minerva;
not recognized by Penelope, he passes the test of the bow and kills the
suitors; finally he is able to convince Penelope that he is not phantom
or a magician but her husband, to whom she has been faithful for
twenty years. Third, there is Penelope: she waits longingly for Ulisse;
she is urged by the suitors to choose one of them for her husband; she
finally promises her hand to the one who can string Ulisse's bow; she
only slowly comprehends, after Ulisse has killed her suitors, that her
sufferings are at an end. In addition, the servant, Melanto, who has a

liason with Eurimaco and tries to convice her mistress to get married, and the parasite, Iro, are tied up with these threads of action; they add, however, a different flavour to the plot: a light, playful atmosphere and a grotesquely comic tone.

In spite of the confusing wealth of scenes and in spite of the jumps in the story, the three acts of the score are so systematically arranged that it seems as if Monteverdi's ordering hand may be behind it. The reduction of the five-act libretto to three composed acts may perhaps be traced back to him. Scenes which depart too far from these threads of action, such as the one in which the dead suitors are led to hell by Mercurio, are left out of the composition. In the score, the entire first act, as an exposition, is filled with the introduction of the characters surrounding Ulisse and Penelope. The second act tells the story of the suitors. The third act proves to be a complement to the first: instead of Penelope's lament at the beginning, there is Iro's parody of a lament, before he kills himself because of hunger; a scene with the gods with a following chorus is then found in both acts; and, instead of Ulisse's disguise and Penelope's refusal to give audience to the suitors, there is the difficult task, which lasts half of the act, of convincing Penelope that the beggar is not disguised as Ulisse, but that Ulisse was disguised as a beggar.

*Il ritorno d'Ulisse*, however, deviates from the early operas primarily in its connection between action and music. The fact that there is any action on stage at all is one of the most important features of the new dramaturgy. *Il ritorno d'Ulisse* presents everything on stage that in a pastoral drama would have been conveyed discreetly in a messenger's report: the stoning of the Phaeacians, with which Neptune wreaks his last vengeance, the suitors' end, Iro's suicide. This tendency towards drastically powerful scenes, albeit effective on the stage, may be observed in all operas from the 1630s and is evidence of the change in the audience's taste.

The connection between the action and the music is manifested in *Il ritorno d'Ulisse* in several ways: in the use of differing types of declamation; in the construction of scenic complexes on a musical level; and in several purely instrumental pieces, which do nothing more than provide time for pantomimic movement. Penelope's first entrance at the beginning of the opera is accompanied by a sinfonia, for which only a two-bar skeleton is notated together with the instruction: 'Questa sinfonia si replica tante volte insino che Penelope arriva in scena' (This sinfonia is to be repeated until Penelope has entered on stage). It is even clearer in the fourth scene of Act I: the Phaeacians' ship approaches the shore; they carry the sleeping Ulisse on shore and sail away. Here again there is a two-bar skeleton together with the instruction: 'Qui esca la Barca de'Feaci che conduce Ulisse che dorme e perchè non si desti si fa la seguente sinfonia toccata soavemente sempre su una corda' (The Phaeacian ship enters here which brings Ulisse who is sleeping; the following sinfonia is to be played softly, always struck on one string, so that he does not awaken). And finally there is the beginning and end of the test with the bow: here, first Ulisse, in disguise, fights with Iro to the sounds of a martial sinfonia until Iro at the end cries out 'son vinto' (I am vanquished); then, later, Ulisse kills the suitors while a *sinfonia da guerra* is played.

Monteverdi also treated the various interwoven threads of action differently. He composed mostly recitatives for the serious characters; for the merry Melanto and her lover he preferred dance-like arias in triple time; for the gods he chose all sorts of 'elevated' declamation—ariettas in triple time, strophic scherzos *alla francese* with instrumental ritornellos, and texts interpreted in a madrigalistic fashion with virtuoso coloraturas. The qualitative difference between recitative and arioso declamation is particularly clear in the music for the suitors. In paying court to Penelope, they try to outdo one another with vainglorious airs, dancing around the queen with arias and ensemble pieces in triple time and attempting to ingratiate themselves with her by means of graceful coloraturas. In the gloomy conspiracy scene, however, when they decide to murder Telemaco, they are quite capable of a recitative declamation. It is even clearer in the test with the bow, where the song itself is turned into drama: a broadly dimensioned plot full of tension, a scene which in its completeness is reminiscent of the cyclical dramaturgy of *L'Orfeo*. It begins with the suitors, certain of their victory, singing a trio in triple time; and before their demise, as they stand petrified with horror that the old beggar has actually been able to string the bow, it ends with almost rhythmically free chords. In between, each of the three suitors tries his luck following the same musical scheme: each takes the bow—sinfonia; confident of victory, each invokes the protection of a godhead—arioso; each has to admit his failure—recitative. Musically the fall of the vain braggarts could not have been more crassly displayed. Ulisse, on the other hand, first stays in a recitative in this scene; only after he has strung the bow does he slip into the broken chords typical for the *genere guerriero*.

Apart from the construction of such musical scenes, Monteverdi's main interest in *Il ritorno d'Ulisse* lay in the recitatives and in the ensemble pieces which resulted from the recitative declamation. Penelope's and Ulisse's entrances, Telemaco's fright when the beggar turns into his father, and Ulisse's attempts to convice Penelope of his identity are all scenes which display the same power of musical expression as Monteverdi's early operas; they reveal in addition the influence of the stylistic features of the later madrigal books. Penelope's plaint at the beginning of the tenth scene of Act I, with its simple chordal bass and declamation close to that of speech (Ex. 6.6a), could just as easily be from *L'Arianna*; her irritated answer to Melanto's panegyric of love, however with its motivic leaps upwards over 'Amor' and its interrupted bass line, shows the further development of the recitative and the instrumental accompaniment (Ex. 6.6b). The duet between the father and the son in the third scene

Ex. 6.6a.   *Il ritorno d'Ulisse*, Act I, sc. x
(Grant me one day, ye gods,
gratification of my desires)

Ex. 6.6b.   *Il ritorno d'Ulisse*, Act I, sc. x
(Amor is a tiny god, Amor is a vagabond godhead)

of Act II, on the other hand, could have come from Book VII. Here, however, the musical conception behind the gradual increase in structural density acquires additional dramatic meaning. Monteverdi composed the first shy, then more and more impulsive advances towards one another, which end in an embrace, with melodically related recitative fragments that get shorter and shorter; these are abandoned after various checks when Telemaco emits a long cry of joy (over a 'walking' bass) at the embrace, where father and son sing together for the first time (Ex. 6.7).

Ex. 6.7.    *Il ritorno d'Ulisse*, Act II, sc. iii
(TELEMACO. O father whom I have sighed for,
glorious parent,
I bow down to you,
O my delight
ULISSE. O son whom I so much longed for,
sweet token of love,
I embrace you)

mio di - let - to      O mio di - let - to

ti___ strin - - - - - - - go ti

*Il ritorno d'Ulisse* was very successful, as Badoaro reported a year later, and was performed frequently. What the audience liked best, however, were not Ulisse and Penelope, but the ridiculous Iro. Like the audience for *L'Arianna*, the Venetians enjoyed being moved to tears, but they preferred even more to laugh at the gluttonous, stuttering gnome. His lament parody is a grotesque exaggeration of the means of the dramatic recitative (Ex. 6.8): the nine-bar long exclamation at the beginning, the trick of the goat-like laughter which turns into a *trillo*, the incessant sighs and the just as endless sequential passages, and finally the inappropriate use of the *ciaccona* bass at the question 'Chi lo consola?' (Who comforts him?).

Before Monteverdi appeared in Venice as a composer of publicly performed operas, Francesco Manelli's opera company had produced *Il ritorno d'Ulisse* in Bologna. Because of its great success in Venice, Monteverdi's friends later desired that it be offered once more in the following year. This summary of events is more than just a report about a series of successes; it also tells something about the origins of

Ex. 6.8.   *Il ritorno d'Ulisse*, Act III, sc. i.
       (O sorrow)

the operatic repertory. Monteverdi's last opera had an important role in its development, as *L'incoronazione di Poppea* was not only played for several years in Venice, but it was also taken on tour. In 1651 it opened a series of publicly performed operas in Naples.

The fate of a repertory opera is revealed more clearly by the state of the sources for *L'incoronazione di Poppea* than for *Il ritorno d'Ulisse*. In addition to several printed and manuscript librettos and scenarios, there exist two manuscripts of the score, in Venice and Naples, which deviate significantly from one another. Both are probably based on an original version by Monteverdi which no longer survives. Although we have no authorized version, and thus are unable to distinguish precisely between Monteverdi's original intentions and later arrangements or even additions, it is less important to lament over this fact than to recognize, as is shown by the confused state of these sources, that a repertory opera and a festive court opera need to be judged according to different standards.

In Francesco Busenello, Monteverdi once again discovered a librettist who, like Alessandro Striggio, was able to incorporate Monteverdi's suggestions and his own ideas in such a manner as to create a text full of drama and tension, variety and unity, literary quality and musical promise. In addition, the financial situation of the opera theatre was an excellent taskmaster for tauter dramaturgy, as may be seen in the following summary:

Act I: Returning home at dawn from a trip, Poppea's husband, Ottone, discovers Nerone's soldiers standing guard outside his house. The suspicion that his highly esteemed emperor is tarrying with his wife, whom he loves more than anything, is confirmed immediately; the soldiers awake and complain about Nerone's escapades and the resultant extra night duty. Finally Nerone and Poppea appear in person, full of the joys of the past night. Nerone assures her that he will get rid of his spouse, Ottavia, and take Poppea as his wife. Poppea feels that the fulfilment of her desires is near, but her nurse, Arnalta, warns her not to place too much trust in love and fortune. In the imperial palace meanwhile, Ottavia bewails her fate as a scorned woman. Neither her nurse, who advises her to return like for like, nor the servant is able to cheer her up. She listens only to the philosopher Seneca, who advocates endurance. Seneca, left alone, reflects upon the ephemeral nature of fortune; Pallas Athene appears and foretells his impending death, promising to send Mercurio as a messenger when his time has come. Seneca attempts in vain to persuade Nerone to abandon his plans; Nerone throws him out in a rage. Ottone overhears an amorous conversation between Nerone and Poppea, in which Poppea immediately uses her charms in order to disarm the inimical Seneca. Nerone orders his death. Ottone then tries to win back Poppea, but without success: the prospect of becoming empress is more enticing than the love of her husband. Despairing, Ottone seeks comfort from Drusilla, a lady-in-waiting.

Act II: On the same day, still in his country house, Seneca receives Mercurio's message presaging his death; a captain of the guard appears immediately with Nerone's command that he die. Seneca calls his household together and asks them to prepare a bath for him, so that he may go gracefully. They sadly try to dissuade him from suicide. In Rome, meanwhile, Ottavia's servant dallies with a maid. After the news of Seneca's death has made its way to Rome, Nerone, together with the poet Lucano, drafts hymns of praise on Poppea's beauty and goes into such raptures at the vision of her lips that his poetry seems too weak to him. Ottone, enraged with himself and his inability to part from her, allows himself to be incited by Ottavia to murder Poppea. Following Ottavia's order that he disguise himself in women's attire, he persuades Drusilla to give him her clothes. In her garden, Poppea rejoices in Seneca's death and believes all obstacles standing in the way of her ascent are now eliminated. She lies down to sleep, and while she sleeps Amore descends from the heavens to protect her. Ottone approaches in Drusilla's clothes; when he raises the dagger, however, Amore sounds an alarm. Poppea, awakened, sees Drusilla flee.

Act III: Drusilla awaits the news of Poppea's death with joy. Instead of this Arnalta appears with the lictors and has her arrested as a murderer. Nerone is furious when he hears of the attempt on Poppea's life. Drusilla wants to sacrifice herself for Ottone, but Ottone reveals himself as the murderer. Nerone, glad to have a pretext now against the empress, bans both of them instead of sentencing them to death. Ottavia is also exiled. While Nerone rushes to Poppea and tells her that she will become empress that very day, Ottavia, full of grief and despair, bids farewell to Rome and her relatives. In Nerone's palace, the consuls and tribunes present Poppea with the imperial crown, and in the heavens Venus and Amore bestow upon her the title of goddess of mortal beauty.

*L'incoronazione di Poppea* no longer has any choruses, has only a few ensemble pieces, and has hardly any scenes with gods and the concommitant stage machinery. It is the first libretto with a historical subject. Gods naturally have less to say there than in a pastoral or mythological context. Even though they still intervene on occasion, they have lost their command over the course of the action. This is perhaps one of the most important innovations of historical subject-matter, as it was equally possible to delineate characters and to portray human behaviour in mythological works as in historical ones. In *L'incoronazione di Poppea* all the main characters are driven by some kind of passion: Nerone by his passion for Poppea, Poppea by her social ambition, Ottone by his love for Poppea, Drusilla by her love for Ottone, Ottavia by revenge, and Seneca by morality. In this carousel of relationships, it is significant that Amore is the only god who does not merely serve as an ornament, but intervenes at a decisive moment in the action.

Limiting the characters involved to mortals had musical consequences. Since the early days of opera, composers had battled with the problem of representing speech credibly in music. This seemed least problematic in Arcadia, where the language itself was almost music. The gods were also allowed to express themselves in closed musical forms and artificial ornaments without forfeiting verisimilitude. The closed form of an aria sung by a Nero or a Poppea still needed justification forty years after the first operas. In *Il ritorno d'Ulisse* the type of declamation was determined by the social status of the characters; this is most obvious with the figure of Ulisse himself, who declaims differently in his disguise as a beggar from the style he uses in his true shape. In *L'incoronazione*, however, Monteverdi goes a step further: here the passions, independent of social status, determine the declamation. Dance-like rhythms, strophic and closed musical forms, are no longer limited to the portrayal of servant roles, but also represent heavenly and earthly joys, the eruption of sensuality, and love. For example, Ottavia, scorned and rejected, expresses herself only in recitatives, with one exception: she changes to triple time for a short passage in which she envisions her husband in Poppea's arms. Seneca, full of virtue, also breaks loose from the recitative only when he sings of fate, of beauty, and of joy. Poppea and Nerone, on the other hand, slip again and again from a recitative to a dance-like declamation and into overflowing coloraturas. Thus, by means of the type of declamation, Monteverdi skilfully gave expression to Poppea's character with its wavering between sensuality and calculation. The way in which Poppea ensnares Nerone and at the same time gets him to promise to marry her is a musical showpiece in the art of seduction. In her first scene Poppea pleads with Nerone to stay; she literally hangs herself around his neck, and Nerone makes it clear to her that he would like to behave discreetly until he has disposed of Ottavia. In the libretto it is a plain passage:

NERONE. La nobiltà de'nascimenti tuoi
    non permette che Roma
    sappia che siamo uniti
    in sin che Ottavia non rimane esclusa
    col repudio da me.
POPPEA. Vanne, ben mio.

NERONE. The nobility of your birth
    does not permit Rome
    to know that we are united
    until Ottavia has been
    repudiated by me.
POPPEA. Go, my love.

Monteverdi, however, gave Poppea the reins: with insistent question-
ing she forces the somewhat hesitant Nerone to complete the crucial
sentence; when she finally has him where she wants him, she breaks
out in a dance-like song in which it is impossible to distinguish
between joy and malice (Ex. 6.9).

Ex. 6.9.    *L'incoronazione di Poppea,* Act I, sc. iii
        (NERONE AND POPPEA. until Ottavia has been repudiated by me
        POPPEA. Go, my love)

Monteverdi treated the next scene, the dialogue between Poppea and Arnalta, her nurse, in a similar manner. Here, too, Monteverdi has taken a passage of the text out of context and constructed a scene with it which once again demonstrates his love for cyclic structures. Poppea reaffirms her confidence, while Arnalta warns her not to raise

Fig. 6.1. *L'incoronazione di Poppea*, Act I, sc. iv

her hopes too high. Each character has her own ritornello; Poppea's optimistic observation:

> no, no, no, non temo di noia alcuna
> per me guerreggia amor e la fortuna

> no, no, no, I am not afraid of any untimeliness
> Amor and Fortuna are fighting for me

is turned into rondo-like connecting links for the entire scene (Fig. 6.1). While the first part of the scene is devoted exclusively to Poppea and her hopes, the second part is dominated by Arnalta's warnings. It is in particular by means of the curtain lecture at the end of the scene, which breaks off in mid-sentence, that Monteverdi has managed to create an effective characterization of this old scold (Ex. 6.10). Arnalta is the most expressive character among the servant roles. She is also the only one who receives a solo scene, in which she, continually wavering between recitative and arioso declamation, takes delight in her social ascent:

Hoggi sarà Poppea di Roma imperatrice. Io che son la nutrice ascenderò delle grandezze i gradi. No no col volgo io non m'abbasso più, chi mi diede del tu hor con nova armonia gorgheggierammi il vostra signoria. Chi m'incontra per strada mi dice fresca donna e bella ancora. E io pur so che sembro delle Sibille il leggendario antico.

Today Poppea becomes the empress of Rome. I, her nurse, ascend the ladder of power. No, I will no longer associate myself with the common people. Anybody who spoke familiarly with me until now will, full of sweet flattery, warble 'Your Excellency'. Anybody who meets me on the street will say: 'What a young lady and still so beautiful'. And I know, however, that I look like a Sibyl from the old legends . . .

Arnalta is one of the prototypes for an endless succession of comic, old nurses in the Venetian opera. These parts, as opposed to the serious role of Ericlea in *Il ritorno d'Ulisse*, were played by tenors and, along with the cheerful young servants and maids, provided comic relief.

Ex. 6.10.  *L'incoronazione di Poppea*, Act I, sc. iv
(You are quite a fool
if you believe that a blind lad and a blind bald woman
can make you contented and safe)

Although closed forms and scenes in *L'incoronazione di Poppea* are mostly a result of the emotional situation, there are three scenes whose disposition is determined by external circumstances: Seneca's farewell scene (II. iii), Nerone's and Lucano's scene as poets (II. vi), and Poppea's festive coronation (III. viii). All three are ensemble scenes; the coronation scene, the final apotheosis, contains instrumental sections which, as in *Il ritorno d'Ulisse*, serve as a background for an action taking place on stage—the entrance of the consuls and tribunes. One can only make conjectures as to whether the instrumental ritornellos in Seneca's farewell scene accompanied any action on stage. The futile attempts on the part of the household to cheer him up and keep him from dying may well have been accompanied by dance interludes, particularly because the middle stanzas are based on the same alternating rhythm found in the dance scene at the beginning of Act II of *L'Orfeo*. Once again this scene has an almost symmetrical structure: it begins with an aria and ends with a recitative of Seneca's; the members of his household give the middle section its shape by means of three musical ideas—the dance stanzas with their alternating rhythms and the ritornello associated with them; a chromatically ascending, imploratory plea (Ex. 6.11*a*); and a diatonically descending, rhythmically more active statement (Ex. 6.11*b*); these two motifs appear in the opposite order after the two dance stanzas.

The vitality of the poets' scene lies in song. The Nerone–Lucano duet is one of Monteverdi's vocal ensemble pieces in the new style: virtuoso, ecstatic, with many slow build-ups, and full of climaxes; the middle section is composed over a tetrachord bass, which provides musically for Nerone's short, passionate objections. It is a piece with a closed musical form, which is not only born of overflowing passions, but also has a dramatic *raison d'être*—the attempt at writing poetry.

*L'incoronazione di Poppea* stands alone in its intent to represent human passions with closed musical forms. Even in the recitative,

Ex. 6.11.  *L'incoronazione di Poppea*, Act II, sc. iii
(Do not die, Seneca)
(I do not wish to die)

however, Monteverdi does not forgo a presentation of the characters that goes far beyond that of *Il ritorno d'Ulisse*. In her scheming calculation Ottavia is quite Poppea's equal. Her rapacious attack on Ottone with the command to murder Poppea is more than *Sprechgesang*: with its short fragments of sentences, repeated at higher and higher pitches, it is an outburst of hate that can hardly be portrayed more exactly in music, and is echoed in Ottone's horrified response (Ex. 6.12). Nerone's invective against Seneca in the *concitato genere* also goes far beyond the usual recitative (Ex. 6.13).

Although *L'incoronazione di Poppea* contains all of the elements which promised success in a public theatre, at the same time it displays much closer connections to Monteverdi's early operas than *Il ritorno d'Ulisse*. *L'incoronazione di Poppea* does not tell a story; there is

Ex. 6.12. *L'incoronazione di Poppea*, Act II, sc. ix
(OTTAVIA: I want your sword to write my conditions with Poppea's blood. I want you to kill her
OTTONE. I must kill whom? Whom?)

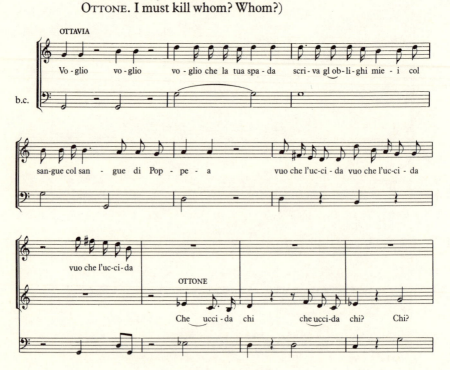

Ex. 6.13. *L'incoronazione di Poppea*, Act I, sc. ix
(You infuriate me)

only one scene really full of suspense—the attack on Poppea—and it can otherwise be reduced to continual variation of the grouping of characters. Even though the alternation between serious and comic scenes, masters and servants, monologues and ensembles speaks for the new requirements, Monteverdi still adhered to what had remained the purport of dramatic music for him: the painstaking representation of human passions, the revelation of hidden characteristics. Monteverdi's last opera is a masterpiece, which is unique in spite of all the external social restrictions. With its idea of a 'passionate' musical language it was, as with so many of his late works, more of a full stop than a beginning. With opera's preference for closed musical forms, independent of the character involved and his or her social position, it soon thereafter took off in other directions.

# 7

# PRIMACY, DATING, AND AUTHENTICITY

A special problem posed by Monteverdi's work is the question of when the compositions were written. It would be less serious if the question of primacy, and thus qualitative judgement, were not linked over and over again with the dating. All attempts to resolve such matters and all painstaking enquiries will certainly advance the state of musicology; they also show, however, the problems of a 'genius' concept, in which the best must always have been the first. Various indications given by Monteverdi's publications in connection with historical sources suggest that prudence should be exercised in all too closely associating chronology and observations of a historically developmental nature. Insoluble problems are presented not only by the works in the posthumous prints. The last two publications actually edited by Monteverdi himself must also be seen as summations of decades of work, whose dating is only possible in a few cases.

The questions cannot be answered, for example, of when the 'Lamento della Ninfa', published in 1638 in the eighth madrigal book, was written, and of whether it was the model for similar ostinato compositions such as those by Sances and Pesenti, or whether, to the contrary, someone else entirely passed on the idea of the tetrachord bass to them. It is equally impossible to establish a chronology for the *ciaccona* bass, which first appeared in print with Domenico Obizzi's 'O sospiro amoroso' (1627) and Monteverdi's 'Zefiro torna' (1632), or for the succession of cantatas on a 'walking' bass that all came out at almost the same time. We have more information about the stage music from other sources: it can be established by means of a letter that *Tirsi e Clori* from Book VII was written in 1615, four years before publication. The *Combattimento di Tancredi e Clorinda*, published in 1638, was performed in 1624 in the Palazzo Mocenigo; when Monteverdi composed this work, however, remains in the realm of speculation. *Il ballo delle ingrate* may be the oldest work in the eighth madrigal book: it was performed in Mantua in 1608, thirty years before its publication. It is doubtful, however, that the published version is identical with the Mantuan composition. Important evidence for this supposition is a short passage in the *genere guerriero* which Monteverdi first employed in the *Combattimento*, and which he characterized as being his own invention in the foreword to Book VIII. As it is improbable that he only revised a couple of bars, presumably other passages (perhaps the duet between Venus and Amor) no longer correspond with the original Mantuan form. We know too little about Monteverdi's theatre music from the 1620s and 1630s to be able to draw conclusions, based on detailed stylistic comparison, about the dating or even about the relationship between the original and revised versions. Just how concerned Monteverdi was with such revisions is shown by the example of *L'Arianna*, which the court in Mantua planned to perform again in 1620. Although Monteverdi sent them the requested copies, it was with the reservation: 'If I had had more time, then I would have looked through it more carefully and perhaps have corrected far more.' Monteverdi revised *Il ballo delle ingrate* for a performance at Ferdinand's court in Graz in 1628, a full ten years before publication.

A similar puzzle is presented by the early madrigal books. Presumably Monteverdi's madrigals circulated for years in manuscript copies before he prepared them for print. In the foreword of Book IV, Monteverdi expressed his regrets that he was unable to present Alfonso d'Este of Ferrara with some madrigals in manuscript as he had originally intended, because the duke had died. Alfonso d'Este died in 1597; at least a portion of the compositions of Book IV must thus have been written before this date. This supposition is corroborated by the printed collection, *Fiori del giardino di diversi* (Nuremberg, 1597), which includes 'Ah dolente partita' from the fourth madrigal book. Artusi's criticism of 1600 is directed also towards compositions which appeared in print only three or five years later respectively. The madrigals which were to become the starting-point for Monteverdi's reflections on the *seconda pratica* must therefore have already been written some time before 1600. The interval between composition and the theoretical underpinning may be explained by the fact that, on the one hand, Monteverdi was a practical musician far more than a theorist, and, on the other, that at first he did not regard his compositions as revolutionary, but rather as links in a long chain extending from Cipriano de Rore to Luzzasco Luzzaschi. It is regrettable that the dating of the madrigals, in particular for this period of revolutionary change, is not known; it is insignificant, however, for the theory—and Monteverdi's and his brother's explanations are among the most important theoretical manifestos of the new style. Although Monteverdi himself repeatedly placed great value in having 'invented' not only the term *seconda practica* but also certain compositional techniques, his work in madrigal composition was not a single, datable event which changed everything. To the contrary, his grappling with the *seconda pratica* in polyphonic music took place at the same time as work on the chordally accompanied solo song, which was equally decisive but easier to date, and in whose development Monteverdi did not participate at first.

The discrepancy between the date of composition and that of publication, as seen in Monteverdi's secular music, is even more prominent in his sacred music. To begin with, only guesses can be made, on the basis of historical sources, of just how much liturgical music for S. Marco, Monteverdi's primary responsibility in Venice, was lost. In addition, dating the fraction which remains is scarcely possible. Only a single composition can be narrowed down to a *terminus ante quem*: the three-voice 'Salve Regina' appeared in Lorenzo Calvi's *Quarta raccolta de sacri canti* of 1629. A connection could be established between the seven-voice Gloria from the *Selva morale e spirituale* and the mass of thanksgiving for the deliverance from the plague which was celebrated on 28 November 1631 in S. Marco; this is likewise true for the following three portions of the Credo, which seem to belong to the same mass. None of the other compositions can be dated. They preclude a stylistic analysis from a point of view of historical development, just as the compositions in Book VIII do. It seems that Monteverdi had neither time nor interest in the publication of his works in Venice. When the two large collections finally appeared in 1638 and 1641, the overview was already a retrospective, the development already passed; none of the later publications was reprinted.

Questions of dating are often closely connected with problems of authenticity, particularly when there are no printed sources, as in the case of Monteverdi's late operas. Probably no subject has aroused the hearts of Monteverdi specialists more than the question of the authenticity of *Il ritorno d'Ulisse*. Standards of quality repeatedly play a role, consciously or unconsciously, in their discussions: the opera is by Monteverdi because it is good, or is not by Monteverdi because it is weak, or is by Monteverdi and some other composer because some portions of it are good and others weak. Explaining the difference in quality between *Il ritorno d'Ulisse* and *L'incoronazione di Poppea* as that between a precursor and a mature late work is, at the very least, doubtful, given the extremely short time interval between the two. Although seven versions of the libretto found by Wolfgang Osthoff do not prove the authenticity of the score in Vienna, they do on the other hand show that the state of the sources is much too confused to be used as a basis for determining authenticity. Even attempting to prove authenticity by buttressing the evidence of the sources with stylistic analysis and by comparison with Monteverdi's other works can be risky in a place like Venice. There the contact among the composers was so close that not even the subject and object of an influence can be clearly named until Monteverdi's surroundings have been studied exactly. Without wanting to intervene further in the discussion concerning the authenticity of *Il ritorno d'Ulisse*, a small example may illustrate this problem and the danger of mixing standards of quality with questions of authenticity.

The readiness to perceive Monteverdi as the creator of modern music, as an outstanding genius far ahead of his time, has occasionally induced musicologists not to view a remarkable work on its own merits, but instead to account for it, from the point of view of later development, as an individual creative achievement which stands on its own. Among these works is the famous final duet 'Pur ti miro' from *L'incoronazione di Poppea* on the tetrachord bass, which is regarded as one of the first *da capo* compositions in the history of opera. In addition, it is seen to be evidence for the consummation of Monteverdi's endeavours to place human fate in the foreground, taking precedence over theatrical splendour. The extraordinary quality of this composition—whether it lies in the disposition, or in the musical and dramatic expression—has been generally praised and shall not be called into question here. It is uncertain, however, whether this final duet is really by Monteverdi or whether it was added to the actual conclusion at a later date. It does not appear in the printed scenario for the performance of 1642, the earliest incontestable source for *L'incoronazione di Poppea*. In addition, its dramaturgical position at the end of the opera—following the coronation scene, which was conceived as the final grand apotheosis—can be explained only with difficulty. It is also impossible to reconstruct the première, as no libretto was printed in 1642. This text did not even appear for the first time in connection with Monteverdi's name, as Alessandra Chiarelli has shown, but at the end of the Bolognese performance of the opera *Il pastor regio* in 1641. Both the text and the music of this opera are by Benedetto Ferrari, a composer from Reggio nell'Emilia, who is regarded in secondary literature as a loyal vassal and imitator of Monteverdi. As the music is lost, one cannot say with any certainty whether the same composition is involved. The possibility cannot be excluded, however, that the duet was added later to the end of *L'incoronazione di Poppea*, perhaps even after Monteverdi's death. The value of the composition is not impaired by these doubts; they merely show the weakness of a chain of argument which logically connects the concepts of genius and innovator, quality and authenticity.

The picture of the grand old master who, sitting among his students, produces strokes of genius, one after the other, which are immediately eagerly gathered up by his devotees and incorporated into their own works—even if not at his level—must be corrected. Monteverdi's music is incomparable not because it is new, revolutionary, or modern, but because it is consummate and a culmination: it unites the musical, literary, and dramatic developments of its time. Only by considering the questions of quality and primacy separately can an evaluation do justice to his music and to that of his contemporaries.

# CONCLUSION

There is no other composer at the transition from the Renaissance to the Baroque whose life and work is seemingly so well documented as that of Claudio Monteverdi. We have a complete series of madrigal books which document the development of the composer from his first efforts to his last years; beyond that we have three collections of sacred music which appeared during his lifetime at roughly thirty-year intervals, as well as a posthumous publication of sacred works. We also possess—and this is a historical feature which cannot be overestimated—approximately 130 of Monteverdi's letters to a diverse set of people: princes, friends, patrons, and discussion partners. What could be more obvious than the conclusion that for the first time in music history we meet in Monteverdi a personality who, above and beyond his music, can be understood, comprehended as a person and artist?

Monteverdi is the first composer about whom enough is known to allow us, with the indiscretion of later times, to look over his shoulder, so to speak, while he is composing. His letters are full of theoretical reflections on the character of his works, full of practical considerations about their disposition; we are not limited to reconstructing his life from lifeless archives, for we also know of his private anxieties from the letters. We appear to know our Monteverdi; we believe we know what he wanted, how he lived, what he felt and thought. In short, Monteverdi, this highly gifted exponent of one of the most exciting periods of music history, was also just a person like you and me, who had difficulties with his employers, felt himself to be badly paid, had troubles with the treasury and the union, experienced the problems of the generation gap with his children, cultivated exotic hobbies such as alchemy, and liked gossiping in society. It is characteristic that the first historical novel about a composer who lived before Bach and Handel (and who, in addition, was not even a noble who murdered his wife) was written about Monteverdi, long before the rediscovery of early music awakened the musical interest of a larger public in his works.

The abundance of information about Monteverdi none the less warps our picture of the composer if we do not delve deeply enough to ask also what this information conceals. Take, for example, his music:

the largest fraction, the central genre, remains the madrigal; in addition there are several operas and a number of sacred works. If, however, we look at his letters, we observe that completely different works are discussed there. *L'Orfeo* is mentioned only once, *L'Arianna* several times, but mostly in connection with revisions that we do not know, and *Tirsi e Clori* is referred to once. The fact that Monteverdi composed madrigals in Mantua is revealed in a single sentence: 'After Easter', Monteverdi wrote to the duke of Mantua on 26 March 1611, 'I will send you two madrigals'. Which works does Monteverdi mention in his letters? There are twenty-seven in all, of which only three are known, namely *L'Orfeo, Tirsi e Clori*, and the seventh madrigal book which came into being in Venice. Everything else is lost or cannot be identified: *L'Arianna*, except for the lament, lost; *Andromeda, Armida, La finta pazza Licori, Mercurio e Marte, Le nozze di Tetide*, intermezzi, ballets, laments—all lost; masses, motets — either not identifiable or identifiable and lost. If one also considers the statement of Monteverdi's brother, Giulio Cesare, from 1607 that Claudio was primarily busy with the composition of music for tourneys, ballets, comedies, and various *concerti*, works of which practically nothing survives, we have to ask ourselves whether the 'everyday' Monteverdi was the same as the Monteverdi of the published madrigal books. And in the Venetian years, in which he mainly had to compose sacred music (most of which must be lost because the late collections contain only a fraction of what he was required by contract to deliver), in his letters he wrote mostly about theatre music.

Take, on the other hand, his life. What do we really know? We know a number of facts, we know the letters—roughly 130 letters for seventy-six years of living, more than a hundred of them written in the years between 1615 and 1628. Before and after that we know only the bare facts. We do not even know, for example, when Monteverdi joined the clergy, to say nothing of why. We do not know why the seventy-five-year-old cleric let himself be drawn to the front of the fray of the newly founded commercial opera, at an age when others know how to appreciate the contemplative life of the refectory. What do we know about his wife, about his short marriage? Why did he prefer to raise his children on his own instead of marrying a second or, like his father, even a third time if necessary, as was customary? Why did Monteverdi lament more about the loss of his wife's salary after her death than about the loss of her presence? We do not know. The picture of Monteverdi, apparently so well documented, turns out to be a mosaic with half of the tiles missing.

Monteverdi, whom we justifiably recognize as the most important exponent of early baroque music, in whose work the literary, musical, and social trends of his time come together, who learned from his contemporaries as well as they from him, was an outsider his whole life, one whose musical interests led him in a direction different from the ordinary course of development. That also explains why he, in contrast to someone like Gabrieli, did not have a school. The sobriquet *oracolo della musica* (and not, for example, *principe della musica* as Josquin or Lassus before him), given to him at the end of his life, thus has a double meaning: on the one hand, Monteverdi was simply the musical authority, and, on the other, his compositions seemed so individual and impossible to copy that, although they were recognized as great art, it was an irritating, a disquieting art.

The other half of the mosaic—and that only as far as the music is concerned—can only be supplemented by turning our eyes from Monteverdi to the music of his contemporaries. Only a study of these works can show us what is special in Monteverdi's music: the economy of the means, the dramatic spirit, the sense of architecture— and an awe-inspiring imagination which we cannot fathom, cannot comprehend, but at best can describe. Monteverdi's greatness, his individuality cannot be revealed by mere analysis or by simply accumulating historical facts and musical scores. What Wolfgang Hildesheimer once said about Mozart is also true for Monteverdi: 'With all of our research we can perhaps come closer to the riddle, but not to the solution.'

# CHRONOLOGICAL LIST OF
# MONTEVERDI'S WORKS

The order of this list is based not on the date of composition, but solely on the date of publication. For this reason, works in manuscripts are listed separately and lost works are not included. A chronology which takes the date of composition and the lost works into account is found in Claudio Gallico, *Monteverdi: Poesia musicale, teatro e musica sacra* (Turin, 1979). Where a publication includes works by other composers, only compositions by Monteverdi are listed. Poets' names are listed where applicable.

1582 *Sacrae Cantiunculae tribus vocibus Claudini Montisviridi cremonensis Egregii Ingegnerii Discipuli*
Venice, A. Gardano; dedicated to Stefano Canino Valcarengo

Lapidabant Stephanum

Veni, sponsa Christi

Ego sum pastor bonus

Surge, propera

Ubi duo vel tres

Quam pulchra es

Ave Maria, gratia plena

Domine pater

Tu es pastor ovium (1st part)
Tu es Petrus (2nd part)

O magnum pietatis (1st part)
'Eli' clamans (2nd part)

O crux benedicta

Hodie Christus natus est

O Domine Jesu Christe (1st part)
O Domine Jesu Christe (2nd part)

Pater, venit hora

In tua patientia

Angelus ad pastores ait

Salve, crux pretiosa

Quia vidisti me, Thoma

Lauda, Sion, Salvatorem

O bone Jesu, illumina

Surgens Jesus

Qui vult venire

Justi tulerunt spolia

1583 *Madrigali spirituali a quattro voci posti in musica da Claudio Monteverde Cremonese, discepolo del Signor Marc'Antonio Ingegnieri* Brescia, V. Sabbio, 'ad istanza di P. Bozzola, libraro in Cremona'; dedicated to Alessandro Fraganesco

Sacrosanta di Dio verace imago

L'aura del ciel sempre feconda spiri (1st part)
Poi che benigno il novo cant'attende (2nd part)

Aventurosa notte, in cui risplende (1st part)
Serpe crudel, se i tuoi primier'inganni (2nd part)

D'empi martiri e un mar d'opprobri varca (1st part)
Ond'in ogni pensier e d'opra santo (2nd part)

Mentre la stell'appar nell'oriente (1st part)
Tal contra Dio de la superbia il corno (2nd part)

Le rose, gli amaranti (1st part)
Ai piedi havendo i capei d'oro sparsi (2nd part)

L'empio vestia di porpora e di bisso (1st part)
Ma quel mendico, d'acerbe piaghe misero (2nd part)

L'human discorso, se Dio è lontan, quanto (1st part)
L'eterno Dio quel cor pudico scelse (2nd part)

Dal sacro petto esce veloce dardo (1st part)
Scioglier m'addita se tal'hor mi cinge (2nd part)

Afflito e scalz'ove la sacra sponda (1st part)
Ecco, dicea, ecco l'Agnel di Dio (2nd part)

De i miei giovenil anni sì ch'a pena (1st part)
Tutt'esser vidi in questo avaro e cieco (2nd part)

(Only the bass part-book is extant).

1584    *Canzonette a tre voci di Claudio Monteverde cremonese, discepolo del sig. Marc'Antonio Ingegnieri . . . libro primo*
Venice, G. Vincenti and R. Amadino; dedicated to Pietro Ambrosini

Qual si può dir maggiore

Canzonette d'amore

La fiera vista e 'l velenoso sguardo

Raggi, dov'è il mio bene?

Vita de l'alma mia, cara mia vita

Il mio martir tengo celat'al cuore

Son questi i crespi crini e questo il viso

Io mi vivea com'aquila mirando

Su, su, che 'l giorno è fore

Quando sperai del mio servir mercede

Come farò, cuor mio, quando mi parto

Corse a la morte il povero Narciso

Tu ridi sempre mai per darmi pene

Chi vuol veder d'inverno un dolce aprile

Già mi credev'un sol esser in cielo

Godi pur del bel sen, felice pulce

Giù li a quel petto giace un bel giardino

Si come crescon alla terra i fiori

Io son fenice e voi sete la fiamma

Chi vuol veder un bosco folto e spesso

Hor, care canzonette

1587    *Madrigali a cinque voci di Claudio Monteverde Cremonese discepolo del Sig.r Marc'Antonio Ingigneri . . . Libro primo*
Venice, A. Gardano; dedicated to Count Marco Verità

Ch'ami la vita mia, nel tuo bel nome

Se per havervi ohimè donato il core

A che tormi il ben mio                    (G. B. Strozzi)

Amor, per tua mercé vattene a quella      (G. M. Bonardo)

Baci soavi e cari                         (G. B. Guarini)

Se pur non mi consenti                    (L. Groto)

Filli cara et amata                       (A. Parma)

Poi che del mio dolore

| | |
|---|---|
| Fumia la pastorella (1st part) | (A. Allegretti) |
| Almo divino raggio (2nd part) | |
| All'hora i pastor tutti (3rd part) | |
| Se nel partir da voi | (G. M. Bonardo) |
| Tra mille fiamme e tra mille catene | |
| Usciam, Ninfe, homai fuor di questi boschi | |
| Questa ordì il laccio | (G. B. Strozzi) |
| La vaga pastorella | |
| Amor, s'il tuo ferire | |
| Donna, s'io miro voi | |
| Ardo, sì, ma non t'amo | (G. B. Guarini) |
| Ardi o gela a tua voglia (response) | (T. Tasso) |
| Arsi et alsi a mia voglia (counter-response) | (T. Tasso) |

1590    *Il secondo libro de madrigali a cinque voci di Claudio Monteverde Cremonese discepolo del Sig.r Ingegneri*
Venice, A. Gardano; dedicated to Giacomo Ricardi

| | |
|---|---|
| Non si levava ancor l'alba novella (1st part) | (T. Tasso) |
| E dicea l'una sospirand'all'hora (2nd part) | |
| Bevea Fillide mia | (G. Casoni) |
| Dolcissimi legami | (T. Tasso) |
| Non giacinti o narcisi | (G. Casoni) |
| Intorno a due vermiglie e vaghe labra | |
| Non sono in queste rive | (T. Tasso) |
| Tutte le bocche belle | (F. Alberti) |
| Donna, nel mio ritorno il mio pensiero | (T. Tasso) |
| Quell'ombra esser vorrei | (G. Casoni) |
| S'andasse Amor a caccia | (T. Tasso) |
| Mentre io miravo fiso | (T. Tasso) |
| Ecco mormorar l'onde | (T. Tasso) |
| Dolcemente dormiva la mia Clori | (T. Tasso) |
| Se tu mi lassi, perfida, tuo danno | (T. Tasso) |
| La bocc'onde l'asprissime parole | (E. Bentivoglio) |
| Crudel, perchè mi fuggi | (G. B. Guarini) |
| Questo specchio ti dono | (G. Casoni) |
| Non m'è grave 'l morire | (B. Gottifredi) |
| Ti spontò l'ali, Amor, la donna mia | (F. Alberti) |
| Cantai un tempo' e se fu dolc'il canto | (P. Bembo) |

1592   *Di Claudio Monteverde il terzo libro de madrigali a cinque voci*
Venice, R. Amadino; dedicated to Vincenzo Gonzaga

| | |
|---|---|
| La giovinetta pianta | |
| O come è gran martire | (G. B. Guarini) |
| Sovra tenere herbette e bianchi fiori | |
| O dolce anima mia | (G. B. Guarini) |
| Stracciami pur il core | (G. B. Guarini) |
| O rossignuol, ch'in queste verdi fronde | (P. Bembo) |
| Se per estremo adore | (G. B. Guarini) |
| Vattene pur, crudel, con quella pace (1st part) | (T. Tasso) |
| Là tra 'l sangu'e le morti egro giacente (2nd part) | |
| Poi ch'ella in se tornò deserto e muto (3rd part) | |
| O primavera, gioventù dell'anno | (G. B. Guarini) |
| Perfidissimo volto | (G. B. Guarini) |
| Ch'io non t'ami, cor mio | (G. B. Guarini) |
| Occhi, un tempo mia vita | (G. B. Guarini) |
| Vivrò fra i miei tormenti e le mie cure (1st part) | (T. Tasso) |
| Ma dove, o lasso me, dove restaro (2nd part) | |
| Io pur verrò là dove sete, e voi (3rd part) | |
| Lumi, miei cari lumi | (G. B. Guarini) |
| 'Rimanti in pace' a la dolente e bella (1st part) | (L. Celiano) |
| Ond'ei di morte la sua faccia impressa (2nd part) | |

1594   *Il primo libro delle canzonette a tre voci di Antonio Morsolino con alcune altre*
Venice, R. Amadino

| | |
|---|---|
| Io ardo si, ma 'l foco è di tal sorte | |
| Occhi miei, se mirar più non debb'io | |
| Quante son stelle in ciel | (S. Cerreto) |
| Se non mi date aita | |

1597   *Fiori del giardino di diversi*
Nuremberg, Kaufmann

*Six madrigals by Monteverdi, among them the then unpublished*

| | |
|---|---|
| Ah dolente partita | (G. B. Guarini) |

1603   *Il quarto libro de madrigali a cinque voci di Claudio Monteverdi Maestro della Musica del Ser.mo Sig.r Duca di Mantova*
Venice, R. Amadino; dedicated to the Accademici Intrepidi di Ferrara

| | |
|---|---|
| Ah dolente partita | (G. B. Guarini) |
| Cor mio, mentre vi miro | (G. B. Guarini) |
| Cor mio, non mori? E mori | |
| Sfogava con le stelle | (O. Rinuccini) |
| Volgea l'anima mia soavemente | (G. B. Guarini) |
| Anima mia, perdona (1st part) | (G. B. Guarini) |
| Che se tu se' il cor mio (2nd part) | |
| Luci serene e chiare | (R. Arlotti) |
| La piaga c'ho nel core | (A. Gatti) |
| Voi pur da me partite, anima dura | (G. B. Guarini) |
| A un giro sol de begl'occhi lucenti | (G. B. Guarini) |
| Ohimè, se tanto amate | (G. B. Guarini) |
| Io mi son giovinetta e rido e canto | |
| Quell'augellin che canta | (G. B. Guarini) |
| Non più guerra, pietate, occhi miei belli | (G. B. Guarini) |
| Sì ch'io vorrei morire | |
| Anima dolorosa | |
| Anima del cor mio | |
| Longe da te, cor mio | |
| Piagne e sospira e quand'i caldi raggi | (T. Tasso) |

1605   *Il quinto libro de madrigali a cinque voci di Claudio Monteverde Maestro della Musica del Serenissimo Sig.r Duca di Mantoa, col basso continuo per il Clavicembano, Chittarone, od altro simile istromento; fatto particolarmente per li sei ultimi, per li altri a beneplacito*
Venice, R. Amadino; dedicated to Vincenzo Gonzaga

| | |
|---|---|
| Cruda Amarilli, che col nome ancora | (G. B. Guarini) |
| O Mirtillo, Mirtillo anima mia | (G. B. Guarini) |
| Era l'anima mia | (G. B. Guarini) |
| Ecco, Silvio, colei ch'in odio hai tanto (1st part) | (G. B. Guarini) |
| Ma se con la pietà non è in te spenta (2nd part) | |
| Dorinda, ah dirò mia, se mia non sei (3rd part) | |
| Ecco piegando le ginocchie a terra (4th part) | |
| Ferir quel petto, Silvio, non bisognava (5th part) | |

| | |
|---|---|
| Ch'io t'ami e t'ami più de la mia vita (1st part) | (G. B. Guarini) |
| Deh bella e cara e sì soave un tempo (2nd part) | |
| Ma tu più che mai dura (3rd part) | |
| Che dar più vi poss'io | |
| M'è più dolce il penar per Amarilli | (G. B. Guarini) |
| Ahi come a un vago sol cortese giro | (G. B. Guarini) |
| Troppo ben può questo tiranno Amore | (G. B. Guarini) |
| Amor, se giusto sei | |
| 'T'amo mia vita', la mia cara vita | (G. B. Guarini) |
| E così a poco a poco (6 pt.) | (G. B. Guarini) |
| Questi vaghi concenti (9 pt.) | |

*I nuovi fioretti a tre voci d'Amante Franzoni mantovano*
Venice, R. Amadino

Prima vedrò ch'in questi prati nascano

1607   *Scherzi musicali a tre voci, di Claudio Monteverdi, raccolti da Giulio Cesare Monteverde suo fratello . . . con la dichiaratione di una lettera, che si ritrova stampata nel quinto libro de suoi madrigali*
Venice, R. Amadino; dedicated to Francesco Gonzaga

| | |
|---|---|
| I bei legami | (G. Chiabrera) |
| Amarilli, onde m'assale | (G. Chiabrera) |
| Fugge il verno dei dolori | (G. Chiabrera) |
| Quando l'alba in oriente | (G. Chiabrera) |
| Non così tosto io miro | (G. Chiabrera) |
| Damigella | (G. Chiabrera) |
| La pastorella mia spietata e rigida | (J. Sannazaro) |
| O rosetta, che rosetta | (G. Chiabrera) |
| Amorosa pupilletta | (A. Cebà) |
| Vaghi rai di cigli ardenti | (G. Chiabrera) |
| La violetta | (G. Chiabrera) |
| Giovinetta | |
| Dolci miei sospiri | (G. Chiabrera) |
| Clori amorosa | (G. Chiabrera) |
| Lidia, spina del mio core | (A. Cebà) |

Deh chi tace il bel pensiero *by Giulio Cesare*     (A. Cebà)
    *Monteverdi*

Dispiegate *by Giulio Cesare Monteverdi*     (A. Cebà)

*De la bellezza le dovute lodi. Balletto*

*Musica tolta dai madrigali di Claudio Monterverde, e d'altri autori, a cinque, et a sei voci, e fatta spirituale da Aquilino Coppini, Accademico Inquieto con la partitura, e basso continuo nella sesta parte per i quattro ultimi canti a sei*
Milan, A. Tradate; dedicated to Cardinal Borromeo

| | *Original Monteverdi work* |
|---|---|
| Felle amaro | Cruda Amarilli |
| Qui pependit in cruce | Ecco Silvio, colei (1st part) |
| Pulchrae sunt | Ferir quel petto (2nd part) |
| Stabat Virgo Maria | Era l'anima mia |
| Sancta Maria | Deh bella e cara (1st part) |
| Spernit Deus cor | Ma tu più che mai dura (2nd part) |
| Maria quid ploras | Dorinda, ah dirò mia |
| Te Jesu Christe | Ecco piegando le ginocchie a terra |
| Ure me Domine | Troppo ben può |
| Gloria tua | 'T'amo mia vita' |
| Vives in corde meo | Ahi come a un vago sol |

1608   *Il secondo libro della musica di Claudio Monteverde e d'altri autori a cinque voci fatta spirituale da Aquilino Coppini regio lettore di retorica, et Accademico Inquieto. Con la partitura*
Milan, A. Tradate; dedicated to Bianco Lodovica Taverna

| | *Original Monteverdi work* |
|---|---|
| O dies infelices | O come è gran martire |
| Florea serta | La giovinetta pianta |
| Te sequar Jesu | Ch'io t'ami |
| Qui regnas | Che dar più vi poss'io |
| Animas eruit | M'è più dolce il penar |
| O mi fili, mea vita | O Mirtillo, Mirtillo |
| Praecipitantur | O primavera, gioventù dell'anno |
| O infelix recessus | Ah dolente partita |

1609   *Il terzo libro della musica di Claudio Monteverde a cinque voci fatta spirituale da Aquilino Coppini regio lettore di retorica, et Accademico Inquieto con la partitura*
Milan, A. Tradate; dedicated to Francesco Gonzaga.

| | |
|---|---|
| Una es | Una donna fra l'altre |
| Amemus te | Amor, se giusto sei |
| Qui pietate | Ma se con la pietà |
| Jesu dum te | Cor mio, mentre vi miro |
| Jesu tu nobis | Cor mio, non mori? |
| Luce serena | Luci serene e chiare |
| Plagas tuas | La piaga c'ho nel core |
| Tu vis a me | Voi pur da me partite |
| Cantemus | A un giro sol |
| Plorat amare | Piagn e esospira |
| Anima quam dilexi | Anima del cor mio |
| Longe a te | Longe da te, cor mio |
| O Jesu, mea vita | Sì ch'io vorrei morire |
| Anima miseranda | Anima dolorosa |
| O stellae | Sfogava con le stelle |
| Ardebat igne | Volgea l'anima mia |
| Domine Deus | Anima mia, perdona (1st part) |
| O gloriose martyr | Che se tu se' il cor mio (2nd part) |
| Rutilante in nocte | Io mi son giovinetta |
| Qui laudes | Quell'augellin che canta |

*L'Orfeo favola in musica da Claudio Monteverde rappresentata in Mantova l'anno 1607*
Venice, R. Amadino; dedicated to Francesco Gonzaga

1610   *Sanctissimae Virgini Missa senis vocibus ad Ecclesiarum Choros ac Vespere pluribus decantandae cum nonnullis sacris concentibus ad Sacella sive Principum cubicula accommodata*
Venice, R. Amadino; dedicated to Pope Paul V (Borghese)

*Missa da Capella a sei voci, fatta sopra il motetto 'In illo tempore' del Gomberti*
*Vespro della Beata Vergine da concerto composto sopra canti fermi*
(inscription at the beginning of the Bassus generalis part-book)

1614   *Il sesto libro de madrigali a cinque voci, con uno dialogo a sette, con il suo basso continuo per poterli concertare nel clavacembano, et*

*altri stromenti. Di Claudio Monteverde Maestro di Cappella della*
*Sereniss. Sig. di Venetia in S. Marco*
Venice, R. Amadino

| | |
|---|---|
| Lasciatemi morire (1st part) | (O. Rinuccini) |
| O Teseo, o Teseo mio (2nd part) | |
| Dove, dove è la fede (3rd part) | |
| Ahi che non pur risponde (4th part) | |
| Zefiro torna e 'l bel tempo rimena | (F. Petrarca) |
| Una donna fra l'altre honesta e bella. Concertato nel Clavicimbalo | |
| A Dio, Florida bella, il cor piagato. Concertato | (G. B. Marino) |
| Incenerite spoglie, avara tomba. Lagrime d'amante al sepolcro dell'amata (1st part) | (S. Agnelli) |
| Ditelo, o fiumi, e voi ch'udiste Glauco (2nd part) | |
| Darà la notte il sol lume alla terra (3rd part) | |
| Ma te raccoglie, o ninfa, in grembo il cielo (4th part) | |
| O chiome d'or, neve gentil del seno (5th part) | |
| Dunque, amate reliquie un mar di pianto (6th part) | |
| Ohimè il bel viso, ohimè il soave sguardo | (F. Petrarca) |
| Qui rise, o Tirsi, e qui ver me rivolse. Concertato | (G. B. Marino) |
| Misero Alceo, dal caro albergo fore. Concertato | (G. B. Marino) |
| 'Batto' qui pianse Ergasto, 'ecco la riva'. Concertato | (G. B. Marino) |
| Presso un fiume tranquillo. Dialogo a 7 concertato | (G. B. Marino) |

1615   *Parnassus musicus Ferdinandeus . . . a Joanne Bonometti . . .*
*congestus*
Venice, G. Vincenti

Cantate Domino
  SS or TT, bc

1617   *Musiche de alcuni eccellentissimi musici composte per La Mad-*
*dalena. Sacra Rappresentazione di Gio. Battista Andreini*
Venice, B. Magni

Su le penne de'venti (Prologue)
  T, five-part ritornello, bc

1619  *Concerto. Settimo libro de madrigali a 1. 2. 3. 4. sei voci, con altri*
      *generi de canti di Claudio Monteverde Maestro di Capella della*
      *Serenissima Republica*
      Venice, B. Magni; dedicated to Caterina Medici Gonzaga

| | |
|---|---|
| Tempro la cetra e per cantar gli honori | (G.B.Marino) |
| T, sinfonia and ritornello for five instruments, bc. | |
| Non è di gentil core | (F.degl'Atti) |
| SS, bc | |
| A quest'olmo, a quest'ombre et a quest'onde | (G.B.Marino) |
| SSAATB, 2 violins, 2 flutes or recorders, bc. | |
| O come sei gentile | (G. B. Guarini) |
| SS, bc | |
| Io son pur vezzosetta pastorella | |
| SS, bc | |
| O viva fiamma, o miei sospiri ardenti | |
| SS, bc | |
| Vorrei baciarti, o Filli | (G. B. Marino) |
| AA, bc | |
| Dice la mia bellissima Licori | (G. B. Guarini) |
| TT, bc | |
| Ah, che non si conviene | |
| TT, bc | |
| Non vedrò mai le stelle | |
| TT, bc | |
| Ecco vicine, o bella tigre, l'hore | (C. Achillini) |
| TT, bc | |
| Perchè fuggi tra salci | (G. B. Marino) |
| TT, bc | |
| Tornate, o cari baci | (G. Marino) |
| TT, bc | |
| Soave libertade | (G. Chiabrera) |
| TT, bc | |
| Se 'l vostro cor, Madonna | (G. B. Guarini) |
| TT, bc | |
| Interrotte speranze, eterna fede | (G. B. Guarini) |
| TT, bc | |
| Augellin che la voce al canto spieghi | |
| TTB, bc | |
| Vaga su spina ascosa | (G. Chiabrera) |
| TTB, bc | |

Eccomi pronta ai baci                                   (G. B. Marino)
  STT, bc

Parlo miser' o taccio                                   (G. B. Guarini)
  SSB, bc

Tu dormi? Ah crudo core
  SATB, bc

Al lume delle stelle                                    (T. Tasso)
  SSTB, bc

Con che soavità, labbra adorate. Concertato             (G. B. Guarini)
  S, 9 instruments

Ohimè, dove'è il mio ben, dov'è il mio core.            (T. Tasso)
    Romanesca a 2 (1st part)
  SS, bc

Dunque ha potuto sol desio d'honore (2nd part)
Dunque ha potuto in me più che'l mio amore
    (3rd part)
Ahi sciocco mondo e cieco, ahi cruda sorte (4th
    part)

Se i languidi miei sguardi. Lettera amorosa.            (C. Achillini)
    In genere rapresentativo
  S, bc

Se pur destina e vole. Partenza amorosa.
    In genere rapresentativo.
  T, bc

Chiome d'oro. Canzonetta concertata
  SS, 2 violins, bc

Amor che deggio far. Canzonetta concertata
  SSTB, 2 violins, bc

*Tirsi e Clori. Ballo concertato con voci et*           (A. Striggio)
*istrumenti a 5*
  ST, SSATB, bc


1620   *Symbolae diversorum musicorum . . . ab admodum reverendo D.*
     *Laurentio Calvo . . . in lucem editae*
     Venice, A. Vincenti

Fuge, anima mea, mundum
  SA, violin, bc

O beatae viae
  SS, bc

*Libro primo de motetti . . . di Giulio Cesare Bianchi. Con un altro*
*a cinque, e tre a sei del sig. Claudio Monteverde*
Venice, B. Magni

Cantate Domino
  SSATTB, bc

Christe, adoramus te
  SSATB, bc

Domine, ne in furore tuo
  SSATTB, bc

Adoramus te, Christe
  SSATTB, bc

1622    *Promptuarii musici concentus ecclesiasticos . . . Pars prima . . .*
        *Collectore Joanne Donfrido*
        Strasbourg, P. Ledertz

        O bone Jesu, o piissime Jesu
          SS, bc

1623    *Lamento d'Ariana del signor Claudio Monteverde maestro di*
        *capella Della Serenissima Republica. E con due Lettere Amorose*
        *in genere rapresentativo*
        Venice, B. Magni.

        *Concerti sacri . . . del P. Pietro Lappi*
        Venice, E. Magni

                                    *Original Monteverdi work*
        Ave regina mundi            Vaga su spina ascosa

1624    *Madrigali del Signor Cavaliere Anselmi . . . posti in musica da*
        *diversi*
        Venice, B. Magni

        O come vaghi, o come cari sono          (G. B. Anselmi)
          TT, bc

        Taci, Armelin, deh taci                 (G. B. Anselmi)
          ATB, bc

        *Quarto scherzo delle ariose vaghezze commode per cantarsi a voce*
        *sola . . . di Carlo Milanuzzi . . . con una cantata e altre arie del*
        *Signor Monteverde, e del Sig. Francesco suo figliolo*
        Venice, A. Vincenti

        Ohimè ch'io cado
          S, bc

La mia turca
  S, bc
Sì dolce è 'l tormento
  S, bc

*Secondo raccolta de sacri canti . . . de diversi eccellentissimi autori fatta da Don Lorenzo Calvi*
Venice, A. Vincenti

Ego flos campi
  A, bc
Venite, sitientes, ad aquas
  SS, bc
Salve o Regina
  T, bc

1625 *Sacri affetti con testi da diversi eccellentissimi autori raccolti da Francesco Sammaruco*
Rome, L. A. Soldi

Ego dormio et cor meum vigilat
  SB, bc

*Ghirlanda sacra scielta da diversi eccellentissimi compositori de varii motetti a voce sola. Libro primo opera seconda per Leonardo Simonetti*
Venice, B. Magni

O quam pulchra es, amica mea
  T, bc
Currite, populi, psallite timpanis
  T, bc
Ecce sacrum paratum convivium
  T, bc
Salve Regina
  T, bc

1627 *Promptuarii musici concentus ecclesiasticos . . . pars tertia . . . Opera et studio Joannis Donfrid*
Strasbourg, P. Ledertz

Sancta Maria, succurre miseris
  SS, bc

*Psalmi de Vespere a quattro voci del Cavalier D. Gio. Maria Sabino da Turi*
Naples, A. Magnetta

Confitebor tibi, Domine
   SATB, bc

1629   *Quarta raccolta de sacri canti . . . fatta da Don Lorenzo Calvi*
   Venice, A. Vincenti

Exulta, filia Sion
   S, bc

Exultent coeli et gaudeant angeli
   SSATB, bc

Salve, o Regina
   ATB, bc

1632   *Scherzi musicali cioè Arie, e Madrigali in stil recitativo, con una Ciaccona a 1. e 2. voci del M.to Ill.re et M.to R.do Sig.r Claudio Monteverde. Maestro di capella della Sereniss. Repub. di Venetia. Raccolti da Bartholomeo Magni*
   Venice, B. Magni; dedicated by Magni to Pietro Capello

Maledetto
   S, bc

Quel sguardo sdegnosetto (1st part)
   S, bc

Armatevi, pupille (2nd part)
Begl'occhi a l'armi a l'armi (3rd part)

Eri già tutta mia
   S, bc

Ecco di dolci raggi il sol armato
   T, bc

Et è pur dunque vero. Con Sinfonia
   S, bc

Io che armato sin hor
   T, bc

Zefiro torna e di soavi accenti. Ciaccona a due   (O. Rinuccini)
   voci
   TT, bc

Armato il cor d'adamantina fede   (O. Rinuccini)
   TT, bc

1634 *Arie de diversi raccolte da Alessandro Vincenti commode da cantarsi nel clavicembalo chitarrone, e altro simile stromento, con le lettere dell'alfabeto per la chitarra spagnola*
Venice, A. Vincenti

Più lieto il guardo
S, bc
Perchè, se m'odiavi
S, bc

1638 *Madrigali guerrieri, et amorosi con alcuni opuscoli in genere rappresentativo, che saranno per brevi Episodij fra i canti senza gesto. Libro ottavo di Claudio Monteverde Maestro di Capella della Serenissima Republica di Venetia*
Venice, B. Magni; dedicated to Emperor Ferdinand III of Austria.

*Canti guerrieri*
Sinfonia—Altri canti d'amor
SSATTB, 2 violins, 4 violas, bc
Hor che il ciel e la terra e 'l vento tace (1st part)          (F. Petrarca)
SSATTB, 2 violins, bc
Così sol d'una chiara fonte viva (2nd part)
Gira il nemico insidioso amore (1st part)
ATB, bc
Nol lasciamo accostar, ch'egli non saglia (2nd part)
Armi false non son, ch'ei s'avvicina (3rd part)
Vuol degli occhi attaccar il baloardo (4th part)
Non è più tempo ohimè ch'egli ad un tratto
(5th part)
Cor mio, non val fuggir sei morto e sento
(6th part)
Se vittorie si belle
TT, bc
Armato il cor d'adamantina fede                              (O. Rinuccini)
TT, bc
Ogni amante è guerrier (1st part)                           (O. Rinuccini)
TT, bc
Io che nell'otio nacqui (2nd part)
B, bc
Ma per quel ampio Egeo (3rd part)
T, bc

Riedi ch'al nostro ardir (4th part)
  TTB, bc

Ardo, avvampo, mi struggo
  SSAATTBB, 2 violins, bc

*Combattimento di Tancredi e Clorinda in genere*          (T. Tasso)
  *rappresentativo*
  STT, 4 *viole da brazzo,* bc

Introdutione al ballo                                      (O. Rinuccini)
  T, 2 violins, bc

*Ballo Movete al mio bel suon le piante snelle*
  SSATB, 2 violins, bc

*Canti amorosi*

Altri canti di Marte e di sua schiera (1st part)          (G. B. Marino)
  SSATTB, 2 violins, bc
Due belli occhi fur l'armi (2nd part)

Vago augelletto che cantando vai                          (F. Petrarca)
  SSATTTB, 2 violins, contrabass, bc

Mentre vaga Angioletta                                    (G. B. Guarini)
  TT, bc

Ardo e scoprir, ahi lasso
  TT, bc

O sia tranquillo il mare
  TT, bc

Ninfa che scalza il piede (1st part)
  T, bc
Qui, deh, meco t'arresta (2nd part)
  TT, bc
Dell'usate mie corde (3rd part)
  TTB, bc

Dolcissimo uscignolo. A 5 voci, cantato a voce           (G. B. Guarini)
  piena, alla francese
  SSATB, bc

Chi vol haver felice. A 5 voci, cantato à voce           (G. B. Guarini)
  piena, alla francese.
  SSATB, bc

Non havea Febo ancora. Rapresentativo                    (O. Rinuccini)
  (1st part)
  TTB, bc
Amor—Lamento della Ninfa (2nd part)
  STTB, bc
Si tra sdegnosi pianti (3rd part)
  TTB, bc

Perchè te 'n fuggi, o Fillide
    ATB, bc

Non partir, ritrosetta
    AAB, bc

Su, su, pastorelli
    SSA, bc

*Il ballo delle ingrate. In genere rapresentativo*     (O. Rinuccini)
    Solo voices: SSSB; chorus: SSSA, 5 *viole da*
        *brazzo, bc*

1641    *Selva morale e spirituale di Claudio Monteverde Maestro di*
        *Capella della Serenissima Republica di Venetia*
        Venice, B. Magni; dedicated to Eleonora Gonzaga, Empress of
        Austria

O ciechi, il tanto affaticar che giova     (F. Petrarca)
    SSATB, 2 violins, bc

Voi ch'ascoltate in rime sparse il suono     (F. Petrarca)
    STTTB, 2 violins, bc

È questa vita un lampo     (A. Grillo)
    SSTAB, bc

Spuntava il dì
    ATB, bc

Chi vol che m'innamori
    ATB, 2 violins, bc

*Messa da capella*
    SATB, bc

Gloria. Concertata
    SSATTBB, 2 violins, 4 *viole da brazzo* or
        trombones (not extant), bc

Crucifixus
    ATTB, bc

Et resurrexit
    SS or TT, 2 violins, bc

Et iterum. Concertato
    AAB, 4 *viole da brazzo* or trombones (not
        extant), bc

Ab aeterno ordinata sum. Motetto
    B, bc

Dixit Dominus (I) concertato
    SSAATTBB, 2 violins, 4 *viole* or trombones
        (not extant), bc

Dixit Dominus (II) concertato con gli stessi
 istromenti del primo
 SSAATTBB, 2 violins, 4 *viole* or trombones
 (not extant), bc

Confitebor (I)
 ATB, SSATB, bc

Confitebor (II) concertato
 STB, 2 violins, bc

Confitebor (III) alla francese
 SSATB, bc, or S, 4 *viole da brazzo*, bc

Beatus vir (I) concertato
 SSATTB, 2 violins, 3 *viole da brazzo* or
 trombones (not extant), bc

Beatus vir (II)
 SATTB, bc

Laudate pueri (I) concertato
 SSTTB, 2 violins, bc

Laudate pueri (II)
 SATTB, bc

Laudate Dominum (I) concertato
 SSTTB, 2 violins, choir, bc

Laudate Dominum (II)
 SSAATTBB, 2 violins, bc

Laudate Dominum (III)
 SSAATTBB, bc

Credidi propter quod locutus sum
 SATB and ATTB, bc

Memento [Domine, David] et omnis man-
 suetudinis
 SATB and ATTB, bc

Sanctorum meritis (I)
 S, 2 violins, bc

Sanctorum meritis (II)
 T, 2 violins, bc

Deus tuorum militum
 T, 2 violins, bc

Iste confessor (I)
 T, 2 violins, bc

Iste confessor (II)
 SS, 2 violins, bc

Ut queant laxis
 SS, 2 violins, bc

Deus tuorum militum
    TTB, 2 violins, bc

Magnificat (I)
    SATB and SATB (A and B of the 2nd choir
        are missing), 2 violins, 4 *viole* (only 2 parts
        extant) or trombones, bc

Magnificat (II)
    SAAB, bc

Salve Regina (I)
    T, echo-T, 2 violins, bc

Salve Regina (II)
    TT or SS, bc

Salve Regina (III)
    AT (or S) B, bc

Jubilet tota civitas
    S, bc

Laudate Dominum
    S or T, bc

Iam moriar mi fili. Pianto della Madonna sopra
    il Lamento d'Arianna
    S, bc


*Erster Theil geistlicher Concerten und Harmonien . . . colligiret*
*durch Ambrosium Profium*
Leipzig, H. Köler

|                        | *Original Monteverdi work* |
|------------------------|----------------------------|
| Jesum viri senesque    | Vaga su spina ascosa       |


*Ander Theil geistlicher Concerten und Harmonien . . . colligiret . . . durch Ambrosium Profium*
Leipzig, H. Köler

|                        | *Original Monteverdi work* |
|------------------------|----------------------------|
| Ergo gaude laetare     | Due belli occhi            |
| Lauda, anima mea       | Due belli occhi            |
| Pascha concelebranda   | Altri canti di Marte       |


1642  *Dritter Theil geistlicher Concerten und Harmonien . . . colligiret . . . durch Ambrosium Profium*
Leipzig, H. Köler

|  | *Original Monteverdi work* |
| --- | --- |
| Haec dixit Deus | Voi ch'ascoltate in rime |
| Heus, bone vir | Armato il cor |
| Spera in Domino | Io che amato sin hor |

1649   *Corollarium geistlicher collectaneorum . . . gewähret durch Ambrosio Profio*
Leipzig, T. Ritzsch

|  | *Original Monteverdi work* |
| --- | --- |
| Alleluja, kommet, jauchzet | Ardo, avvampo |
| Dein allein ist ja | Così sol d'una chiara fonte |
| Freude kommet, lasset uns | Ardo, avvampo |
| Longe, mi Jesu | Parlo miser o' o taccio |
| O du mächtiger Herr | Hor che 'el ciel e la terra |
| O Jesu lindere | Tu dormi? Ah crudo core |
| O rex supreme | Al lume delle stelle |
| Resurrexit de sepulcro | Vago augelletto |
| Veni, soror mea | Vago augelletto |

1650   *Messa a quattro voci et Salmi a una, due, tre, quattro, cinque, sei, sette, et otto voci, Concertati, e parte da cappella, con le Letanie della B.V. del Signor Claudio Monteverdi già Maestro di Cappella della Serenissima Republica di Venetia*
Venice, A. Vincenti; dedicated to Don Odoardo Baranardi

*Messa da capella*
  SATB, bc
Dixit Dominus (I)
  SATB and SATB, bc
Dixit Dominus (II)
  SATB and ATTB, bc
Confitebor (I)
  S, 2 violins, bc
Confitebor (II)
  ST, 2 violins, bc
Beatus vir
  SSAATTB, 2 violins, bc
Laudate pueri Dominum
  SAATB, bc
Laudate Dominum
  B, bc

Laetatus sum (I)
  SSTTBB, 2 violins, 2 trombones, 1 *fagotto*,
  bc
Laetatus sum (II)
  SATTB, bc
Nisi Dominus (I)
  STB, 2 violins, bc
Nisi Dominus (II)
  SSATTB, bc
Lauda Jerusalem (I)
  ATB, bc
Lauda Jerusalem (II)
  SATTB, bc
Laetanie della Beata Vergine
  SATTTB, bc


1651 *Madrigali e canzonette a due e tre voci del signor Claudio Monteverde già Maestro di Cappella della Serenissima Republica di Venetia . . . Libro nono*
Venice, A. Vincenti; dedicated to Gerolamo Orologio

Bel pastor dal cui bel guardo                      (O. Rinuccini)
  ST, bc
Zefiro torna e di soavi accenti. Ciaccona          (O. Rinuccini)
  TT, bc
Se vittorie si belle
  TT, bc
Armato il cor d'adamantina fede                    (O. Rinuccini)
  TT, bc
Ardo e scoprir, ahi lasso
  TT, bc
O sia tranquillo il mare
  TT, bc
Alcun non mi consigli
  ATB, bc
Di far sempre gioire
  ATB, bc
Quando dentro al tuo seno
  TTB, bc
Non voglio amare
  TTB, bc

Come dolce hoggi l'auretta (1st part)         (G. Strozzi)
Gl'amoretti l'aura fanno (2nd part)
Ride il bosco, brilla il prato (3rd part)
Entri pur nel nostro petto (4th part)
  SSS, bc

Alle danze, alle gioie, ai diletti
  TTB, bc

Perchè se m'odiavi
  TTB, bc

Si si ch'io v'amo occhi vaghi, occhi belli
  TTT, bc

Su su su pastorelli vezzosi
  TTB, bc

O mio bene, o mia vita
  TTB, bc

*Racolta di motetti a 1, 2, 3 voci di Gasparo Casati et de diversi altri*
Venice, B. Magni

En gratulemur hodie
  T, 2 violins, bc

### WORKS IN MANUSCRIPTS

*Lamento di Olimpia*
  Voglio, voglio morir, voglio morire (1st part)
  Anzi che non amarmi (2nd part)
  Ma perchè, o ciel, invendicato lasso (3rd part)
  S, bc
London, British Museum, Add. 30491
(The attribution to Monteverdi is doubtful.)

Ahi, che si partì il mio bel sole adorno
  SST, bc
Modena, Biblioteca Estense

Gloria in excelsis Deo
  SATB and SATB, bc
Naples, Archivio dei Filippini, S.M. IV–2–23a

Voglio di vita uscir
  S, bc
Naples, Archivio dei Filippini, S.M. IV–2–23b
(The attribution to Monteverdi is doubtful.)

*L'incoronazione di Poppea*
Naples, Conservatorio S. Pietro a Maiella

*L'incoronazione di Poppea*
Venice, Biblioteca di S. Marco, MS It. cl. 4 n. 439

*Il ritorno d'Ulisse in patria*
Vienna, Nationalbibliothek, MS. 18763

# SELECT BIBLIOGRAPHY

THIS bibliography does not attempt to be complete. It contains a selection of the most important publications on Monteverdi, as well as works dealing with his social and historical environment. In addition it has been chosen, wherever possible, with the English-speaking reader in mind. The publications have been ordered systematically according to chapter. The most complete Monteverdi bibliography at this time may be found in K. Gary Adams and Dyke Kiel, *Claudio Monteverdi : a Guide to Research* ('Garland Composer Resource Manuals', XXIII; New York & London, 1989). Reasonably full bibliographies may also be found in Denis Arnold and Nigel Fortune (eds.), *The New Monteverdi Companion* (London, 1985), 340–51, and in Paolo Fabbri, *Monteverdi* (Turin, 1985), 439–46.

## EDITIONS

*Tutte le opere di Claudio Monteverdi*, ed. Gian Franceso Malipiero (16 vols.; Asolo, 1926–42); 2nd edn. with revisions by Denis Arnold in vols. 8, 15, and 16 (Vienna, 1954–68); supplementary vol. 17 (Venice, 1966).

*Claudio Monteverdi: 12 composizioni vocali profane e sacre (inedite)*, ed. Wolfgang Osthoff (Milan, 1958; 2nd edn., 1978).

*Claudio Monteverdi: Opere omnia*, ed. Fondazione Claudio Monteverdi (Instituta et monumenta, Monumenta, 5; Cremona, 1970–).

## SOURCE MATERIALS

ADEMOLLO, ALESSANDRO, *La bell'Adriana e altre virtuose del suo tempo alla corte di Mantova* (Città di Castello, 1888).

DE' PAOLI, DOMENICO (ed.), *Claudio Monteverdi: Lettere, dediche e prefazioni* (Rome, 1973).

FABBRI, PAOLO, 'Inediti monteverdiani', *Rivista italiana di musicologia*, 15 (1980), 71–86.

SOLERTI, ANGELO, *Gli albori del melodramma* (3 vols.; Milan, 1904; repr. Hildesheim, 1969).

—— *Le origini del melodramma* (Turin, 1903; repr. Hildesheim, 1969).

—— *Musica, ballo e drammatica alla corte Medicea dal 1600 al 1637* (Florence, 1905; repr. Bologna, 1969).

STEVENS, DENIS (ed.), *The Letters of Claudio Monteverdi* (London, 1980).

## BIOGRAPHIES AND COMPREHENSIVE WORKS

ABERT, ANNA AMALIE, *Claudio Monteverdi und das musikalische Drama* (Lippstadt, 1954).

ARNOLD, DENIS, *Monteverdi* (The Master Musician Series; London, 1963; 2nd rev. edn., 1975).

BARBLAN, GUGLIELMO, GALLICO, CLAUDIO, and PANNAIN, GUIDO, *Claudio Monteverdi sul quarto centenario della nascita* (Turin, 1967).

DE' PAOLI, DOMENICO, *Claudio Monteverdi* (Milan, 1945).

—— *Claudio Monteverdi* (Milan, 1979).

FABBRI, PAOLO, *Monteverdi* (Turin, 1985).

GALLICO, CLAUDIO, *Monteverdi: Poesia musicale, teatro e musica sacra* (Turin, 1979).

MALIPIERO, FRANCESCO, *Claudio Monteverdi* (Milan, 1929).

PESTELLI, GIORGIO, 'Le poesie per la musica monteverdiana: Il gusto poetico di Monteverdi', in Raffaello Monterosso (ed.), *Claudio Monteverdi e il suo tempo* (Verona, 1969), 349–60.

PIRROTTA, NINO, 'Scelte poetiche di Monteverdi', *Nuova rivista musicale italiana*, 2 (1968), 10–42, 226–54; Eng. trans. as 'Monteverdi's Poetic Choices', in Nino Pirrotta, *Music and Culture in Italy from the Middle Ages to the Baroque* (Studies in the History of Music, 1; Cambridge, Mass., and London, 1984), 271–316.

PRUNIÈRES, HENRY, *La Vie et l'œuvre de Claudio Monteverdi* (Paris, 1924; Eng. trans., Marie D. Mackie, New York, 1972).

REDLICH, HANS FERDINAND, *Claudio Monteverdi: Ein formengeschichtlicher Versuch*, I. *Das Madrigalwerk* (Berlin, 1932).

—— *Claudio Monteverdi: Leben und Werk* (Olten, 1949; Eng. trans., rev., London, 1952).

SARTORI, CLAUDIO, *Monteverdi* (Brescia, 1953).

SCHNEIDER, LOUIS, *Un précurseur de la musique italienne aux XVIe et XVIIe siècles: Claudio Monteverdi: L'homme et son temps* (Paris, 1921).

SCHRADE, LEO, *Monteverdi, Creator of Modern Music* (New York, 1950; repr. 1964).

—— 'Monteverdi—ein Revolutionär der Musikgeschichte', *Neue Zeitschrift für Musik*, 123 (1962), 153–7.

STATTKUS, MANFRED H., *Monteverdi: Verzeichnis der erhaltenen Werke*, Kleine Ausgabe (Bergkamen, 1985).

STEVENS, DENIS, *Monteverdi: Sacred, Secular and Occasional Music* (Cranbury, NJ, and London, 1978).

VOGEL, EMIL, 'Claudio Monteverdi', *Vierteljahrsschrift für Musikwissenschaft*, 3 (1887), 315–450.

## GENERAL LITERATURE

BIANCONI, LORENZO, *Il seicento* (Turin, 1982). English translation, David Bryant, *Music in the Seventeenth Century* (Cambridge, 1987).

BRAUN, WERNER, *Die Musik des 17. Jahrhunderts* (Wiesbaden, 1981).

BUKOFZER, MANFRED, *Music in the Baroque Era* (New York, 1947).

CAFFI, FRANCESCO, *Storia della musica sacra nella già cappella ducale di San Marco in Venezia dal 1318 al 1797* (2 vols.; Venice, 1854–55; repr. 1931 annotated edition by Elvidio Surian, Florence, 1987).

EINSTEIN, ALFRED, *The Italian Madrigal* (3 vols.; Princeton, NJ, 1949).

GROUT, DONALD J., *A Short History of Opera* (2 vols.; 2nd edn., New York, 1965). Third edition, D. J. Grout and H. W. Williams (New York, 1988).

HAAS, ROBERT, *Die Musik des Barocks* (Potsdam, 1928).

MOORE, JAMES H., *Vespers at St. Mark's: Music of Alessandro Grandi, Giovanni Rovetta and Francesco Cavalli* (2 vols.; Ann Arbor, 1981).

PALISCA, CLAUDE V., *Baroque Music* (2nd edn., Englewood Cliffs, NJ, 1981).

WORSTHORNE, SIMON TOWNELEY, *Venetian Opera in the Seventeenth Century* (Oxford, 1954; reprinted 1968 with bibliographical supplement).

### FURTHER LITERATURE TO THE INDIVIDUAL CHAPTERS

*Chronology*

CANAL, PIETRO, *Della musica in Mantova* (Venice, 1881; rep. 1978).

DAVARI, STEFANO, *Notizie biografiche del distinto maestro di musica Claudio Monteverdi* (Mantua, 1884).

FENLON, IAIN, *Music and Patronage in Sixteenth-century Mantua* (2 vols.; Cambridge, 1980–2).

—— 'Mantua, Monteverdi and the History of *Andromeda*', in Ludwig Finscher (ed.), *Claudio Monteverdi: Festschrift Reinhold Hammerstein* (Laaber, 1986), 163–73.

REINER, STUART, 'La vag' Angioletta (and others) Part I', *Analecta musicologica*, 14 (1974), 26–88.

—— 'Preparations in Parma 1618, 1627–28', *Music Review*, 25 (1964), 273–301.

SANTORO, ELIA, *La famiglia e la formazione di Claudio Monteverdi* (Cremona, 1967).

*A Change in Style*

ARNOLD, DENIS, ' "Seconda pratica": A Background to Monteverdi's Madrigals', *Music and Letters*, 38 (1957), 341–52.

BLUME, FRIEDRICH, 'Begriff und Grenzen des Barock in der Musik', in *Manierismo, Barocco, Rococò: Concetti e termini. Convegno internazionale Roma 12–24 Aprile 1960* (Rome, 1962), 377–84.

DAHLHAUS, CARL, '*Ecco mormorar l'onde*: Versuch, ein Monteverdi-Madrigal zu interpretieren', in Heinrich Poos (ed.), *Chormusik und Analyse* (Mainz, 1983), 139–54.

FORTUNE, NIGEL, 'Monteverdi and the *seconda prattica*, ii. From Madrigal to Duet', in Denis Arnold and Nigel Fortune (eds.), *The New Monteverdi Companion* (London, 1985), 198–215.

FRIEDRICH, HUGO, *Epochen der italienischen Lyrik* (Frankfurt, 1964).

GALLICO, CLAUDIO, 'La *Lettera amorosa* di Monteverdi e lo stile rappresentativo', *Nuova rivista musicale italiana*, 2 (1967), 287–302.

GARIN, EUGENIO, *Italian Humanism: Philosophy and Civic Life in the Renaissance* (Eng. trans., Peter Munz, Oxford, 1965).

HAMMERSTEIN, REINHOLD, 'Versuch über die Form im Madrigal Monteverdis', in Ludwig Finscher (ed.), *Claudio Monteverdi: Festschrift Reinhold Hammerstein* (Laaber, 1986), 9–33 (a shorter version appeared in *Sprachen der Lyrik: Festschrift für Hugo Friedrich zum 70. Geburtstag* (Frankfurt am Main, 1975) ).

HATHAWAY, BAXTER, *The Age of Criticism: The Late Renaissance in Italy* (Ithaca, 1962).

LEICHTENTRITT, HUGO, 'Claudio Monteverdi als Madrigalkomponist', *Sammelbände der Internationalen Musikgesellschaft*, 11 (1909–10), 255–91.

LEOPOLD, SILKE, 'Kontrapunkt und Textausdruck', *Funkkolleg Musikgeschichte* (Radio Lectures on Music History, Studienbegleitbrief 4; Weinheim and Basel, 1987), 11–45.

MACE, DEAN T., 'Tasso, *La Gerusalemme Liberata* and Monteverdi'. *Studies in the History of Music* 1 (New York, 1983), 118–56.

MASSERA, GIUSEPPE, 'Dalle "imperfezioni" alle "perfezioni" della moderna musica', in Raffaello Monterosso (ed.), *Claudio Monteverdi e il suo tempo* (Verona, 1969), 397–408.

PALISCA, CLAUDE V., 'The Artusi–Monteverdi Controversy', in Denis Arnold and Nigel Fortune (eds.), *The Monteverdi Companion* (London, 1968), 133–66.

—— 'Vincenzo Galilei's Counterpoint Treatise: A Code for the "Seconda Pratica" ', *Journal of the American Musicological Society*, 9 (1956), 81–96.

STEVENS, DENIS, 'Madrigali guerrieri, et amorosi', in Denis Arnold and Nigel Fortune (eds.), *The Monteverdi Companion* (London, 1968), 227–52.

TOMLINSON, GARY, *Monteverdi and the End of the Renaissance* (Oxford, 1987).

—— 'Madrigal, Monody, and Monteverdi's *via naturale alla immitazione*', *Journal of the American Musicological Society*, 34 (1981), 60–108.

WHENHAM, JOHN, *Duet and Dialogue in the Age of Monteverdi* (2 vols.; Ann Arbor, 1982).

—— 'The Later Madrigals and Madrigal-books', in Denis Arnold and Nigel Fortune (eds.), *The New Monteverdi Companion* (London, 1985), 216–47.

WÖLFFLIN, HEINRICH, *Renaissance und Barock. Eine Untersuchung über Wesen und Entstehung des Barockstils in Italien* (Munich, 1888).

*Pastoral Themes*

ABERT, ANNA AMALIE, 'Monteverdi e lo sviluppo dell'opera', *Rivista italiana di musicologia*, 2 (1967), 207–16.

DONINGTON, ROBERT, *The Rise of Opera* (London and Boston, 1981).

—— 'Monteverdi's First Opera', in Denis Arnold and Nigel Fortune (eds.), *The Monteverdi Companion* (London, 1968), 257–76.

FENLON, IAIN, 'Monteverdi's Mantuan Stage Works', in Denis Arnold and Nigel Fortune (eds.), *The New Monteverdi Companion* (London, 1985), 251–87.

HANNING, BARBARA RUSSANO, *Of Poetry and Music's Power: Humanism and the Creation of Opera* (Ann Arbor, 1980).

HELL, HELMUT, 'Zu Rhythmus und Notierung des *Vi ricorda* in Claudio Monteverdis *Orfeo*', *Analecta musicologica*, 15 (1975), 87–157.

JUNG, HERMANN, *Die Pastorale: Studien zur Geschichte eines musikalischen Topos* (Berne and Munich, 1980).

LEOPOLD, SILKE, 'Der schöne Hirte und seine Vorfahren', in *Festschrift Helmut Hucke* (in preparation).

—— 'Die Hierarchie Arkadiens: Soziale Strukturen in den frühen Pastoralopern und ihre Ausdrucksformen', *Schweizer Jahrbuch für Musikwissenschaft*, 1 (1981), 71–92.

—— 'Lyra Orphei', in Ludwig Finscher (ed.), *Claudio Monteverdi: Festschrift Reinhold Hammerstein* (Laaber, 1986), 337–45.

—— 'Madrigali sulle egloghe sdrucciole di Jacopo Sannazaro: Struttura poetica e forma musicale', *Revista italiana di musicologia*, 14 (1979), 75–127.

—— 'Orpheus in Mantua—und anderswo', *Concerto*, 1 (1983), 35–42.

MONTEROSSO VACCHELLI, ANNA-MARIA, 'Elementi stilistici nell'*Euridice* di Jacopo Peri in rapporto all'*Orfeo* di Monteverdi', in Raffaello Monterosso (ed.), *Claudio Monteverdi e il suo tempo* (Verona, 1969), 117–27.

PETRICONI, HELLMUTH, 'Das neuen Arkadien', *Antike und Abendland*, 3 (1948), 187–200.

PETROBELLI, PIERLUIGI, '*Ah dolente partita*: Marenzio, Wert, Monteverdi', in Raffaello Monterosso (ed.), *Claudio Monteverdi e il suo tempo* (Verona, 1969), 361–76.

PIRROTTA, NINO, 'Monteverdi e i problemi dell'opera', in Maria Teresa Muraro, *Studi sul teatro veneto fra rinascimento ed età barocca* (Florence, 1971), 321–43; Eng. trans. as 'Monteverdi and the Problems of Opera', in Nino Pirrotta, *Music and Culture in Italy from the Middle Ages to the Baroque* (Studies in the History of Music, 1; Cambridge, Mass., and London, 1984), 235–53.

PIRROTTA, NINO, and POVOLEDO, ELENA, *Li due Orfei* (Turin, 1969; rev. 2nd edn., 1975); Eng. trans., Karen Eales, as *Music and Theatre from Poliziano to Monteverdi* (Cambridge, 1982).

ROSAND, ELLEN, (ed.), *Aureli-Sartorio: Orfeo*, facs. edn., intr. (Drammaturgia veneta, 6; Milan, 1983).

SNELL, BRUNO, 'Arkadien: Die Entdeckung einer geistigen Landschaft', *Antike und Abendland*, 1 (1945), 26–41.

STERNFELD, FREDERICK W., 'Aspects of Echo Music in the Renaissance', *Studi musicali*, 9 (1980), 45–57.

—— 'The Birth of Opera: Ovid, Poliziano, and the *lieto fine*', *Analecta Musicologica*, 19 (1979), 30–51.

SZWEYKOWSKI, ZYGMUNT, '*Ah dolente partita*: Monteverdi, Scacchi', *Quadrivium*, 12/2 (1971), 59–76.

TOMLINSON, GARY, 'Twice bitten, thrice shy: Monteverdi's "finta" *Finta pazza*', *Journal of the American Musicological Society*, 36 (1983), 303–11.

VOSSLER, KARL, 'Tassos *Aminta* und die Hirtendichtung', *Studien zur vergleichenden Literaturgeschichte*, 6 (1906), 26–40.

WHENHAM, JOHN (ed.), *Claudio Monteverdi: 'Orfeo'* (Cambridge Opera Handbooks; Cambridge, 1986).

*Ostinato and Other Bass Models*

EINSTEIN, ALFRED, 'Die Aria di Ruggiero', *Sammelbände der Internationalen Musikgesellschaft*, 13 (1911/12), 444–54.

HERMELINK, SIEGFRIED, 'Das rhythmische Gefüge in Monteverdis Ciaccona *Zefiro torna*', in Raffaello Monterosso (ed.), *Claudio Monteverdi e il suo tempo* (Verona, 1969), 323–34.

HUDSON, RICHARD, 'Further Remarks on the Passacaglia and Ciaccona', *Journal of the American Musicological Society*, 23 (1970), 302–14.

MÜLLER, REINHARD, 'Basso ostinato . . . *Poppea*', *Archiv für Musikwissenschaft* (1983), 1–23.

OSTHOFF, WOLFGANG, *Das dramatische Spätwerk Claudio Monteverdis* (Tutzing, 1960).

—— 'Die frühesten Erscheinungsformen der Passacaglia in der italienischen Musik des 17. Jahrhunderts', *Atti del congresso internazionale di musiche populari mediterranee* (Palermo, 1959), 275–88.

RIEMANN, HUGO, 'Der "Basso ostinato" und die Anfänge der Kantate', *Sammelbände der Internationalen Musikgesellschaft*, 13 (1911/12), 531–43.

WALKER, THOMAS, 'Ciaccona and Passacaglia: Remarks on their Origin and Early History', *Journal of the American Musicological Society*, 21 (1968), 300–20.

WALTER, LOTHAR, *Die Ostinatotechnik in den Chaconne- und Arienformen des 17. und 18. Jahrhunderts* (Wurzburg, 1940).


*The Lament*

DANCKWARDT, MARIANNE, 'Das Lamento d'Olimpia *Voglio voglio morir*—eine Komposition Claudio Monteverdis?', *Archiv für Musikwissenschaft*, 41 (1984), 149–75.

EPSTEIN, PETER, 'Dichtung und Musik in Monteverdis *Lamento d'Arianna*', *Zeitschrift für Musikwissenschaft*, 10 (1927/8), 216–22.

GALLENI LUISI, LEILA, 'Il *Lamento d'Arianna* di Severo Bonini (1613)', in Raffaello Monterosso (ed.), *Claudio Monteverdi e il suo tempo* (Verona, 1969), 573–82.

GALLICO, CLAUDIO, 'I due pianti d'Arianna di Claudio Monteverdi', *Chigiana*, 24 (1967), 29–42.

HORSLEY, IMOGENE, 'Monteverdi's Use of Borrowed Material in *Sfogava con le stelle*', *Music and Letters*, 49 (1978), 316–28.

MURATA, MARGARET, 'The Recitative Soliloquy', *Journal of the American Musicological Society*, 32 (1979), 45–73.

ROSAND, ELLEN, 'The Descending Tetrachord: An Emblem of Lament', *Musical Quarterly*, 65 (1979), 346–59.

WESTRUP, JACK A., 'Monteverdi's *Lamento d'Arianna*', *Music Review*, 1 (1940), 144–54.


*Church Music*

ADRIO, ADAM, *Die Anfänge des geistlichen Konzerts* (Berlin, 1935).

ARNOLD, DENIS, 'A Background Note on Monteverdi's Hymn Settings', *Scritti in onore di Luigi Ronga* (Milan, 1973), 33–44.

ARNOLD, DENIS, 'Formal Design in Monteverdi's Church Music', in Raffaello Monterosso (ed.), *Claudio Monteverdi e il suo tempo* (Verona, 1969), 187–216.

BONTA, STEVEN, 'Liturgical Problems in Monteverdi's Marian Vespers', *Journal of the American Musicological Society*, 20 (1967), 87–106.

FERRARI BARASSI, ELENA, 'Il madrigale spirituale nel Cinquecento e la raccolta monteverdiana del 1583', in Raffaello Monterosso (ed.), *Claudio Monteverdi e il suo tempo* (Verona, 1969), 217–52.

HUCKE, HELMUT, 'Die fälschlich so genannte "Marien"-Vesper von Claudio Monteverdi', in Christoph-Hellmuth Mahling and Siegrid Wiesmann (eds.), *Bericht über den internationalen musikwissenschaftlichen Kongress Bayreuth 1981* (Cassel, 1984), 295–305.

KURTZMAN, JEFFREY, *Essays on the Monteverdi Mass and Vespers of 1610* (Rice University Studies, 44/4; Houston, 1978).

—— 'Some Historical Perspectives on the Monteverdi Vespers', *Analecta musicologica*, 15 (1975), 29–86.

ROCHE, JEROME, *North Italian Church Music in the Age of Monteverdi* (Oxford, 1984).

—— 'Monteverdi and the *Prima Prattica*', in Denis Arnold and Nigel Fortune (eds.), *The Monteverdi Companion* (London, 1968), 167–91.

RORKE, MARGARET ANNE, 'Sacred Contrafacta of Monteverdi Madrigals and Cardinal Borromeo's Milan', *Music and Letters*, 65 (1984), 168–75.

SMITH BRINDLE, REGINALD, 'Monteverdi's G Minor Mass: An Experiment in Construction', *Musical Quarterly*, 54 (1968), 352–60.

STEVENS, DENIS, 'Claudio Monteverdi: *Selva morale et spirituale*', in Raffaello Monterosso (ed.), *Claudio Monteverdi e il suo tempo* (Verona, 1969), 423–34.

—— 'Where are the Vespers of Yesteryear?', *Musical Quarterly*, 47 (1961), 315–30.

*The Musician in Society*

ABERT, ANNA AMALIE, 'Die Opernästhetik Claudio Monteverdis', in Raffaello Monterosso (ed.), *Claudio Monteverdi e il suo tempo* (Verona, 1969), 35–44.

BEAT, JANET E., 'Monteverdi and the Opera Orchestra of his Time', in Denis Arnold and Nigel Fortune (eds.) *The Monteverdi Companion* (London, 1968), 277–301.

BENVENUTI, GIACOMO, 'Il manoscritto veneziano della *Incoronazione di Poppea*', *Rivista musicale italiana*, 41 (1937), 176–84.

BERTOLOTTI, ANTONIO, *Musici alla corte dei Gonzaga in Mantova dal secolo XV al XVIII* (Milan, 1890; repr. 1969).

BIANCONI, LORENZO, and WALKER, THOMAS, *Seventeenth Century Italian Opera: Two Essays in Social History* (Cambridge, 1982).

DAMERINI, GINO, 'Venezia al tempo di Monteverdi', *Musica*, 2 (1948), 105–20.

FANO, FABIO, '*Il combattimento di Tancredi e Clorinda* e *L'incoronazione di Poppea* di Claudio Monteverdi', in Maria Teresa Muraro (ed.), *Studi sul teatro veneto fra rinascimento ed età barocca* (Florence, 1971), 345–71.

HAAS, ROBERT, 'Zur Neuausgabe von Claudio Monteverdis *Il ritorno d'Ulisse in Patria*', *Studien zur Musikwissenschaft*, 9 (Vienna, 1922).

MOLMENTI, POMPEO, *La storia di Venezia nella vita privata* (5 vols.; Bergamo, 1908–11).

ORTOLANI, GIUSEPPE, 'Venezia al tempo di Monteverdi', *La rassegna musicale*, 2 (1929), 469–82.

OSTHOFF, WOLFGANG, 'Die venezianische und die neapolitanische Fassung von Monteverdis *Incoronazione di Poppea*', *Acta musicologica*, 26 (1954), 88–113.

—— 'Maske und Musik: Die Gestaltwerdung der Oper in Venedig', *Castrum Peregrini*, 65 (1964), 10–49.

—— 'Neue Beobachtungen zu Quellen und Geschichte von Monteverdis *Incoronazione di Poppea*', *Die Musikforschung*, 11 (1958), 129–38.

—— 'Zu den Quellen von Monteverdis *Ritorno d'Ulisse in patria*', *Studien zur Musikwissenschaft*, 23 (1956), 67–78.

ROSAND, ELLEN, 'Seneca and the Interpretation of . . . *Poppea*', *Journal of the American Musicological Society*, 38 (1985), 34–71.

SOLERTI, ANGELO, 'Un balletto musicato da Claudio Monteverde sconosciuto ai' suoi biografi', *Rivista musicale italiana*, 9 (1904), 24–34.

STROHM, REINHARD, 'Osservazioni su *Tempro la cetra*', *Rivista italiana di musicologia*, 2 (1967), 357–64.

WALKER, THOMAS, 'Gli errori di *Minerva al tavolino*', in Maria Teresa Muraro (ed.), *Venezia e il melodramma del Seicento* (Florence, 1976), 7–20.

WOLFF, CHRISTOPH, 'Zur Frage der Instrumentation und des Instrumentalen in Monteverdis Opern', in Ludwig Finscher (ed.), *Claudio Monteverdi: Festschrift Reinhold Hammerstein* (Laaber, 1986), 489–98.

*Primacy, Dating, and Authenticity*

BIANCONI, LORENZO, and WALKER, THOMAS, 'Dalla *Finta pazza* alla *Veremonda*; storie di Febiarmonici', *Rivista italiana di musicologia*, 10 (1975), 379–454.

CHIARELLI, ALESSANDRA, '*L'incoronazione di Poppea* o *Il Nerone*: Problemi di filologia testuale', *Rivista italiana di musicologia*, 9 (1974), 117–51.

MAGINI, ALESSANDRO, 'Le monodie di Benedetto Ferrari e *L'incoronazione di Poppea*: Un rilevamento stilistico comparativo', *Rivista italiana di musicologia*, 21 (1986), 266–99.

# INDEX